OSKAR
KOKOSCHKA

Fig. 1. Poster for *Murderer Hope of Women*,
Vienna Kunstschau, 1909, colored lithograph,
48 × 31¼ in. (122 × 79.5 cm.). Courtesy
Verlag Galerie Welz, Salzburg.

OSKAR KOKOSCHKA

THE PAINTER AS PLAYWRIGHT

by Henry I. Schvey
LEIDEN UNIVERSITY

Wayne State University Press, Detroit, 1982

Library of Congress Cataloging in Publication Data

Schvey, Henry I., 1948–
   Oskar Kokoschka, the painter as playwright.

   Includes three plays, Murderer the women's hope, Sphinx and strawman, and Job, by Kokoschka.
   Bibliography: p.
   Includes index.
   1.   Kokoschka, Oskar, 1886–   —Criticism and interpretation.   I.   Kokoschka, Oskar, 1886–
II.   Title.
PT2671.O37Z86   832'.912   82-2871
ISBN 0-8143-1702-2   AACR2

Grateful acknowledgment is made to the National Endowment for the Humanities for financial assistance in publishing this volume.

To Patty and Aram

A play of Kokoschka's is only a variation on his paintings, and vice versa. The tone and melody, rhythm and gesture of his words are parallel to those of his paintings. He confronts the chaos of the world as though he were the first man, and invents technique and form ingenuously, as though he were the first artist. The people of his dramas are as huge and simple as the colossus of a mountain, and as natural as a landscape.

Paul Kornfeld
Program note to the premiere
of Kokoschka's plays, 1917

Contents

Illustrations

Preface

The death of Oskar Kokoschka on February 22, 1980, just before his ninety-fourth birthday, was a loss not only to followers of this extraordinary artist but to those interested in the history of art in this century as well. He was an innovative painter and playwright, but he was also something even more rare: a uniquely perceptive human being. As he aged, he never lost what he called the "spark," the ability to see the world with the freshness and fantasy that link the artist with the child.

At his School of Seeing, which he founded in Salzburg in 1953, he made no promises to turn his students into artists. (Art, he felt, could not be taught.) He did, however, offer them something ultimately more significant: the ability to see the world and to understand the function of art. As he said in the brochure for his school: "There is always the hope that in the class there will be some young student who will come to realize in his innermost being that he possesses the gift of learning how to see with his own eyes—the eyes of an artist."

In August 1973 I was granted a week of interviews with Kokoschka in his home in Switzerland. As I sat in his living room with trepidation, I heard his booming voice sound from the top of the stairs: "No need to get up, Mr. Schvey, I'll be right down." In the hours of discussion that followed, many topics were touched upon, but the one I remember most clearly was how much this man, then eighty-seven, loved life—how precious it was to him and how much he wanted to continue experiencing and seeing the world around him. "It goes so fast," he said, snapping his fingers, "and then it's over." Then he wheeled around, stared at my wife, and asked with extraordinary bluntness: "How old do you think I am?" Not waiting for a response, he answered himself in a loud voice: "I am *three hundred years old,* and I am only now just starting to learn how to paint." Then he quickly added, with a smile: "But I'm lucky. I started young."

As we parted, he presented me with a copy of his autobiography, *My Life.* Later I read the inscription: "To friend Henry I. Schvey, if you do not read this book with interest I am going to kill you; because you have the vocation and the understanding."

I did read it with interest. As a result of it, and of my meeting with him in Switzerland, I would like to think that Kokoschka helped me to see and to value perception in a fresher, more meaningful way. The present book is offered to his memory as an indication that he did.

As the title suggests, *Oskar Kokoschka: The Painter as*

Playwright is an interdisciplinary study of the relationships between Kokoschka's plays and his work in the visual arts. As such, it is exclusively concerned neither with literary criticism nor with art history. Rather, by revealing the extraordinary degree of interpenetration in his approach to writing and painting, it bridges the gap between previous studies of Kokoschka the dramatist and those of Kokoschka the painter and graphic artist. Kokoschka's plays are, above all, visual theater. It is, therefore, the nonverbal aspects of his approach to the stage—scenic imagery, color, and light symbolism—that this book examines most closely.

Within the text, translation of Kokoschka's *Murderer Hope of Women* (sometimes translated as *Murderer the Women's Hope*) is by Michael Hamburger (Appendix B); *Sphinx and Strawman,* by Victor H. Miesel (Appendix C); and *Job,* by Walter H. Sokel and Jacqueline Sokel (Appendix D). All other translations within the text are mine.

Appendix A lists the versions of each of the plays and of their various editions, both in German and, where available, in translation.

Acknowledgments

My deepest thanks to Oskar Kokoschka and to his wife Olda for their generosity, constant encouragement, and invaluable comments and suggestions about the manuscript. Meeting them at their home in Villeneuve, Switzerland, for a week of interviews in 1973 and again in 1977 provided me with important insights into Kokoschka's art and life and was a source of continuing inspiration.

In the preparation of the manuscript, I owe a debt to two professors of comparative literature at Indiana University: Ulrich Weisstein, for his constant encouragement and attention to detail; and Breon Mitchell, for his many insights. Those friends and colleagues at Leiden University with whom I discussed portions of the book deserve special mention: A. G. H. Bachrach, C. C. Barfoot, J. A. van Dorsten, M. Horne, and Alastair Hamilton. I am also grateful to J. A. A. Spiekerman and A. J. M. Hoenselaars for their assistance with my translations. At the Wayne State University Press, I would like to thank Bernard Goldman, Jean Owen, and Richard Kinney for their enthusiasm and kindness and my editor, Jean Spang, for her unstinting efforts on my behalf.

Thanks are due the individuals, publishers, museums, and archives who supplied the photographs used here and to Olda Kokoschka and Cosmopress for allowing reproductions and translations of Kokoschka's work. I appreciate the willingness of Michael Hamburger, Victor H. Miesel, and Walter H. Sokel and Jacqueline Sokel to let me include their translations of Kokoschka's plays.

A part of the first chapter was published in slightly different form in Dutch, in *Forum der Letteren*, vol. 17, no. 2 (1976), under the title "Oskar Kokoschka en de wederzijdse verheldering der kunsten," and in *Literature and the Other Arts*, vol. 3 of *Proceedings of the Ninth Congress of the International Comparative Literature Association* (Innsbruck, 1981), under the title "The Playwright's Eye: The Visual Drama of Oskar Kokoschka." My thanks to both these publishers for their permission to allow publication here.

My foremost debt is to my wife, Patty. She provided enthusiasm and forbearance through the whole of the writing project. It was Patty who initially proposed writing to Kokoschka, offered critical insights, interpretation, and helped type and prepare the manuscript. To her, my gratitude, appreciation, and love.

Fig. 2. *Hans and Erika Tietze*, 1909, oil on canvas, 30⅛ × 53⅝ in. (76.5 × 136.2 cm.). Collection The Museum of Modern Art, New York, Abby Aldrich Rockefeller Fund.

13

Fig. 3. *Lovers with Cat*, 1917, oil on canvas, 37 × 54 in. (93 × 137 cm.). Collection Kunsthaus, Zurich.

Fig. 4 *The Slave Girl*, 1920, oil on canvas, 43 × 31 in. (110 × 80 cm.). Collection Mr. and Mrs. Morton D. May, St. Louis.

Fig. 5. *The Tempest*, 1914, oil on canvas, 71 × 87 in. (181 × 220 cm.). Collection Kunstmuseum, Basel.

Introduction

*this I shall do by printing in the infernal method, by corrosives,
which in Hell are salutary and medicinal, melting apparent
surfaces away, and displaying the infinite which was hid.*

William Blake
The Marriage of Heaven and Hell

The plays, paintings, and graphics of the Austrian artist Oskar Kokoschka are expressions of a single symbolic language. As he wrote in 1953:

> The plastic arts are a language of images, visible or tangible signs, graspable reflections of experience and knowing, through which the artist's vision takes on, for those close in time and for coming generations, the impact of a common existence and humanity. If the content of what is being stated is to get across, literature as well as the arts must express this content in meaningful symbols.[1]

The connection between Kokoschka's dramatic and pictorial work is evident in five plays he wrote between 1907 and 1972: *Murderer Hope of Women, The Burning Bush, Job, Orpheus and Eurydice,* and *Comenius.* Each play is significant not only for its literary content but for its unique use of visual elements: the unconventional design of the stage itself and the use of color and light symbolism, as well as gesture and pantomime, to communicate a stark vision of an intense experience. Thus, these five plays form an indivisible unity with Kokoschka's work in the visual arts and confirm him as one of the foremost innovators of the twentieth-century theater, the first German Expressionist dramatist.

The early artistic works of Kokoschka were forged in a spirit of rebellion against authority, convention, and the prevailing decorativeness of Viennese *Jugend-*

stil, the art nouveau movement that emphasized the stylized conventions of art for ornamentation. His first charge at the establishment was made in 1908—during an exhibition of Viennese art, the Kunstschau, where the "neo-classical, art-deco phase of the Viennese aesthetic movement celebrated its greatest triumph" and where "even the most serious painting and sculpture was reduced to decorative functions."[2] In this competition, Kokoschka, then a student at the Vienna School for Arts and Crafts, entered *Self-Portrait as Warrior* (Fig. 6), a painted clay bust with its mouth agape in an impassioned cry.

More at home in an ethnology museum than in a museum of art, Kokoschka had spurned the intricately ornamented surfaces of the style of the Viennese Secessionists (the Austrian followers of *Jugendstil*) in favor of the instinctive, emotional immediacy inspired by primitive art. "Seeing a Polynesian mask with its incised tattooing, I understood at once, because I could feel my own facial nerves reacting to cold and hunger in the same way,"[3] he said. *The Warrior,* then, had been the outgrowth of this inspiration, which was to affect all Kokoschka's future work and ultimately the art of his generation as well.

His challenge to the contemporary art world had begun deviously. He had been permitted to exhibit his

Fig. 7. Kokoschka, 1909. Photograph courtesy F. Bruckmann KG, Munich.

Fig. 6. *Self-Portrait as Warrior*, 1908, clay and polychrome, 16 in. (40 cm.). Collection Museum of Fine Arts, Boston.

work at the Kunstschau in 1908 only because he had locked the door to his studio, preventing the organizers of the exhibit, including its president, Gustav Klimt, the leader of the Secessionists, from seeing his work in advance. To the Viennese public, Kokoschka's room at the exhibit became known as the "Chamber of Horrors," while he himself was dubbed "Chief Savage" (*Oberwildling*) by one prominent critic. For the Kunstschau of 1909, Kokoschka defiantly shaved his head (Fig. 7) as a rebuttal to the hostile press of the previous year, where he had seen himself "treated as a criminal."

But in making a forced entry into the Viennese art world, Kokoschka had fulfilled a remarkable prophecy that Hermann Bahr, an editor of a leading journal of the Viennese Secession, had made ten years earlier: "One must know how to make oneself hated. The Viennese respects only those people whom he despises. . . . The Viennese painters will have to show whether or not they know how to be agitators."[4] Indeed, Kokoschka knew how to be an agitator; defiance of convention was to characterize his artistic innovations throughout his long career.

In 1908, the same year in which he burst upon the Viennese art scene, a small book by Kokoschka appeared, *The Dreaming Youths (Die träumenden Knaben),* which he had designed the previous year. He had been commissioned by the Vienna Workshops (Wiener Werkstätte) to create a picture book for children which was to be displayed at the Kunstschau exhibition commemorating "The Art of the Child."

But Kokoschka followed his teachers' instructions in only a single colored lithograph, that depicting a young girl with long blonde hair nestled amid a field of flowers (Fig. 8). Rather than a picture book, he created a picture-poem devoid of conventional structure, punctuation, and capital letters, the first example of the stream-of-consciousness technique in German. The focus was on an adolescent boy awakening to sexual desire for the first time:

> anxious hours i dream sobbing and quivering
>   like children
> who rise pubescent from their beds
>
> not the events of childhood pass through me
>   nor of manhood
> but those of adolescence
> a trembling desire
> the groundless shame before adults
> and companions
> the overflowing and the isolation
> i discovered my self and my body
> and i sank down and dreamed love.[5]

In addition to the one "acceptable" illustration of the young girl, the book included seven colored and two black-and-white lithographs. Each illustration in the book demonstrated the Secession influence, the delicate arrangement of complementary colors and decorative patterning especially suggestive of Austrian peasant art. Significantly, too, the book was dedicated to Secession leader Gustav Klimt "with admiration."

Nevertheless, there is an aura of scarcely concealed tension about the lithographs, suggested by the presence of red fish with gaping jaws in five of the illustrations and the fact that Kokoschka's adolescents often look lost, insecure, and frightened in their peaceful Eden. This sense of isolation is especially true of the last lithograph (Fig. 9), in which the girl and boy are depicted as cut off from one another, gazing within themselves, awkwardly and self-consciously touching their thin, undeveloped bodies. But if the *form* of the illustrations points backward to a style from which the young artist was already emerging, the poem itself, lacking spatial and temporal continuity, forcefully portrays in extraordinary images the fierce desires of adolescence.

Fig. 8. *The Sleeping Girl*, from *The Dreaming Youths*, 1908, colored lithograph, 9 × 11 in. (24 × 29 cm.). Courtesy Verlag Galerie Welz, Salzburg.

Fig. 9. *The Girl Li and I*, from *The Dreaming Youths*, 1908, colored lithograph, 9 × 11 in. (24 × 29 cm.). Courtesy Verlag Galerie Welz, Salzburg.

As one critic characterized *The Dreaming Youths,* it was a "fairy tale . . . but not for the children of philistines."[6] The book was a nightmarish fantasy because of the stark contrast between the violent content of the poem and the fairytale quality of the lithographs, a combination of lyricism and violence that prefigures Kokoschka's early plays. Indeed, turbulent emotions abound in the poem:

red little fish
little fish red
stab yourself with the triple-edged knife dead
slit yourself with my fingers in two
that the silent circles may be through

red little fish
little fish red
my knife is red
my fingers are red
in the bowl a little fish sinks dead
. . . . . .
do you feel the excited warmth of the trembling tepid air
—i am the circling werewolf—
. . . . .
my unbridled body
my erect body swollen with blood and color
creeps into your bower
swarms through your villages
creeps into your souls
swarms into your wombs

out of the most solitary stillness
before you wake pierces my howl.[7]

Clearly, these images, which seem dredged from the artist's subconscious, convey the sense of visionary intensity characteristic of Expressionism.

The term Expressionism, however, must be applied to Kokoschka's work with caution, since he vehemently opposed such classification throughout his career: "There is no such thing as German, French or Anglo-American Expressionism: there are only young people

trying to find their bearings in the world,"[8] he said. Unlike the artists gathered around Herwarth Walden's Expressionist periodical *Der Sturm,* for which Kokoschka served as Viennese editor and in which he published his first play and several drawings in 1910 and 1911, Kokoschka "took little interest in their formal problems or in their moral ideas. [He] contributed no manifestoes, not even a signature. [He] was not going to submit [his] hard-won independence to anyone else's control."[9]

While he liked the work of Emil Nolde, Ernst Ludwig Kirchner, Erich Heckel, and Max Pechstein because of its vibrant use of color, and while he exhibited with the artists of Die Brücke (perhaps the only Expressionist group with a true commonality of goals and programs) in the New Secession Exhibit of 1911, the influence other Expressionist painters had on his individualistic nature was largely a confirmation of his own direction, which was at this time psychological portraiture. Thus, Kokoschka was "able to achieve stature as an artist, going far beyond expressionism as a trend or style."[10]

His uneasy relationship to the movement was succinctly articulated by the contemporary composer Arnold Schoenberg: "Kokoschka is one of those strong natures who can afford to express *themselves,* aware that they are thereby making their contribution to the expression of everyone and everything: the universe itself. This is without doubt the task of the great artist. Even if the lesser ones, and the public, call it Expressionism."[11] But it was in an essay on the painter Edvard Munch that Kokoschka carefully formulated his own ideas of Expressionism without pigeonholing his own accomplishments under that label:

Expressionism . . . shapes life into true experience. What marks off true experience from all grey theory (Goethe's phrase) is this: that something which is of this world

22

embraces something which lies beyond it—a single moment appearing in the guise of eternity—and that the dull edge of human desires in itself sets off the divine ray of light, just as silence is broken by a cry, or as the dullness of habit is broken by the unexpected. Expressionism is the forming of experience, and as such it requires a medium; it is a message from the I to the Thou. Like love, it takes two. True Expressionism does not live in an ivory tower; it addresses itself to a fellow being whom it awakens.[12]

The essay on Munch defines two attributes of Expressionist art: its visionary quality, "a single moment appearing in the guise of eternity," and its intensity, "a silence broken by a cry." The "cry" alludes to Munch's masterpiece *The Scream* (1893), but a cry is also characteristic of Expressionist drama—from Kokoschka's own *Murderer Hope of Women* to Reinhard Goering's *Naval Battle* (1917), both of which begin with an anguished cry.

As Ulrich Weisstein has observed, "what Expressionist art seeks to render visible . . . are soul states and the violent emotions welling up from the innermost recesses of the subconscious."[13] Despite Kokoschka's personal dissociation from the term, his conception of Expressionism as intensely communicated visionary experience shows much of his work, both visual and dramatic, against the broader background of German Expressionist art which sought, in its rebellion against the premises of realist art, not to reproduce the visible but to "make visible, in images, a reality that could not be perceived by the senses."[14]

Kokoschka's earliest plays, *Murderer Hope of Women* and *Sphinx and Strawman,* both of which date from 1907, when the artist was twenty-two years old, are exuberant yet hostile gestures of youthful anxiety. Both are jarring revolts against conventional dramatic form, cast in indelible images for the theater. By reducing the stage to nameless elemental types instead of individu-

alized characters, and by filling the air with sentence fragments and screams instead of carefully polished dialogue, Kokoschka prefigures both the technique and the telegrammatic style of later Expressionist dramatists: Reinhard Goering, Georg Kaiser, Walter Hasenclever, and Ernst Barlach. But, as his friend the poet Albert Ehrenstein said, Kokoschka was not an "Expressionist—he was an Explosionist."[15]

Yet the violence, concentration, and compression of *Murderer Hope of Women* (only a few pages long, with more than half the text consisting of stage directions), the use of grotesquely comic distortion in *Sphinx and Strawman* and *Job* (1917), and the concern with myth and the theme of spiritual regeneration in *The Burning Bush* (1911) indicate that Kokoschka's plays are of historical importance as the first German Expressionist dramas. Coming to the stage unencumbered by the conventions of nineteenth-century realism in the drama, Kokoschka wrote plays as he perceived the world around him—with his eyes. The visual spectacles that resulted were the cause of riots in the theaters where they were first performed, shocking even audiences familiar with the "expressionistic" plays of August Strindberg or Frank Wedekind, with their anti-realist bias and interest in the grotesque. Kokoschka's creations as a dramatist, his expressions of the playwright's "eye," therefore, are inextricably related to his works as one of the great painters of the twentieth century.

Kokoschka's plays written from 1907 to 1918 concern his obsession with the relationship between the sexes, a focus which suggests the influence of the Swedish playwright August Strindberg. Indeed, as one critic boldly (and erroneously) claimed: "Certainly Kokoschka knew Strindberg and had read all his plays, in addition to attending productions in Vienna."[16]

Strindberg was undoubtedly the most influential force on early German Expressionist drama. Between

1913 and 1915 over one thousand performances of twenty-four of his plays were performed in Germany alone.[17] In works such as *To Damascus* (1898–1903) and *A Dream Play* (1902), he foreshadowed not only the Expressionist thematic preoccupations with man's transformation and regeneration but the formal developments of later Expressionist drama: the reduction of the *dramatis personae* to nameless types, and the employment of a succession of short scenes or *Stationen* to denote stages in the central character's journey toward spiritual renewal. Yet there is no clear evidence of Strindberg's influence on Kokoschka.

Instead, Kokoschka's early interest in the theater was nonliterary and based on his visual orientation toward the world. Of his first work for the stage he said, "My play is not for reading. It must be spoken, acted and lived, as an antidote to the torpor that, for the most part, one experiences in the theater today."[18] Thus, rather than Strindberg's *The Father* or *The Dance of Death* influencing Kokoschka's *Murderer Hope of Women*, there are affinities between Strindberg's and Kokoschka's works. Both playwrights externalize their obsessions with the power struggle between men and women, which they see as the Captain in Strindberg's *The Father* does: "To eat or be eaten, that is the question! If I do not eat you, you will eat me; and you have already bared your teeth to me!"[19]

Kokoschka's early plays about the war between the sexes are reminiscent of the ideas of Viennese psychologist Otto Weininger, who, in his 1902 treatise *Sex and Character (Geschlecht und Charakter)*, postulated the opposition between the "male principle," responsible for all the positive achievements in human history, and the "female principle," responsible for all those that are negative. Although, for Weininger, these principles did not exist in a pure form, they provided a basis for explaining human behavior since all humans are androgynous, containing a mixture of these antithetical principles in varying proportions.

An analogy between Weininger's thesis and Kokoschka's attitude toward the sexes in the earliest versions of *Murderer Hope of Women* and *Sphinx and Strawman* would be simple, but the argument that Weininger "made a deep and lasting impression" on Kokoschka lacks evidence.[20] In the autobiographical essay "From Experience" ("Vom Erleben," 1935), Kokoschka, in most un-Weiningerian terms, said that "in my first play I had taken a swipe at the thoughtlessness of our male-oriented society, advancing the fundamental notion that man is mortal and woman immortal."[21] For Kokoschka, woman was immortal because she could bear children. Indeed, horror and grief accompanied his discovery in 1915 that his mistress, Alma Mahler, had aborted their child. "You wish to know exactly why I paint? I'll tell you. It's because I cannot have children," he said in 1973.[22]

The proto-Expressionist plays of Frank Wedekind, such as *Spring's Awakening (Frühlings Erwachen*, written in 1890–91) and *The Earth Spirit (Erdgeist*, 1893), also present analogies with the work of Kokoschka, particularly in the treatment of the relation between the sexes. However, Wedekind's mordant interest in caricature, the grotesque, and satire finds its partial equivalent in but one of Kokoschka's plays, *Job*, and cannot be said to be representative of his dramatic style as a whole.

Therefore, although there are links between Kokoschka's interest in the battle between the sexes and the same theme in the works of Strindberg, Weininger, and Wedekind, there is no evidence that any of these three had a direct influence on him. But to see Kokoschka's dramas within the context of German Expressionism or its precursors does not obscure the specifically Austrian aspects of his work.

As a child, Kokoschka's passion for the stage was first kindled by his father's gift to him of a marionette theater, and was later enriched by the tradition of nineteenth-century Austrian popular theater as found in the works of Ferdinand Raimund and Johann Nepomuk Nestroy. Although the plays of Raimund and Nestroy were (and are) often accepted by the Viennese public as merely witty satires on the bourgeoisie, Kokoschka viewed their work, where fantasy reigned supreme and good and evil were clearly defined, in a different light. To him, "these two, poets of humorous fairyland as well as of bitter farce, peopled the already magical world of the Baroque with the figures of their own imagining, tragicomic characters who aspire to ever-greater heights, reaching even to the spirit kingdom."[23]

Kokoschka the painter drew heavily upon the sources of the Austrian Baroque, its fantasy, whirling intensity, dramatic spectacle, and painterly approach to color. As he said, "It was the Baroque inheritance I took over, unconsciously still. Just as it offered itself to my dazzled eyes as a boy singing in choir in the Austrian cathedrals, I saw the wall painting of Gran, the Kremser Schmidt, and of the outspoken extremist among them, Maulpertsch."[24] Similarly, Kokoschka the playwright was excited by the fairytale world of Raimund and Nestroy which he adapted to his own ends.

Thus, it was not proto-Expressionists, such as Munch, Strindberg, or Wedekind, with whom Kokoschka's work is most likely to be compared, who influenced his work as an artist-dramatist. Rather, it was the Austrian Baroque tradition in art and the Viennese popular theater that had the greatest impact on his development.

Additional parallels to the underlying concerns of Kokoschka's work are found in the works of fellow Austrians, like Karl Kraus, the moralist, satirist, and editor of *Die Fackel;* the composer Arnold Schoenberg; and the architect Adolf Loos. Each was in sympathy with the young painter's aims of rebellion against all that was smug, complacent, and merely "pretty" in the art of the period. Kraus, perhaps more than anyone else, took it upon himself in his satirical essays and pithy aphorisms to reveal the hypocrisy and spiritual lassitude behind the pleasant facade of *fin de siècle* Vienna, which he called "a proving ground for world destruction."[25]

Kraus fought bitterly against the devaluation of language in modern life, and was a fierce opponent of the Viennese press. Kokoschka painted and drew Kraus many times and was in frequent attendance at the coffee-house discussions over which Kraus presided. After Kraus's death, Kokoschka wrote of him with a conciseness that even the aphorist Kraus would have appreciated: "When Kraus died, independence of thought in Austria died with him."[26]

Another of Kokoschka's contemporaries was Adolf Loos, who lived his life as a spiritual crusade. What purification of language was for Kraus, purity of architectural form was for Loos. An opponent of the Kunstschau ideal of decorative beauty, Loos advocated functionalism in architecture, as is evidenced by his Steiner House (1910), one of the first private homes in which concrete was used as a building material, and by his essay on Secession style, "Ornament and Crime," written in 1908, the year of Kokoschka's stormy entrance into the Viennese art world.

Loos's attack on the Secession style was based on a strict utilitarian rationale which might seem to be antithetical to Kokoschka's interest in psychological portraiture as a means of delving beneath the calm facade of the sitter. However, the interests of the two were complementary. Loos insisted that while architecture must serve utility, art must not: "The work of art wants to shake people out of their comfortableness. The house must serve comfort. The artwork is revolutionary, the house conservative."[27] Loos therefore was in sympathy with Kokoschka's attack on the Secessionist aesthetic of art as ornamentation, an ideal embodied in the comment by Oscar Wilde which was used as an epigraph to the section on painting in the 1908 Kuntschau catalogue: "Art must never express anything but itself."

A third contemporary with whom Kokoschka can be compared is the composer Arnold Schoenberg. As Carl Schorske has observed, Schoenberg's development, from the song cycle *The Book of the Hanging Gardens* (1908), based on a series of poems by Stefan George on the theme of adolescent sexuality, through the Expressionist monodramas *Expectation* (*Erwartung*, 1909) and *The Fortunate Hand* (*Die glückliche Hand*, 1910–13), offers a parallel to Kokoschka's maturation. Both the composer and the artist turned to literature—specifically, to drama—early in their careers, which indicates not only their versatility but the multiple talents which flourished during the Expressionist period, as well as the specifically Austrian consideration that "whatever was vital in Austrian culture ultimately had to express itself in theater."[28]

Schoenberg's liberation of dissonance, like Kokoschka's introduction of sexual violence into plays, struck a blow at the *fin de siècle* ideal of the beautiful. Just as distortion of form and color are hallmarks of Expressionist art, so Schoenberg's early Expressionist musical dramas employ "a wide dynamic range, strong accentuation, sharp dissonance, and a jagged improvisatory overall effect."[29]

As in Kokoschka's early dramatic works, Schoenberg's monodrama *Expectation* has as its central theme the quest of a woman for her lover, which is presented in a dreamlike atmosphere, using types ("Man," "Woman") and a chorus instead of individualized char-

acters. It is significant that in a projected film version of *The Fortunate Hand* Schoenberg wanted Kokoschka to design the sets "with apparitions of color and form."[30]

While Kraus, Loos, and Schoenberg can be compared with, and had influences on, Kokoschka's work, an important key to Kokoschka's early works is found in the sexually repressive atmosphere of turn-of-the-century Vienna. It was a world where, as Stefan Zweig notes in his autobiography, *The World of Yesterday*, "the true lines of the body of a woman had to be so completely hidden that even her bridegroom at the wedding banquet could not have the faintest idea whether his future life-partner was straight or crooked, whether she was fat or lean, short-legged, bow-legged, or long-legged."[31] Inevitably, instead of de-emphasizing the chemistry of sexual attraction, the suppression of normal instincts led to heightened sexual awareness. "By its unpsychological method of concealment and reticence, the society of that time achieved the directly opposite effect. . . . Everywhere the suppressed sought by-ways, loopholes and detours. In the final analysis that generation, to whom all enlightenment and all innocent association with the opposite sex was prudishly denied, was a thousand times more erotically inclined than the younger generation of today with its greater freedom of love."[32]

Kokoschka wrote, "An inner voice tormented me, like a hermit in the wilderness, with imaginings about the female sex."[33] Thus, like that of many of his contemporaries, such as Gustav Klimt and Egon Schiele, Kokoschka's work was filled with references to the erotic power of the female.

Although Klimt often chose to portray society ladies in static poses against ornamental backgrounds, in many of his finest paintings, such as *Judith and Holofernes* (1901) and *Salome* (1909), he explored his complex anxieties about the opposite sex. Often, women in his paintings appear as both sensuous and castrating creatures, which is suggested, for example, in the contrast between the warm, full body and the claw-like hands of Salome. As Schorske observed, Klimt's attitude toward women was a mixture of his resistance to the restrictive attitudes of his day, and a fear of what liberation might bring: "In his exploration of the erotic, Klimt banished the moral sense of sin that had plagued the righteous fathers. But in its place arose a fear of sex that haunted many of the sensitive sons."[34]

The work of Kokoschka's younger contemporary, Schiele, was even more overtly erotic than Klimt's. Klimt used delicate arabesques and ornamentation to suggest his preoccupation with the female, but Schiele depicted his sexual anxieties and fantasies openly in his work; in fact, in 1912 his erotic drawings were the cause of his imprisonment.

The women in Klimt's work are often threatening, as in his paintings *Gold Fish* and *Watersnakes,* or in his drawing *Fish Blood* (1898), in which they float about "in a liquefied world, where the male would quickly drown, like sailors seduced by mermaids."[35] By contrast, women in paintings by Schiele, such as his *Girl in the Green Stockings* (1914), are far more arrogant about their own magnetic eroticism: "There is an openness, almost a brazen directness about their expressions . . . seeing their powerful sexuality as a tool."[36]

If painters like Klimt and Kokoschka reacted to a repressive cultural climate, their responses were different. In Klimt's portraits, there is little attempt to delineate psychological states. Instead, the model becomes part of a stylized setting. As in his portrait of Adele Bloch-Bauer (1907), "she graces the interior as it frames her. . . . Such a portrait belongs in an art-deco room; and such a room deserves as its centerpiece a portrait so sublimely stylized."[37] By contrast, Kokoschka's early "black portraits," as he himself called them, were

painted "with the scalpel," in an attempt to liberate the inner self from the encumbrance of the fleshly surface.

As a young art student, instead of posing his models in passive stylized positions, Kokoschka encouraged them to move about and to talk, thus enabling him to establish "an essential image of the kind that remains in memory or recurs in dreams."[38] Kokoschka trained himself in this method of dramatic portraiture by using children from a circus family as models so that he could learn to capture the essence of their wiry bodies in flashes of twisting movement.

The process by which Kokoschka tried in his portraits to capture the subconscious fears and desires of a personality can be compared with the technique employed by his spiritual brother Sigmund Freud in *The Interpretation of Dreams* (1900). Just as Freud delved into the turbulent world of repressed sexuality and hostility in his patients, Kokoschka explored the innermost psyches of his models. He said that his early portraits originated "in Vienna before the World War; the people lived in security yet they were all afraid. I felt this through their cultivated form of living. . . . I painted them in their anxiety and pain."[39]

Nell Walden's account of Kokoschka's portrait of her offers a clear example of his method. Kokoschka began work by squeezing the paint out of a tube and scratching around in it with a fingernail, saying that "one shouldn't be afraid to use a hammer if necessary" since what was important was to create something convincing, regardless of the tools. In the completed picture, all her beauty had been stripped away:

> He captured my likeness by lifting off all the top layer revealing the face of a fairly desperate convict underneath. And this was another example of "the eye of God," for he had no means of knowing that I had done twenty months in prison some years before. . . . this is by the way and just to give some really concrete example of

the fantastic, one might almost say, demonic ability, of this artist.[40]

Thus, Kokoschka's portraits often revealed his gift of "second sight," a power of seeing into the future which frequently resulted in his making his sitters appear some twenty years older than they actually were when they had their portraits painted.

If Kokoschka's art, particularly his early portraits, reveals a tearing away of the surface of an individual to expose the raw psyche beneath, his dramas offer a world of archetypes rather than of individuals. Yet such a distinction between his work in both media is superficial since he externalized the anxieties and fears of an individual in one medium (painting) and of a culture in another (plays), but "from both he tore away the mask and discovered his own obsessions underneath."[41]

The key to this process of penetrating beneath the surface is Kokoschka's visual imagination, evident in both his pictorial and dramatic works. While much critical attention has been focused on the visual elements of his paintings and graphics, there have been few detailed examinations of the visual elements of Kokoschka's dramatic works—although critics have perceived their significance: "Kokoschka's pictorial and poetic works derive from a single artistic source; the same spiritual process in which image and word carry the same expressive weight, unlock the same world and come together to form a unity."[42] Among the earliest reviewers of Kokoschka's plays, one, aside from objecting on moral grounds to their eroticism, dismissed his dramas as mere "screaming images" (schreiende Bilder).[43] Another noted with reservation that "he works from a painterly conception." A third exclaimed, "wonderful, but only in the way it's staged."[44] And others referred to the plays as "hybrid[s] of words and images,"[45] or as "verbally supported pantomime."[46]

Nevertheless, in studies of Kokoschka, the artist and the dramatist have been kept distinct, which suggests a division within his *oeuvre* and distorts the relationship between his paintings, graphic works, and plays. The most important studies of Kokoschka's visual work[47] make little mention of his dramas other than to cite them as the "curious by-products of a great painter."[48] Even Hans Maria Wingler, who, as the editor of Kokoschka's writings, is conversant with his career as a dramatist, pinpoints few relationships between his plays and paintings.

This one-sided approach is also true of the few attempts to examine Kokoschka's dramatic works from a literary perspective. Even though several critics have noted the unity between Kokoschka's literary and visual works, none have advanced the detailed analyses necessary to prove the relationship.[49] In criticism of *Murderer Hope of Women,* in particular, the focus is on his role as innovator and as an originator of German Expressionist drama, rather than on the play's visual aspects.[50] Because of this focus, there has been a paucity of secondary literature devoted to *Job* (1917), and especially *Orpheus and Eurydice* (1918) and *Comenius* (1936–38, 1972), three plays in which Kokoschka can be viewed within the Expressionist framework least successfully, but in which he remains eminently fascinating as a visual dramatist.

The reluctance to make connections between the work of Kokoschka the dramatist and Kokoschka the visual artist is an indication of the scepticism with which the parallels between the arts have been considered until recently. René Wellek in his and Austin Warren's influential *Theory of Literature,* for example, states that "the various arts—the plastic arts, literature and music—have each their individual evolution, with a different tempo and a different internal structure of elements." He concludes that "the artist does not conceive in general mental terms" and the parallels that are drawn between them usually "amount to the assertion that this picture or poem induces the same mood in me."[51] Even in the case of "double talents" (*Doppelbegabungen*), Wellek argues that there is no reason to assume significant analogies between a single artist's productions in different media:

> The comparison of the poetry and the paintings of Blake or of Rossetti, will show that the character—not merely the technical quality—of their painting and poetry is very different, even divergent. A grotesque little animal is supposed to illustrate "Tyger! Tyger! burning bright." Thackeray illustrated *Vanity Fair* himself, but his smirky caricature of Becky Sharp has hardly anything to do with the complex character in the novel.[52]

This assertion about the division between art forms is at variance with both the theory and the practice of an artistic movement such as Expressionism. Expressionists sought to emphasize the visionary character of their creations and minimized the distinction between subjective perception and objective reality. Therefore, a change of medium need not imply a change in the character of the art. That such outstanding figures as Ernst Barlach, Wassily Kandinsky, Paul Klee, Oskar Kokoschka, Alfred Kubin, and Arnold Schoenberg all practiced, to varying degrees, more than one art form illustrates that the Expressionist artist's technical and formal concerns were subordinated to the intensity of the artistic drive.

Kandinsky observed in his essay "Concerning the Spiritual in Art" that "form is the external expression of inner meaning."[53] If the artist is the "hand which, by playing this or that key purposely vibrates the human soul," then to change the artistic medium is no more than a "change of instrument . . . because the force that drives [the artist] to . . . work remains the same, namely an internal pressure."[54]

Consequently, the plays of Kokoschka are worthy

of critical attention not only as dramatic texts but because their visual images are central to all his plays, suggesting an important link with his work in the visual arts. Clearly, "painter and poet are an indivisible unity in Kokoschka. Just as in his paintings there is always something poetically lyrical, or more properly dramatic, so in his poetic work there is much that is pictorial. Word and visual expression are united and rendered inseparable."[55]

Kokoschka's career began in rebellion and amid critics' distaste. His art, however, continued to develop after he left Vienna in 1909. Although his plays continued to incite riots whenever they were performed, he was gradually accorded the status of a young master. As one German critic wrote upon first seeing his work in 1912, "Kokoschka, a most original young man, is the first Viennese painter in whom one can say there is genius. . . . possibly Germany has seen nothing so wild and fantastic since the death of Grünewald."[56]

In 1911, after the period of his "black portraits," Kokoschka returned from Berlin to Vienna. The result was a stylistic beginning nearly as dramatic as the earlier break with the *Jugendstil*. A calm entered his work, evident both in the religious subjects he chose to paint and in the increased use of light and delicate texture in his canvases. His second play, *The Burning Bush,* with its theme of reconciliation and harmony, written in the same year, contrasts with the brutal violence of *Murderer Hope of Women* in a way that parallels the stylistic changes in his paintings and graphic works. In the works of 1911 and 1912, the jagged lines change to a new emphasis on a modeled whole and on the uses of light.

His later work was to show the influences of the major events of his life. In 1914 the tumultuous relationship between Kokoschka and Alma Mahler, his mistress since 1912, came to an end. His resultant inner crisis is apparent in the renewed emotional intensity of his works of that period, such as the painting *The Tempest (Die Windsbraut)* and the graphic work *The Bach Cantata (O Ewigkeit, Du Donnerwort)*, which deal explicitly with the unhappy fate of that love affair.

Following the First World War, in which he was seriously wounded while serving with the Austro-Hungarian army in 1915, Kokoschka convalesced in Dresden. There he completed his third play, *Job*, in 1917, a grotesque tragicomedy which reveals his disillusionment and despair over his relationship with the opposite sex. The sardonic humor with which these emotions are expressed is also apparent in the illustrations for the play and in his other graphic work at the time.

Still haunted by his affair with Alma Mahler, he returned to the theme of the relations between the sexes in his fourth play, *Orpheus and Eurydice,* in 1918. He also made etchings and an oil painting on the same theme, demonstrating both its obsessive hold over him and, once more, the intimate connections between the literary and the visual in his work.

After this last attempt to come to terms with the past, the emotional necessity to write for the stage was gone. Kokoschka did not complete another play for over fifty years. His break with the past is commemorated in the painting *The Woman in Blue* of 1919, a portrait of a life-size doll, modeled according to his ex-mistress's measurements, which he obtained from her dressmaker. In this work, the tortured brushstrokes of the 1917 and 1918 convases, with their writhing, worm-like forms are replaced by large, bright color patches, a technique well suited to the many landscapes to which Kokoschka then turned his attention in the wide-ranging travels which absorbed him until 1934.

In 1934, Kokoschka moved to Prague. There, in the homeland of Jan Amos Comenius, he rekindled a life-long interest in the seventeenth-century Czech peda-gogue, theologian, and author of the *Orbis Pictus.* A commissioned portrait of President Thomas G. Masaryk of Czechoslovakia, in which Comenius appears, was the first of many such symbolic or allegorical paintings. Immediately following this work in 1936, Kokoschka began another drama, *Comenius,* a political play, never finished, about the life and sufferings of Comenius, with allegorical references to the horrors of Nazi Germany.

In 1938, just before the Nazi invasion of Czechoslovakia, Kokoschka fled Prague for London. There he continued to work on *Comenius,* while painting works in his allegorical style for the remainder of the war years. After the war the dramatic impulse in his work is to be found in large, mythical-historical canvases such as his *Prometheus-Saga* (1950) or *Thermopylae* (1956) triptychs, rather than in works for the stage.

However, in 1972, at the age of eighty-six, Kokoschka rewrote his earlier play about the life of Comenius, now emphasizing the martyrdom of the humanist rather than political allegory. His continuing interest in history is also evident in paintings such as *Herodotus* (1960–63). Both the later *Comenius* and Kokoschka's late paintings share a calm monumentality, strongly different from his earlier work, which, while constantly changing in style, maintains a sense of agitated intensity.

Kokoschka's artistic development, then, moves from the extraordinary energy and iconoclasm of the early plays and paintings toward the somber humanism discovered in *Comenius* and in his essays and late paintings. Throughout his long and spectacular career, however, despite constant change, the cross-fertilization between word and image never ceased. It was far stronger than an occasional overlapping of particular stylistic traits or even a common use of symbols. His plays, paintings, and graphics are all expressions of a single language, a language of images.

1. The Tower and the Cage
Murderer Hope of Women

But occasionally the intensity of the vision of its own ecstasies or horrors, combined with a mastery of word and rhythm, may give to a juvenile work a universality which is beyond the author's knowledge of life to give, and to which mature men and women can respond.

T. S. Eliot
"Cyril Tourneur"

On July 4, 1909, Oskar Kokoschka produced *Murderer Hope of Women* at a small outdoor theater in Vienna, close to the Kunstschau, an exhibition of contemporary Viennese art to which he had contributed a number of paintings.[1] Permission for the twenty-two-year-old student to produce his play was granted by the Kunstschau authorities on provision that there be no cost to the management. The play attracted a full house, both because of the notoriety the young student had attracted with his *Self-Portrait as Warrior* at the previous year's Kunstschau and because of the strange poster he had designed as the play's advertisement: a flayed, bloody body of a dead man held in the lap of a death-like woman with black hair, chalky skin, cavernous eyes, bared teeth, and blood-red lips (Fig. 1).

The actors Kokoschka chose for the performance were drama students. As there was no money for costumes, they were dressed in rags and bits of cloth. Inspired by South Sea masks which he had seen in the ethnology museum in Vienna as a child, Kokoschka painted the actors' faces to suggest extreme expressions of horror, grief, surprise, and fear. Upon their arms and legs he painted nerves, veins, and muscles. As there was no prepared script, the lines were distributed to the actors on scraps of paper the evening before the performance; the playwright simply demon-

strated to them the intonation, rhythms, and gestures with which the lines were to be delivered. To accompany the action, an "orchestra" of drums, pipes, clarinets, and a pair of cymbals came from a nearby cafe.

As the first performance began, a troop of Bosnian soldiers stationed nearby gathered along the balcony overlooking the stage. They watched as two groups of actors with masklike faces approached one another slowly, some carrying torches. Suddenly a tall blonde woman in red was seized by a group of men, her costume torn open, and her flesh branded. Pounding drumbeats and shrill pipes accompanied this action, while the audience began to scream and jeer at the actors, and then to push and shove among themselves. At this point, the soldiers left the balcony, entered the audience, and began fighting with the crowd in the aisles. Order was finally restored by the police.

Kokoschka, the young playwright responsible for this mayhem, would certainly have been arrested had not two reknowned men, Adolf Loos and Karl Kraus, been present to speak in his behalf. However, as a result of the fracas, the young "scourge of the bourgeoisie" (*Bürgerschreck*, a name given Kokoschka by Viennese critics at the Kunstschau of 1909), was asked to leave the School for Arts and Crafts. Soon after, under the patronage of Loos, Kokoschka left Vienna

Fig. 10. Title page of *Der Sturm,* July 14, 1910, with illustration to *Murderer Hope of Women,* line-block and letter-press, 15 × 11¼ in. (38.2 × 28.5 cm.). Courtesy Count Reinhold Bethusy-Huc, Vienna, and The Stedelijk Museum, Amsterdam.

Zeichnung von Oskar Kokoschka zu dem Drama
Mörder, Hoffnung der Frauen

for Berlin, where he became a regular contributor to Herwarth Walden's avant-garde periodical *Der Sturm*.[2]

His play, with the first of what would later be four illustrations, was published in *Der Sturm* on July 14, 1910.[3] Between 1907 and 1917, Kokoschka wrote four versions of it.[4] The text of the final version was only six-and-a-half pages long.[5]

Murderer Hope of Women has only a single scene without division; two characters, "Man" and "Woman"; and a chorus of men and women, called "Warriors" and "Maidens." The time is given simply as "Antiquity." The scenery consists of a tower with a large iron cage door set against the backdrop which, in both the 1909 Kunstschau debacle and in the 1917 production (see Fig. 11) at the Albert-Theater in Dresden, was painted by Kokoschka himself. (In the latter performance, the backdrop depicted the sun emerging from behind clouds to eclipse the moon. On the right, a sea was painted; on the left, two towerlike structures.) The setting is dark, lit only by the torches of the Warriors; the black stage floor is raked upward toward the tower.

The action begins with the Man, with a white face, a bandage covering a wound on his forehead, and dressed in blue armor, entering in the company of his Warriors, who are trying to restrain him. They carry their torches high and are shouting loudly. As the Man breaks free from them, they utter a cry which grows increasingly highpitched, and chant: "We were the flaming wheel around him, We were the flaming wheel around you, assailant of locked fortresses!" The Maidens enter with their leader, the Woman, from stage left. The Woman is tall with long blonde hair, and is dressed in red. She asserts her sexual power: "My eye collects the jubilation of the men, their stammering lust prowls around me like a beast." She demands to see the Man. As they meet, however, the Woman grows frightened and the Man seems dazed and confused.

The chorus inflames their sexual passion, and the Woman confesses her desire for, yet fear of, the Man. Suddenly the Man awakens from his lethargy and orders the Warriors to brand her with his sign. They do. She shrieks in pain from the wounding, but manages to free herself and stab the Man in the side with a knife. The semi-conscious Man is carried on a bier by several Warriors into the barred cage within the tower, his bleeding wound visible.[6] The Warriors then leave him and go off to join their companions, who are now lying on the floor with the Maidens enjoying themselves at the right of the stage.

Except for a faint light, it is now dark on stage. The Woman, alone, crawls in a circle around the stage, threatening and taunting the wounded Man, desperately trying to reach him. Gradually he stirs, dragging himself up one hand at a time. As he recovers, the Woman grows weaker, yet continues her furious verbal assault. The Man regains his full strength; the Woman, now drooping, drapes her body upon him, separated by the bars of the cage. She slowly slides to the floor as the Man, now erect, wipes his eyes and throws open the door. He touches her outstretched hand with his own; she falls, utters a slowly dying scream, and knocks a torch from the hands of an old Warrior who has remained beside the cage, showering the entire stage with sparks. The Man now emerges from the cage and stands above the men and women of the chorus, who flee from him in terror as the tower suddenly blazes behind him. He slaughters them all, and rushes off through the fire. In the distance a cock crows.

Kokoschka's first play depicts the sexual war between man and woman in the simplest possible terms. Recently an adolescent himself, the young author still viewed the opposite sex with an uncertain mixture of curiosity, fear, and lust: "I was now an adult in every

33

sense, and different from before, but my curiosity remained unassuaged. An inner voice tormented me, like a hermit in the wilderness, with imaginings about the female sex."[7]

Kokoschka said of his first play, "It was just what I had dreamed about women when I was younger. . . . I am the stronger! I wouldn't be swallowed by her."[8] That Kokoschka should compare the writing of *Murderer Hope of Women* with a dream is hardly accidental, since its effect is closer to witnessing a dream than to viewing a theatrical action. Rather than a realistic portrayal of a conflict between two individuals, the play is a symbolic battle between elemental urges. Indeed, "the people in his dramas are as majestic and simple as the colossus of a mountain, and as natural as a landscape."[9] Since such archetypal figures do not converse in lucid discourse, the language of Kokoschka's play is primarily sentence fragments, exclamations, and screams. The author portrays a world of irrational violence; thus his characters do not act logically. For example, suddenly, without motivation, the Man awakens from his lassitude and orders the warriors to brand the Woman. Later, after her retaliation and his imprisonment, he regains his strength and kills her by touching her outstretched hand with his fingers.[10] Nothing prepares the audience for any of these actions or explains them; they happen with the spontaneity of a dream.

Fundamentally a demonstration of the love-hate between the sexes, "the quarrel [which] is incomprehensible and lasts an eternity," *Murderer Hope of Women* explodes on the stage with all the violence of a chemical reaction: "Man and Woman crash against one another solely because irreconcilable opposition is inherent in their sexual natures. Just as salt and base react, must react to one another, so they search for and flee from, unite and decompose from, one another."[11] The conflict between the Man and the Woman may be seen as an allegory in the manner of a medieval morality play in which the Man represents the spirit and the Woman the body. The Man's dazed condition when he is first confronted by the Woman ("what did the shadows say?") reveals the weakness and lassitude of the spirit in the face of the temptations of the body. Attempting to lift himself out of his torpor, the Man tries to assert his superiority over the Woman by branding her, but instead he sinks back even further into weakness and despair as he is wounded by her in turn. This shift from false potency to exhaustion and despair is mirrored by a shift in the Man's language from command ("My men, now brand her with my sign, hot iron into her red flesh!") to a lyrical monologue which is sung: "Senseless craving from horror to horror, unappeasable rotation in the void. Birth pangs without birth, hurtling down of the sun, quaking of space. The end of those who praised me. Oh, your unmerciful word."

The depression into which the Man falls suggests a martyrdom of the spirit which is conveyed by allusions to the betrayal and crucifixion of Christ. Thus, after the Man receives the knife wound in his side (reminiscent of the spearing of Christ by the soldier in John 19:34), he is betrayed by his companions ("we do not know him"), reminiscent of Peter's denial of Christ in Matthew 26:74, which, like that of the Warriors, is also followed by a cock crowing. Even as the Man sinks to his lowest level of strength, his subsequent rebirth is foreshadowed by the analogies with Christ. The cock crow which echoes the Man's betrayal by his companions also points to the resurrection of the spirit at the end of the play.

Having almost caused the death of the Man after his assault on her, the Woman grows helpless without him. On one hand, the body seeks the imprisonment of the spirit. On the other, the body is dependent on the spirit for its sustenance ("open the gate; I must be with him"). Finally, as she grows more helpless, he opens the door to the cage, and the reborn spirit triumphs over the now enfeebled body. After killing the Woman and the chorus, the victorious Man rushes from the burning stage as the cock crows a third time, signaling his victory, symbolized by the dawn of the new day.

Murderer Hope of Women may be seen as an illustration of the view of Austrian philosopher Otto Weininger, who believed that the polarity between sexes is a battle between a higher, spiritual essence ("Factor Man") and a lower, animal essence ("Factor Woman"). Such an interpretation sees the play's culmination in the male's dominance over the female as the triumph of the spirit over sexuality.[12]

However, interpretation of Kokoschka's first play is not only dependent on a reading of the text but also on which text is used. In the *Sturm* version (1910) emphasis is placed upon the dominance and ultimate triumph of the Man. This focus is particularly evident when the animal imagery with which the Woman is associated in that version is examined: "She creeps round the cage like a panther . . . hissing maliciously like an adder. . . . Woman covers him entirely with her body; separated by the grille, to which she clings high up in the air like a monkey . . . writhes on the steps like a dying animal, her thighs and muscles convulsed." In the final version (1917) these animal images are eliminated: "Woman covers him entirely with her body; separated by the grille, slowly closes the gate." There is thus a greater sense of ambiguity about the outcome, suggesting that man and woman are both puppets in a struggle which leads ultimately to chaos, symbolized by the burning stage, from which nothing escapes.

The tendency toward the greater ambiguity of the last version is illustrated by a comparison of the final stage directions in all four versions which describe the

Man as he leaves the fiery stage at the end of the play. In the two earliest versions, the Man strides off in victory. He "goes forth red," the color red identified with life in Kokoschka's *oeuvre*. In the third version (1916), the Man hurries "like the morning" through the blaze, whereas in the final version he flees from the stage: "The Man hurries off, through the path of fire." Thus, "hurries off" suggests terror and uncertainty rather than triumph.[13] Given these variations among the different versions of the play, added to the uncertainty surrounding the dreamlike actions themselves, it becomes clear that an unambiguous interpretation of the play is not possible. Yet *Murderer Hope of Women* conveys with power the mutual attraction and repulsion of the sexes:

> There were no thoughts or feelings depicted, but the word-pictures and sound-rhythms conveyed thoughts and feelings in a mysterious way, revealed the world of destructive powers. . . . This poetry operates as a self-consuming lust with a power hardly rivalled by that of any of its contemporaries. The unmasking of pure sexuality in its hellish lust has here come to pass.[14]

The hostile response to the play when it was performed in 1917 along with two other of Kokoschka's plays, *The Burning Bush* and *Job,* is revealing. Even an audience familiar with the innovations of August Strindberg and the German Expressionists found Kokoschka's visual conception of drama shocking. "The word has become an accessory; screams, spectacle and images predominate," the influential critic Bernhard Diebold wrote in a review in the *Frankfurter Zeitung*.[15] In his book *Anarchy in Drama*, the same critic used the expression "screaming images" to attack visually oriented theater, and *Murderer Hope of Women* in particular:

> Far more significant than the mere renunciation of the word out of the inability to articulate emotion is the pretentious Decoration Drama that without characters, with-

out language, and even without a clear direction simply offers screaming images to the public to interpret.[16]

Robert Breuer, commenting upon the same performance for *Die Schaubühne*, was more enthusiastic about the play's visual aspects, but had reservations concerning the reduced role of language: "the words, which were simultaneously spoken, are remembered only as the subtitles under extremely powerful images. . . . he works from a painterly conception, and when he writes prose or verse, changes the medium, but not the perspective, from which he conceives the world."[17] The playwright Paul Kornfeld, who wrote the program notes for the same performance in Dresden, was the most excited critic, judging Kokoschka's plays not by conventional literary standards but as a revolutionary breakthrough in the conception of theater: "We suspect a new possibility in style, perhaps even a new art form, which comes closest to that of opera: verbally supported pantomime."[18] Clearly, these critical responses to the first public performances, after the 1909 debacle in Vienna, reveal, in their extremes of condemnation and enthusiasm, just how profoundly original Kokoschka's visual conception of the theater was.

Even before a single word is spoken, the audience is barraged by colors, lights, noises, screams, gestures, and movements. The stage directions indicate:

> Night sky. Tower with large red iron grille as door; torches the only light; black ground, rising to the tower in such a way that all the figures appear in relief.

> The Man in blue armor, white face, kerchief covering a wound, with a crowd of men—savage in appearance, gray-and-red kerchiefs, white-black-and-brown clothes, signs on their clothes, bare legs, long-handled torches, bells, din.

The actor's painted faces and bodies add to the effect of total visual spectacle. The dominant stage image in *Murderer Hope of Women* is the tower with its enormous cage door (Fig. 11), and so vital is it to Kokoschka's overall conception that the play may well be considered as the sum of the metamorphoses of this image. It can therefore hardly have been accidental that Kokoschka insisted in the stage directions that the stage floor should be raked upward toward the tower, emphasizing its importance.

This central image is made up of fused opposing elements: the tower as a phallic symbol and the cage as a vaginal symbol. The first part of the play culminates with the Man being carried semi-conscious into the cage, an action reinforcing his "defeat" by the Woman in visual terms. As she grows weaker because of his absence, the Man regains his strength and rises within the cage, with the Woman draping her body over his, although separated by the iron bars. The image becomes a metaphor for the paradox around which the play has been constructed: the sexes are mutually attracted to one another, but also need to dominate and to destroy each other. As the Woman drapes her body over the Man's, a rare equilibrium has been achieved between the rising Man and the falling Woman. Even now, however, the bars which separate them indicate the impossibility of real union between the sexes. The next moment, the cage door is opened, but the balance that has precariously existed for an instant is gone. The Man murders the Woman and, as she falls, she sets fire to the object which has been the visual representation of the entire conflict: "The flames catch hold of the tower and tear it apart from the bottom to the top." Thus Kokoschka's vision of the conflict between the sexes, from the imprisonment of Man to his liberation and triumph, is reflected in the manipulation of the tower, the central stage image.

In addition to using stage images, Kokoschka also employs color to suggest visually the sexual conflict in the play. On a superficial level, opposition between the sexes is revealed through the colors red and blue: the Woman's costume, red, the color of blood, and a traditional representation for the flesh; and the Man's armor, blue, the color of the sky, likewise a familiar representation for the spirit. In the early versions of the play the color symbolism was even more specific: the cage door was to be painted red, and when Man was imprisoned, the stage directions specify that the stage was to be dark except for a faint blue light shining within the cage. It is probable that the tendency toward greater ambiguity in the final versions of the play necessitated the elimination of this obvious use of color.

But the color symbolism in all versions of the play operates at a more subtle level as well. In the opening stage directions, the Man's face is described as white. From the beginning of the play until after his imprisonment, the Man is associated with whiteness and paleness: "Lead us, pale one! . . . Who is the pallid man? . . . He is completely white. . . . He is pale as a corpse." However, toward the conclusion, as the Man grows stronger and the Woman weaker, it is she, previously associated with the color red, who is described as "completely white." In the original version, this transference of colors was made explicit by the stage directions which state that, at the end of the play, the Man "leaves red behind."

For Kokoschka, red is the color of life and white that of death.[19] The transference of colors on stage suggests that the war between the sexes is a continual movement from death to life and from life to death, a state of perpetual vampirism which is explicitly suggested by the dialogue in the *Sturm* version:

m1n: Who suckles me with blood? I devour your melting flesh.
wom1n: I will not let you live, you vampire, piecemeal you feed on me, weaken me.

Fig. 11. Kokoschka's stage design for *Murderer Hope of Women*, Albert-Theater, Dresden, 1917. Photograph from *Die Neue Bühne,* ed. Hugo Zehder (Dresden: Rudolf Kaemmerer Verlag, 1920).

Kokoschka also depicts the conflict between the sexes as a symbolic struggle between light and dark. The Woman, who is associated with night, darkness, and the moon, is clearly ascendant as she enters the darkened stage, and her power eclipses that of the Man, who is associated with day, light and the sun: "With my breath I fan the yellow disc of the sun." Conversely, the Man is introduced in the past tense by his chanting, torch-bearing Warriors (who represent the rays of the sun), suggesting the absence of light at the beginning of the play: "We were the flaming wheel around him."

As the play opens, the stage is illumined only by the torches of the Warriors. When the Man is stabbed, imprisoned, and betrayed by them, it grows even darker until it is black except for a faint light within the cage. As the Woman is attracted to the Man, the cock crows and it begins to grow light in the background, suggesting the eventual return of light and the growing ascendancy of the Man, emphasized by the painted backdrop for the 1917 performance in which the sun is depicted as eclipsing the moon (see Fig. 11).

As the Man gains his release from the cage, his words emphasize the correspondence between the sexual polarity and the symbolic use of light and dark: "Stars and Woman! Dream or awake, I saw a singing creature brightly shine. Breathing, dark things become clear to me." Moments later he sees "a span of timid light," while the Woman pleads desperately for a return to night: "Man, sleep with me." As the Man flees the burning stage, the cock crows for a third time, promising the return of daylight to the darkened world. As in two later plays by Kokoschka, *The Burning Bush* and *Orpheus and Eurydice*, the flames which engulf the stage at the play's end are intended both as a symbol for the self-destructive passion between the sexes and as a means of purging that passion in preparation for the spiritual dawn which will follow the night of sexual torment.

The poster (Fig. 1) which Kokoschka executed in 1908 to advertise the first performance of his play in Vienna not only employs the same subject matter as the play, but echoes its violent style and symbolism as well. Depicted is the chalkwhite figure of the Woman holding the scarlet body of the dead Man in her arms, while behind them, against a dark blue background, the sun and moon shine simultaneously.

This grotesque Pietà is the visual equivalent of the central paradox set forth in Kokoschka's play: the living Woman holds the body of the dead Man in her arms, yet it is she who is painted in white, the color of death, while the dead Man is painted in red, the color symbolizing life for the artist. Through this apparent reversal of the play's color symbolism, Kokoschka suggests both the Woman's sexual power over the Man and her lifelessness without him.

Such is the bitter nature of the sexual conflict for Kokoschka, which offers a basis for the interpretation of the ambiguous title of the play: the Man, bearer of the spirit, is enslaved by the body, while the Woman who possesses him can only be redeemed by the spiritual powers contained within the Man—which she herself is instrumental in suppressing. As the title of the play suggests, the Woman's only "hope" is to be "murdered" and thus spiritually redeemed by the Man. If this interpretation is weighted towards the spirit-matter duality which is dominant in the *Sturm* version, it is justifiable since Kokoschka conceived of the title with this earliest version in mind. Further, the only reference to the word *hope* in the play follows a meeting between the Man and the Woman in which she feels captivated by his devouring light, which nonetheless fills her with renewed life: "Why do you bind me, man, with your gaze? Ravening light, you confound my flame! Devouring life overpowers me. Oh, take away my terrible hope." Man is both a murderer and a bearer of hope for woman, since the act of physical destruction is also an act of spiritual liberation.[20]

That the conflict is tragic for both man and woman is suggested in the poster, just as in the play it is indicated by the allusion to the martyrdom of Christ implicit in the Pietà. The light and dark symbolism of the play is also conveyed in the poster by means of the simultaneous presence of the sun and moon, suggesting the solar-lunar conflict between male and female forces struggling for supremacy.

Like the poster, the illustrations (see Figs. 10, 12–14) which Kokoschka produced for his play (and which were also published weekly in *Der Sturm* in July 1910[21]) do not merely "illustrate" individual moments of the action, but seek to re-create its essence in graphic terms. The primitive violence of the play is suggested by means of the networks of spiky lines which radiate outwards from the figures of the Man and Woman, naked from the waist up, who are engaged in scenes of primitive combat. In addition to these lines of force, Kokoschka drew muscles and veins upon the bodies of the figures themselves, as he did in his production of the play. As he later said, "I wanted, in fact, to turn the figures [of the actors] inside out, to make the inner man visible, and did exactly the same in the illustrations to the play."[22] The effect of all these jagged, intersecting lines is to create the impression of fierce, uncontrolled energy which appears both to emanate from, and to engulf, the struggling participants themselves: "In the filigreed net of woven lines there are trapped demons who are threatening—Kokoschka has cast the net masterfully, and the lament of the demons, like tormented souls, is terrifying."[23]

In addition to drawing on the skin of his figures in both media, Kokoschka, in the illustrations to the play, also attempted to create elemental types rather than individuals. However, instead of basing his designs on South Sea masks, as he did with the makeup for the actors in his play, Kokoschka stripped all excess flesh from his figures, leaving their faces mere skulls with horribly gaping eyes and mouths.[24] These elemental forces are further distorted by the combining of profile and full face, giving them an even more barbarous, subhuman aspect.

In the first of the illustrations (see Fig. 10), which was published in the same issue of *Der Sturm* as the text of *Murderer Hope of Women*, the Man is shown attacking the fallen Woman with a knife, his right hand pressed down upon her grimacing mouth, his foot planted beneath her breast. She lies with all her weight on one elbow, one flailing hand drawing attention to the stylized, rootlike design which Kokoschka has used to accentuate the Man's genitals. In the background, three figures, also with skull-like heads, watch from underneath a curtain and serve a function analogous to that of the chorus in the play. In the upper lefthand corner, a strange chimerical doglike creature, not mentioned in the play, laps up a pool of blood which heightens the scene of bestial violence in the foreground.

In the second drawing (Fig. 12), the Man and Woman are depicted within a barred structure analogous to the cage in the play. The Woman wears an expression of sadness, conveyed by the slanting lines over her eyes, and although she touches the wound on the Man's chest precisely as in the *Sturm* version ("Woman slides her arm through the bars and prods his wound"), she does not appear as violent as she does at the same point in *Murderer Hope of Women*. Similarly, while at this point in the play the Man is at his lowest ebb, in the drawing he appears in full pos-

Fig. 13. Illustration to *Murderer Hope of Women, Der Sturm*, 1910, wash drawing in India ink, 9½ × 7⅓ in. (24.7 × 18.2 cm.). Courtesy Count Reinhold Bethusy-Huc, Vienna, and The Stedelijk Museum, Amsterdam.

Fig 12. Illustration to *Murderer Hope of Women, Der Sturm*, 1910, wash drawing in India ink, 10 × 7 in. (26 × 19 cm.). Courtesy Count Reinhold Bethusy-Huc, Vienna, and The Stedelijk Museum, Amsterdam.

Fig. 15. *Running Amuck*, 1907–8, gouache, 9 × 6⅓ in. (23 × 16.5 cm.). Collection Museum für Kunst und Gewerbe, Hamburg. Photograph from *Oskar Kokoschka* [catalogue] (New York: Marlborough-Gerson Gallery Inc., Oct.–Nov. 1966).

Fig. 14. *Sacred and Profane Love,* fourth illustration to *Murderer Hope of Women, Der Sturm,* 1910, wash drawing in India ink, 11 × 11 in. (29 × 27 cm.). Courtesy Count Reinhold Bethusy-Huc, Vienna, and The Stedelijk Museum, Amsterdam.

41

session of his powers, leering down at the Woman through clenched teeth, while grabbing her wrist with one hand and clutching a knife in the other. Between the two protagonists is the form of the hyenalike creature of the previous drawing.

In the third illustration (Fig. 13) the couple is seen wrestling, as in the first drawing. The Woman, with enormous head and powerful neck, is shown being crushed beneath the Man, and looking up at him with clenched teeth from the level of his chest. She continues to resist his onslaught, and, with an outsized left arm, attempts to pin back his smaller right one. In this drawing, the figures are also marked by veins and sinews, and, as in the poster, sun and moon are shining simultaneously, heightening the tension and mirroring the human struggle in cosmic terms.

The fourth illustration has a separate title, *Sacred and Profane Love* (Fig. 14), suggesting a reference to the Titian painting and reinforcing the interpretation of the play as a dialectic struggle between spirit (Man) and matter (Woman). In this drawing the battle continues, but even though the Woman beside the Man is now erect, it is clear that he is ascendant. The Woman's expression, with her eyes raised upward, now is one of supplication, and the curved position of her left hand suggests a futile effort to embrace a lover rather than to destroy him. By contrast, the Man's expression remains fierce and is heightened by the cruelty of the mouth. His right arm is held aloft and poised to strike another blow. Were there any doubt remaining of the Man's victory, it would be dispelled by the fact that in the upper lefthand corner the sun surges upward with lines of force emanating from it, giving the impression of an erect phallus, while the moon is now no longer visible. Although not an attempt to depict a specific moment from the play, this illustration reveals the shift of power from the Woman to the Man and foreshad-

ows the Woman's demise. Each of the illustrations portrays a different point in the violent struggle. Together, they demonstrate the pattern of rise and fall that is discernible in the play, which opens with a shrill, high-pitched scream and closes with a dying cry.

The link between Kokoschka's play and his visual works is not only evident in the works inspired by *Murderer Hope of Women*. In the gouache *Running Amuck* (Fig. 15), executed in 1907–1908, a horribly grimacing man, encircled by flames, races down a street. In the one hand, he holds a dagger; in the other, a flaming torch. The arm that is bared reveals a tattoo with the initials OK and LL, the former referring to the artist, the latter to Lilith, the young Swedish girl he loved at the time and who also inspired his early poem about adolescent sexuality, *The Dreaming Youths*. In the background stand panic-stricken men and women, one of whom—evidently the possessed man's victim—is naked. In its subject matter (the violent conflict between the sexes) and in its symbolism (the fiery street, the torches, and the rising sun in the background), *Running Amuck* has much in common with the world of Kokoschka's play, although its style is more eclectic than that of either the illustrations or the poster, and still reveals Kokoschka's early interest in the Japanese print.

Another work of this period, done slightly later, in the summer of 1908, and exhibited to widespread outrage at the 1908 Kunstschau, shows Kokoschka capable of expressing the violent, destructive fury of his play in a visual style all his own. The work, the previously mentioned polychrome clay bust *Self Portrait as Warrior* (see Fig. 6), reveals the face of a man much older than the twenty-one-year-old artist. The face is distorted with bumps and hollows and the mouth is agape with an impassioned cry similar to the faces of the actors in his first play. With its sunken eyes, blue-veined cheeks, and hostile yet terrified expression, it conveys the same mixture of confusion, fear, and brutality as the Man (also a "Warrior") in *Murderer Hope of Women.*

The oil paintings which Kokoschka executed at about the same time (1908–10) have often been described as examples of psychological portraiture. This evaluation places them at a great distance from the elemental types which appear in *Murderer Hope of Women.* However, none of the "black portraits," as the artist himself called them, are merely psychological studies. Rather, these paintings are lyrical transcriptions of emotions which reside within the artist himself and for which the subject forms only the raw material or "poetic possibility" of the painter's visionary response.[25]

"Interior portraiture" is described by Kokoschka in a chapter on his early paintings in his autobiography:

> When I paint a portrait, I am not concerned with the externals of a person—the signs of his clerical or secular eminence, or his social origins. . . . What used to shock people in my portraits was that I tried to intuit from the face, from its play of expressions, and from gestures, the truth about a person, and to recreate in my own pictorial language the distillation of a living being that would survive in my memory. . . . In a face I look for the flash of an eye, the tiny shift of expression which betrays an inner movement.[26]

Of the controversial early portraits, Kokoschka said that "for me it was just natural, I made them [his subjects] like they really were . . . the face of a man or woman—I saw the death already. I always see the death."[27] For this reason, in one of his earliest oil paintings, *Father Hirsch* (1907) (Fig. 16), Kokoschka reproduces not the external likeness of an old man but rather the essence of what lies beneath. The face has the appearance of a crumbling mask: lusterless eyes have sunken deep into two cavernous pits, the false teeth seem about to drop from the mouth, and on the gnarled bony hands there are greenish streaks of de-

composition. The man's flesh is only a thin covering for the real subject of the painting: the imminence of death. *Father Hirsch* is not so much a psychological study of a living person as a corpse into which life has, for an instant, been breathed.

A famous example of the artist's "second sight," by which he seemed to see into the future of his subjects, is his portrait of the noted biologist and entomologist Auguste Forel (Fig. 17). Kokoschka's completed portrait of Forel looked older and more haggard than its model. Indeed, the sitter and his family indignantly refused to buy the finished work, with its drooping right eye and gnarled, twisted hands. Then, some months after the completion of the portrait, Forel suffered a serious stroke which paralyzed the right side of his body and gave his features the deep sadness revealed in Kokoschka's study.

Karl Kraus, who sat for several of Kokoshcka's works, gave a brilliant description of Kokoschka's method of visionary portraiture, however cryptic it may seem at first reading: "Kokoschka has done a portrait of me. It is quite possible that those who know me will not recognize me. But certainly those who do not know me will recognize me."[28]

During this period Kokoschka was almost exclusively engaged in commissioned portraits. There was only one painting, a double portrait of a man and a woman, in which he had the opportunity to explore on canvas his obsession with the conflict between the sexes in a way comparable to that which he had chosen in his first play. In 1909, just four months after the abortive performance of his play in Vienna, Kokoschka was asked to paint a portrait of the art historians Hans and Erika Tietze (see Fig. 2).

The bodies of Dr. Tietze and his wife are drawn at right angles to one another, so that the man is seen in profile and the woman in full face, creating a subtle

Fig. 16. *Father Hirsch*, 1907, oil on canvas, 27 × 27 in. (68 × 68 cm.). Collection Neue Galerie der Stadt Linz, Wolfgang Gurlitt Museum, Linz. Photograph by Franz Michalek.

Fig. 17. *Auguste Forel*, 1910, oil on canvas, 28 × 23 in. (70 × 58 cm.). Collection Städtische Kunsthalle, Mannheim.

tension between them. The woman stares straight ahead with a vacant but sad expression, while the man is more energetic, concentrating his view upon the meeting of their left hands and drawing the viewer's eyes to that point as well. The treatment of the hands is the most arresting part of the painting. Although the woman stares ahead as if in a trance, her left hand moves upward to meet the hands of her husband, which are moving anxiously toward hers. The hands are just at the point of making contact, yet fail to do so. In this striking pose, Kokoschka creates an image of combined attraction and repulsion that is comparable to the near contact of the bodies of the Man and Woman in *Murderer Hope of Women,* which are separated by the bars of the cage, or to the death of the Woman resulting from the mere touch of the Man in the same play. In the painting, the feeling of unrest and even potential violence in this confrontation is also suggested by the differences in the painter's execution of the hands: the man's hands are rough, gnarled, and suffused with harsh reddish tones; those of the woman are smooth, pale, and white, echoing the red and white color symbolism of the play.

The feeling of incipient conflict is further conveyed by Kokoschka's use of color in the painting. Reds, yellows, and angry orange tones behind the darkly clad figures suggest the fiery passion implicit in the sexual conflict, which has its parallel in the fire with which the play ends. Conflict is also suggested in the play by the countless tiny lines which radiate outward from the meeting hands like lines of force, identical to the techniques employed to accentuate the violence in Kokoschka's illustrations for his play. Some idea of the artist's involvement with the subject matter of the work, as well as his bizarre technique (reminiscent of Nell Walden's account of her portrait) is evident from a statement by Mrs. Tietze herself: "When Kokoschka began to paint, he worked with a brush; however, he soon gave it up and continued with his finger tips, scratching wondrous lines in the background with his fingernails."[29]

These networks of lines, which might easily be dismissed as meaningless scribbling, offer the key to the entire painting. Behind the man there is an exploding sun, while embedded in the extreme upper righthand corner on the canvas beside the woman is a moonlike crescent, thus forming the equivalent of Kokoschka's representation of the Man and the Woman in his play as elemental, antagonistic forces and offering explicit evidence of the relationship between his dramatic and pictorial art.[30]

In his portrait of the Tietzes, Kokoschka grafts the individual visage of his subjects onto a personal emotion which tends toward archetype. In the double portrait of the art historian and his wife there is the same explosive world of sexual conflict encountered in *Murderer Hope of Women,* providing a clear example of how Kokoschka's visual imagination in both media reveals an ideal instance of artistic interpenetration.

2. **Woman Redeemed**
The Burning Bush

And always, she was gone before he came. As he came, she drew away, as he drew away, she came. Were they never to meet? Gradually a low, deep-sounding will in him vibrated to her, tried to set her in accord, tried to bring her gradually to him, to a meeting, till they should be together, till they should meet as the sheaves that swished together.

D. H. Lawrence
The Rainbow

Kokoschka's second play, *The Burning Bush (Der brenn-ende Dornbusch),* was begun in Vienna in 1911 following his return from Berlin, where he had been working as a member of the editorial staff of *Der Sturm.* The premiere was planned for the evening of June 5, 1913. But for "unknown reasons," not entirely surprising in the light of the initial production of *Murderer Hope of Women* in 1909, the censor prohibited the performance of *Schauspiel (Spectacle),* as the play was then called.[1] Nevertheless, the play was published in the same year[2] and was finally performed, together with *Murderer Hope of Women* and *Job,* at the Albert-Theater in Dresden on June 3, 1917, in a revised version under its new title, *The Burning Bush* (Fig. 18).[3]

Like *Murderer Hope of Women, The Burning Bush* presents the subject of male-female relations as a continuous struggle leading to the death of one of the partners, although this time it is man who is killed by woman. In addition, as in the earlier play, Kokoschka uses types ("Man," "Woman," "Mother," "Boy") who often speak to one another in disconnected fragments. As in *Murderer Hope of Women* there is no plot in the conventional sense, and, although *The Burning Bush* is a much longer work, consisting of five scenes instead of one and covering twenty pages instead of six and

one-half, the scenes and events are not causally or chronologically linked.

Despite these similarities, the two works are quite different. In *Murderer Hope of Women,* Kokoschka set out to demonstrate the mutual destructiveness and polarity of the sexes. In *The Burning Bush* his purpose is to suggest how that polarity may be overcome. In the former work, Kokoschka's vision of the sexual conflict as a battle of irreconcilable forces ends in chaos; in the latter, the conflict is ultimately resolved, and the Man's murder is metamorphosed into a symbolic act of redemption for both man and woman.

Kokoschka's first play concluded with a blazing fire, symbolizing the destructiveness of male-female relations. But in the very title of his second play, *The Burning Bush,* Kokoschka suggests the motif of redemption through the biblical allusion (Exodus 3:2) to the burning bush in which Moses recognized the presence of God: "and, behold, the bush burned with fire and the bush was not consumed." However, in this play Kokoschka is not concerned with the discovery of God. Rather, he examines the process of self-discovery which ultimately frees man and woman from the bondage of the tormenting physical relationship which was portrayed in his first play.

Fig. 18. Käthe Richter and Ernst Deutsch in *The Burning Bush,* Dresden, 1917. Photograph courtesy F. Bruckmann KG, Munich.

Woman Redeemed

The opening scene is set at night in the room of the Woman, who is dressed for bed. She cannot sleep, however, and her long opening monologue reveals the great excitement which she feels at the anticipated arrival of the Man. At the conclusion of her monologue the Man enters with a candle. But they do not actually converse; their speeches are filled with exclamations and sentence fragments, reminiscent of the dialogue in *Murderer Hope of Women*: "Help—my powerlessness is flowing into your strength. Oh God!"[4] Following this interchange, without explanation, the Man takes a cloth and covers the Woman with it, leaving only her head visible, and walks unsteadily out of the door. Grabbing a candle which is extinguished by the draught of air coming in through the open door, the Woman tries to follow him. The Man returns, and the Woman confesses her weakness and dependence upon him. The Man insists upon her asserting her independence ("Arise, awaken your soul to its birth") and once more covers her with the cloth, this time closing her eyes, then covering her head as well, before rushing away. Starting in confusion, the Woman rouses her drunken admirers, who are sleeping below, and orders them to capture the Man, who barely manages to escape their wild pursuit.

The beginning of the second scene is almost identical with that of the first: the action takes place at night and in the Woman's room. But the atmosphere of longing and expectancy of the opening scene has given way to a frenzied mood of frustration and confusion. In the Woman's opening monologue the lyrical images of desire and hoped-for fulfillment of the first scene are replaced by half-articulated remarks in broken syntax, which reveal her despair:

Isn't it better not to be, than to be wicked? Since wickedness begets appearance and thence reality?

At the conclusion of her speech, the audience is aware of the Man lying in another room, "singing in a strange tone without moving." He does not respond to her speech but offers a verse monologue of his own, at first describing a world in which there is no love:

The deep slept
The mountain stood shadowless
And there was no time
And no beast heard
And no fire warmed
And no flame burned
When love did not exist

Then, in the antistrophe, the Man describes a bestial world in which violent sexual love has appeared:

And the beast slew man, and devoured him and spewed him forth. And flames beat red wounds whenever love became sweet to Man and Woman.

Following the second part of the Man's narration the Woman's voice grows tender and sad and her breathing is hardly audible, while he stares transfixed in her direction, unable to turn his eyes away from her. She staggers toward the door of her room but falls and calls for help, as the Man, rousing himself from his trance, again urges her towards independence: "Let hope raise you up! Soon you will go out of the house."

In the third scene the location switches to a forest. The Woman, desperately searching for the Man, is ill. She groans as though in childbirth, but nevertheless continues walking blindly ahead. Along her way she meets three men and women, who form a chorus at the end of the scene, and who are used to externalize and articulate the Woman's search. Finally she realizes the futility of her quest: "A graveyard will be my bridal bed and a sob my bridal cry." She collapses in the middle of the stage, lying there motionless as the three men from the chorus suggest three possible directions she can follow.

The first two possibilities suggest the Man's grief and disappointment in the Woman: "I see a man weeping on the ground." The Woman chooses the third direction, where she rescues both herself and the Man from the animal in whose body she is imprisoned and to which the Man is bound:

> I see a metallic man fastened to a beast in heat. But have you seen that the beast ate from his heart. He stirs. His taut chain rattles. His glittering hand triumphs in the uncertain struggle. His metallic call awakens the Woman who steps from the belly of the beast. Woman, you who trample the snake, your heart swells with the joy of motherhood.

All three images contain allusions to the Passion of Christ in their depiction of the Man. But, only in the final image is the Woman seen to transcend her role as tormentor of the male in the allusion to her as the Virgin Mary treading on a serpent, as seen in medieval or renaissance sculpture:

> He thirsts because you reached up the sponge soaked in vinegar. . . . With you, he took the body from a chalice— and you have blasphemed . . . Woman, you who trample the snake, your heart swells with the joy of motherhood.

The final vision of the Woman's surmounting her physical nature, symbolized by her climbing out of the skin of the animal in which she has been contained, although narrated by the chorus, is intended to reveal a process which is taking place within the Woman herself. This transcendence is made clear by the stage directions which follow ("radiant heart, agitated din, men and women snatch at open hands, shouting, sobbing; one catches glimpses of many open hands"), as well as by the psalm sung by the chorus in the background, "I believe in the resurrection within me."

Following this moment of pure ecstasy, the stage slowly grows dark. Then, in the place where the Woman should be, there is a young girl, who symbolizes the spiritual rebirth of the Woman from animal desire to virginal innocence.

The fourth scene, also not causally connected with the previous ones, depicts the Man and Woman again in conflict. They stand on two precipices, with the chorus seen indistinctly against the dark background. They hurl violent insults at one another, the Woman aggressively and powerfully, the Man defensively. Finally she throws a stone at him, hitting him in the chest, eventually killing him. But instead of aggravating the battle between the sexes, this act of violence is really a source of liberation from the world of physical torment. With the word *Mercy! (Barmherzigkeit)*, which the Man utters as he is struck, their relationship is transformed from one of mingled hate and desire into the purest spiritual love:

> Mercy!
> You, through whom I am released,
> you give me pain.
> Sister, dry my brow!

Whereas moments before the Man was her "hated enemy and jailer," with the negation of the world of appearance and physical desire she comforts him with maternal warmth.

In the final scene at the Man's deathbed, the transformation of the physical into the spiritual is completed. The Woman and the dying Man she is holding form a Pietà, which, unlike the Pietà poster advertising *Murderer Hope of Women,* expresses resolution rather than conflict. As the Man dies, a corona of light forms above the Man and Woman, suggesting that the Man's physical death is a symbol for the spiritual rebirth of them both, as is expressed in the Man's words shortly before he dies: "Let me live—*you* and *I.*"

The Burning Bush revolves around the quest for self-knowledge, which ultimately moves the elemental sexual conflict to a higher plane. In the final speech of the play the chorus gives a general formulation of this process:

> Coerced, a vision, a world appears to consciousness. And then again the creation, from the image which constrained it, frees itself. Space takes shape like water, air and earth. Fire burns it forever and consumed it.[5]

But these crucial lines cannot be understood without reference to "On the Nature of Visions," a lecture delivered by Kokoschka at a meeting of the Academic Association for Literature and Music in Vienna on January 26, 1912, while he was writing *The Burning Bush*. There he describes the perception of visions as a state of heightened consciousness in which one sees the world in a fresh way through the release of the cognitive faculty:

> The consciousness of visions is not a mode of perceiving and understanding existing objects. It is a condition in which we experience the visions themselves. . . . This state of alertness of the soul or consciousness, expectant and receptive, is like an unborn child whose own mother might not be aware of it and to whom nothing of the outside world slips through. And yet, what affects his mother . . . becomes a part of him; just as if he could use his mother's eyes, the unborn absorbs visions even though he himself is unseen.[6]

What Kokoschka describes in his lecture is the creative process itself: the artist's method of perceiving reality. In this context, it is significant that the image he chooses to represent the creative imagination is that of an oil lamp:

> I search, guess, question. And with what sudden eagerness must the lamp-wick seek its nourishment, for the flame leaps before my eyes as the oil feeds it. . . . My vision is like this: unintentionally I draw something out of the world. But then I become nothing more than one of the world's imaginings. Thus in all things, imagination is that which is perfectly natural. Thus, imagination is nature, vision, life itself.[7]

If this statement is applied to *The Burning Bush* it becomes clear that the concluding speech by the chorus is also a description of the creative process: a vision is formed through the transcendence of everyday reality ("water, air and earth") by the spirit; "fire burns it forever and consumed it."[8] Further, in the original version of the play, the final line reads: "The fantasy, fire, burns it forever and consumes it."

In her study of Kokoschka's dramas, Regina Brandt uses "On the Nature of Visions" as the key to Kokoschka's plays, suggesting that not only the final chorus of *The Burning Bush* but the entire play, and Kokoschka's other dramas as well, should be seen from the essay's perspective. The danger inherent in this viewpoint is that the theme of sexual conflict, so central to the play, is seen only as an exemplum of the process of self-discovery: "The theme of 'love,' the Man-Woman problem, can only have an exemplary, symbolic function in Kokoschka's plays."[9] According to Brandt, the image of fire in the play should be seen as one with the concept of love, both functioning to form an image of "creative power." But such an assumption oversimplifies Kokoschka's symbolism, especially in *The Burning Bush* where the distinction between fire and light is crucial. The miracle of the burning bush of the title is that, although it burns, miraculously it is not destroyed. Similarly, the disembodied, spiritualized love which is forged at the end of the play (the "Woman and Man speak in a trance, in high, unfamiliar tones so that every sound is stressed") gives off *light*, but does not emit the fiery heat of a mutually destructive, sexual love: "Something has been fanned into flame; let's hope it is light, and not smoking fire, which causes the eye to overflow. Fire burns to ashes, light looks so friendly at long last!" Therefore, *The Burning Bush* should be seen as the evolution of spiritual from carnal love, as is suggested in the Salvation Army hymn which concludes scene 1:

> He who has the key to divine love,
> can never die.
> Earthly love is but agony,
> a rose thorn on the path
> to Golgotha.

The Burning Bush is essentially a play about the transformation of physical desire into spiritual light. Thus, it is hardly surprising that light is the dominant visual element and that the use of stage design and color symbolism are of comparatively minor importance and are never completely divorced from Kokoschka's use of light symbolism.

Two of the play's stage images are closely related. In the second scene, following the Woman's monologue, the audience becomes aware that the Man is in an adjoining room. He lies on a couch with the door open, unable to turn his eyes from the Woman, yet equally unable to join her. In this image of combined attraction and separation, Kokoschka suggests the perpetual discord which exists between the sexes. As he does so often in this play, he uses light to enhance the dramatic tension of the image of the sexes desperately seeking to make contact, yet unable to do so: "rays of light from the two rooms cross and seek one another on high in the center of the stage." As the Man begins to speak of love to the Woman, the lights "rise, meet, and come to rest" before fading in the Woman's room as her breathing grows weak. Unable to resist her desire for the Man, she staggers weakly toward the door of the room, but falls before any contact betweem them is possible. In this stage image Kokoschka suggests the impossibility of contact between the sexes.

A similar image is found in the fourth scene, where the Man and the Woman stand opposite one another on two precipices, speaking to each other with mingled love and hate:

> Enter in to me, release and redeem me. . . . I know you wish to be my wooer and liberator . . . and are my hated enemy and jailer.

As with the previous stage image of the adjoining rooms, the precipices confirm Kokoschka's thesis of the mutual attraction and repulsion of the sexes. Both images are reminiscent of the nearly touching hands in the Tietze portrait, and of Kokoschka's use of the cage in *Murderer Hope of Women,* where for one instant the bodies of the rising Man and falling Woman are in contact but for the bars of the cage.

The second stage image is also enhanced by lighting, but this time it is by colored lights, which echo the red-white color symbolism present in *Murderer Hope of Women* and the poster for that play: "As long as he is speaking, white light, which is mixed with red as soon as she answers."

As in *Murderer Hope of Women,* the use of red and white suggests that the sexual conflict is a state of perpetual vampirism. But more importantly, the flickering red and white is reminiscent of *fire.* It is as a human flame that the Woman, burning with uncontrollable desire for the Man, appears:

> My body is a burning bush,
> You my man. Nourishing wind!
> My breasts two tongues of flame, . . .
> My hands not wings,
> My legs burning coals—
> White and red—white and red I burn;
> in a fiery garment of long pain, glowing in shame,
> I burn but am not consumed.

So, in the color symbolism in the play, Kokoschka suggests that the Woman, not yet redeemed by the sacrificial death of the Man which turns her love to light, is literally burning with desire. By doing so, he has created an extraordinary image which combines all three visual elements: a symbolic use of the stage, lighting, and color.

The final stage image in *The Burning Bush* is the placement of the figures of the Woman and the dying Man in the form of a Pietà in the fifth scene, where Kokoschka suggests the final triumph of divine over earthly love. As in *Murderer Hope of Women*, where the Man suffered a wound in his side at the hands of the Woman, in *The Burning Bush* the stone which strikes him in the chest makes him a Christian martyr like St. Stephen: "Ah, see how my life ebbs away in martyrdom." The Woman is similarly cleansed by her martyrdom. It purges her of fleshly desire ("My Man shall remain untouched! I suffer with you") and enables her to take the role of the Virgin Mary in the Pietà, a role which was prefigured in the third scene when the Woman was transformed into an innocent virgin.

Kokoschka's symbolic use of light and dark in *The Burning Bush* is all-pervasive from the opening of the first scene to the close of the play. When not conveyed through the visual elements themselves, it is expressed by means of the discourse. The purpose of the symbolism is to dramatize the Woman's search for self-realization, from the darkness of her complete dependence on the Man for fulfillment, which she sees in purely physical terms, to the light of spiritual rebirth at the end of the play. Although the scenes are not arranged chronologically, they follow a general movement from darkness toward light, with the third scene functioning as a microcosm of the play as a whole.

But the various uses of light in the play must be carefully differentiated. In the first scene, the Woman cannot sleep because she is drawn towards the moonlight flickering in through her window. But this light, coming from outside, does not have the same function as, for example, the candlelight which appears in her room later in the scene, or the oil lamp mentioned in "On the Nature of Visions." Instead of representing the Woman's awakening consciousness, the light of the moon arouses her sexually and increases her dependence on the Man:

> Where do the new rays come from?
> They attract me,—awaken me with all their might . . .
> Man in the moon,—turn away, don't look in here.
> Your radiance releases so much power that it follows me up the stairs and into my room . . .
> Tonight a man will blow his breath into me and believe in the image.

As in *Murderer Hope of Women*, the Man is represented as the bearer of light in *The Burning Bush*. This role is visually depicted at his entry when he carries a burning candle into the Woman's room. The Woman, who describes herself as a "flower in the darkness," tries to draw him with her into the darkness: "My desire wants to draw you into the darkness. I hunger for love." The Man's mission is to make her look within, which Kokoschka suggests visually by having him cover her with a cloth, shutting out the external light and forcing her not to look at him but to know herself.[10] Afraid of her isolation, she attempts to follow him, but the candle which she uses to light her way is blown out in the open doorway, symbolizing her inability to control the light, that is, her spiritual weakness. The Woman, used to the darkness of her physical existence, is terrified of the process of self-awareness toward which the Man is trying to guide her: "O Master—I am afraid, I am so weak, so dependent upon you."

Not unsympathetic toward her position, the Man returns and, kneeling before her, allows her to light her candle from his. At the same time, he urges her to develop her own resources instead of maintaining her dependence upon him. His final speech in the first scene reveals how completely Kokoschka's use of light as a visual element is interwoven with his use of literary symbolism:

> Now you kindle your own light as it were by my love, and your body will sustain it! . . . Arise, awaken your soul to its birth. And if the separation makes you melancholy, my image will be mirrored in the night. And the glow of your self-love will again be kindled by the tender night vision.

After this speech, he places the cloth over her head again and gently shuts her eyes. But no sooner has he fled into the corridor than she calls to the men below for his capture.

Although the second scene is set, as before, in the Woman's room on a moonlit night, the greater sense of confusion and desperation that the Woman now feels is conveyed not only through her language with its exclamations and outcries but also by means of light. In the first scene, when the Woman believed in the arrival of the Man, the stage directions referred to the "electric brightness of the moon." In the second scene, however, the eerie atmosphere of tension and anxiety is reflected in the shadows on the windowpane, which "change and flood the floor with shapes." As the scene ends, following the Woman's collapse as she nears the door of her room, the lights which have previously been "crossing and seeking" one another now go out in her room. The Man's speech urging her towards self-sufficiency and rebirth is also heavily imbued with light symbolism, reminiscent of the lamp used in "On the Nature of Visions":

> As you wear yourself out, the dreary light fades. . . . Already the color of life pales! Wingbeat that you are, blow on the wick.

In the third scene, again by means of light and darkness, Kokoschka depicts the painful process of self-discovery undergone by the Woman. Unlike the previous two scenes, where the Woman's darkened room was permeated by moonlight or shadows, the third scene is set in a forest in which there is absolutely no light ("tree stumps black, sky black") except for the reflected light of the white ground. In this scene of austere darkness the Woman is forced to search for the inner light toward which the Man has been guiding her in vain. Along her way she meets the members of the chorus, who also employ the language of Kokoschka's light symbolism: "with lanterns we light the way through the hazy forest."

After the Woman's collapse, the medium of light is again used to depict the process through which she will attain salvation for herself and for the Man. The possible paths are revealed to her as three successive images illuminating the darkness. After the third image, which depicts the Woman as liberator of both herself and the Man, a "radiant heart" gleams, prefiguring, by means of light, the final triumph over the physical which is enacted at the end of the play.

At the end of the third scene, it is once again through the medium of light that Kokoschka symbolizes the Woman's psychic rejuvenation. Following the appearance of the radiant heart, the stage again grows dark as the chorus chants a psalm. When it has become completely dark, a spotlight from above slowly focuses on the middle of the stage, where the Woman had been lying. The moment of her spiritual rebirth is thus depicted in the gradual shift from total darkness to light. As such, the third scene reveals the course of the entire drama in miniature.

Although Kokoschka relies upon the stage image of the Pietà to suggest the transformation of physical hate and desire into spiritual love in the first scene, he makes ample use of light symbolism as well. The darkness with which the first three scenes began is now replaced by light: "The corona of light has in the meantime formed above the main group." However, this corona is not ordinary daylight but a light emanating from *within* the Man and Woman, as is made clear by the stage directions that specify "the sun goes down." The dying sun symbolizes the world of physical reality which, at the end of the play, is superseded by light from within.

The completed transition from the darkness and fire of sexual conflict to pure light is also revealed through a final allusion to the image of the burning bush. Whereas earlier in the play the Woman referred to the bush to suggest the torment of her desire for the Man ("my body is a burning bush"), now the burning bush is used as a symbol of the metamorphosis of fire into light:

A bush has burned suddenly. The aridity is at once snatched from the worm. God lets the light rise to him on high.

Kokoschka did not execute illustrations for *The Burning Bush,* but, in the same year in which the play was published (1913), a cycle of twelve lithographs appeared under the title *Columbus Enchained (Der gefesselte Kolumbus)* which have a close thematic relationship with his play.[11] The accompanying text for the lithographs was a prose poem Kokoschka wrote in 1908, *The White Slayer of Beasts (Der weisse Tiertöter),*[12] which was intended as a sequel to his earlier poem *The Dreaming Youths* (1907). Both chronologically and stylistically, *The White Slayer of Beasts* is a transitional piece between the *Jugendstil*-oriented technique of *The Dreaming Youths* and the more mature style of *The Burning Bush.* Like the former work, the poem is about the sexual initiation of an adolescent. Yet in the poem Kokoschka uses

many of the same visual symbols which appear in the play, notably the identification between the expectant Woman and the moon: "On the moon was the lifelike figure of a woman, clearly in the attitude of someone waiting." In addition, the Woman is compared to a bird, as she is in the first and third scenes of *The Burning Bush;* and fire and thorns are used as symbols for violent sexual desire, as they are in the play:

With the leaping mountains of fire which bark at the moon . . . barked this, my horrible love . . . How can I scold your lust! My sides are already bloody as though by thorns from your clumsy hands!

The links between the play and the lithographs are even more specific. *The Face of the Woman* (Fig. 19), the frontispiece for *Columbus Enchained,* is a portrait of Alma Mahler, the widow of the composer Gustav Mahler, whom Kokoshcka met in 1912 in Vienna and who was to dominate his life and art for the next few years. That the portrait is entitled *The Face of the Woman* indicates that in the *Columbus* lithographs Kokoschka was thinking of himself and Alma Mahler as the archetypal man and woman of his play. However, the frontispiece shows the face of a determined and strong-willed woman who is closer to the domineering, aggressive character in the fourth scene than the weak, dependent Woman of the opening scenes of *The Burning Bush.*

The second lithograph, *The New Columbus and St. George* (Fig. 20), depicts the chained Columbus of the title of the series and suggests the central paradox found in the character of the Man in both the play and the cycle of lithographs. He is both independent and heroic (thus the reference to Columbus); he seems to be free, yet is in fact enslaved by his physical desire for the Woman. This lithograph portrays the artist, kneeling and in chains, looking back over his right shoulder toward the figure of St. George, who is carrying a spear, while the woman of the frontispiece kneels down beside him to kiss his hands. In the background two volcanoes are erupting, and a sun, marked by a cross, shines overhead.

While not illustrating any specific moment of the play, the illustration reveals its basic pattern. The woman is now shown as the dependent creature of the opening scenes, while the man, despite his longing for freedom, represented by the herioc image of St. George, whom he hails with his left hand, is fettered by his sexual desire. As in the play, "he stirs. His taut chain rattles." The implicit violence of the conflict between freedom and desire in the male is suggested by the twin volcanoes. The sun with the cross reveals that, despite his ascendancy, he is doomed to become a sacrificial victim to the liberation of the woman—as he was in the play.

The third and fourth lithographs create images of torment and despair which reflect upon the condition of the man and woman, rather than referring to particular images found in the play. In the third drawing, *Judgment Day*, a dancing Death embraces an open coffin. In the fourth, *The Way to the Grave*, the couple are tossed adrift in a stormy sea, while a striped, wolflike creature, reminiscent of a similar animal in the illustrations to *Murderer Hope of Women*, looks on, emphasizing the hopelessness of their plight. In the right foreground another representation of the artist faces the viewer, his hands raised upward in desperation. The background is a desolate landscape littered with graves.

The fifth lithograph, *The Pair by Candlelight* (Fig. 21), represents the couple in a room. The woman, who is seated on a bed, points with her left hand toward an open door through which moonlight is flickering. Her other hand is pointing toward a lighted candle which stands on a table before her. The man looks on, his left hand raised to his face, his expression an uncertain mixture of apprehension and hope. It would be difficult to construct any more precise analogy to the first scene of *The Burning Bush* than this. Not only is the couple situated in a room with bed, table, and candle, as they are in the play, but the light symbolism of the first scene has been perfectly realized in the lithograph. As in the play, there are two possibilities for the woman: sexual fulfillment, symbolized by the shimmering moon, or spiritual fulfillment, symbolized by the candle. Her simultaneous gestures toward both suggest her own uncertainty as to her choice, which is also registered in the expression of the man.

In *The Apple of Eve*, the sixth illustration, the man and the woman (again bearing the features of Kokoschka and Alma Mahler) are seated on opposite sides of a table in an empty landscape. Their isolation is emphasized by the use of heavy black outlines with very little shading in comparison with the earlier drawings. As the woman offers the apple of Eve to him, the man hesitantly extends one hand to accept it, while with the other he tries to shield his eyes. This illustration emphasizes the woman's role as sexual temptress, as in the play. In addition, the man appears unable to resist her power over him, as in the play's first scene, when he says, "my potency dissipated, completely sucked up by you."

In *At the Crossroads* (Fig. 22) Kokoschka once again employs the light symbolism of the play. The man is walking out of the open doorway leading from the woman's room holding a large burning candle, whose flame he shields with his hand. The woman, her hand held up to her head, seems undecided whether or not to follow him. The resemblance between the illustration and the play's opening scene is so strong that

Fig. 19. *The Face of the Woman*, frontispiece, from *Columbus Enchained*, 1913, chalk lithograph, 9¼ × 7¾ in. (23.7 × 19.3 cm.). Courtesy Verlag Galerie Welz, Salzburg.

Fig. 20. *The New Columbus and St. George*, from *Columbus Enchained*, 1913, chalk lithograph, 12⅔ × 12¾ in. (32.5 × 32.8 cm.). Courtesy Verlag Galerie Welz, Salzburg.

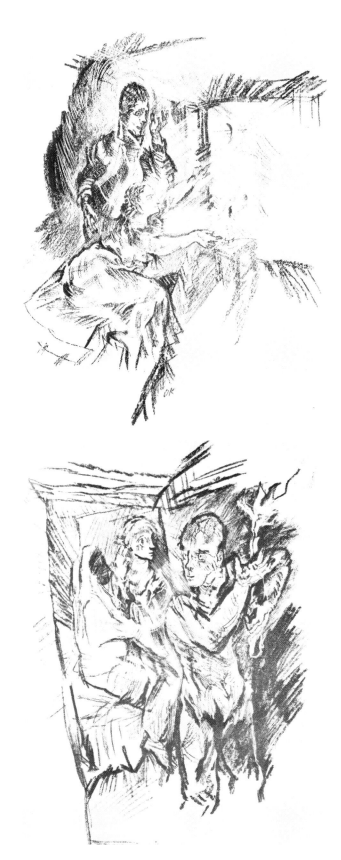

Fig. 21. *The Pair by Candlelight,* from *Columbus Enchained,* 1913, chalk lithograph, 13 × 10½ in. (32.9 × 26.7 cm.). Courtesy Verlag Galerie Welz, Salzburg.

Fig. 23. *Meeting,* from *Columbus Enchained,* 1913, chalk lithograph, 12¼ × 11½ in. (30.9 × 29.5 cm.). Courtesy Verlag Galerie Welz, Salzburg.

Fig. 22. *At the Crossroads,* from *Columbus Enchained,* 1913, chalk lithograph, 14¼ × 10⅓ in. (36.3 × 26.5 cm.). Courtesy Verlag Galerie Welz, Salzburg.

Fig. 24. *Woman Bent over Shadow,* from *Columbus Enchained,* 1913, chalk lithograph, 12 × 8½ in. (30.4 × 22.2 cm.). Courtesy Verlag Galerie Welz, Salzburg.

Fig. 25. *The Woman Triumphs over the Dead,* from *Columbus Enchained,* 1913, chalk lithograph, 12 × 10 in. (31 × 25.5 cm.). Courtesy Verlag Galerie Welz, Salzburg.

Fig. 26. *The Pure Vision,* from *Columbus Enchained,* 1913, chalk lithograph, 8 × 13¼ in. (20.7 × 33.6 cm.). Courtesy Verlag Galerie Welz, Salzburg.

Kokoschka could be quoting his own stage direction: "Man hesitantly starts to leave, it grows dark, she takes her candlestick from the table in order to follow him, but the open door extinguishes her light."

In *The Man with Raised Arms and the Figure of Death* the man is prostrate on the edge of an embankment, his arms raised in a gesture of despair, while the figure of Death lurks behind on a rock. Suggesting, if not illustrating, the Man's wounding at the end of the fourth scene of the play, the drawing shows the moon rising while the sun sets. Significantly, the sun's rays are in the shape of a cross, indicative of the man's Christ-like martyrdom, as in the play.

The ninth illustration, *Meeting* (Fig. 23), portrays the man and woman together nude in a rocky landscape. Despite the title, which suggests a meeting between them, the figures, although staring at one another, seem by the positions of their bodies and feet to be heading past and not toward each other. As in the second and fourth scenes of the play, when Kokoschka portrayed them in adjoining but separate rooms or on opposite cliffs, this lithograph reveals the separation of, as well as the attraction between, the sexes: "No picture more expressive of the polarity of man and woman can be imagined than this drawing, in which the man's body is of a darker shade than the woman's, and both seem at once to strive towards each other, simultaneously attracted and repelled; they are in a permanent state of suspense, a unity and yet two opposed parts."[13]

In *Woman Bent over Shadow* (Fig. 24) the woman bends over the phantom projection of her own sexual desire. The face of the male figure is vague and ill-defined, in sharp contrast to the dark eyes and vivid features of the woman, whose amorous attention and powerful grip on the passive figure of the shadow in her arms suggests the predatory violence of *Murderer*

Hope of Women or the beginning of the fourth scene of *The Burning Bush*, where the Woman describes her body as "a burning bush."

In the penultimate lithograph, *The Woman Triumphs over the Dead* (Fig. 25), the man, again with Kokoschka's features, is lying on a bier with hands folded, while the woman, no longer recognizable as Alma Mahler, is in the act of covering his face with a sheet. Her expression is one of sadness and her left hand is raised in lamentation, yet her left foot is planted upon the body in triumph. This paradoxical mixture of grief and victory is precisely the effect which the Man's death has upon the Woman in Kokoschka's drama. She grieves over his loss, yet because of his sacrifice she is finally able to triumph over the restrictions of her physical being: "I lost myself—and I regained myself."

The final lithograph is symmetrically balanced with the first; it too is a portrait of a woman, but not of Alma Mahler. In this last illustration, *The Pure Vision* (Fig. 26), the woman is shown in her purified state—as at the end of Kokoschka's drama. Kokoschka clearly suggests this symmetrical relationship between the first and last lithographs (as well as the Woman's transformation) in the double meaning of the German word *Gesicht* in the titles of the two illustrations. In the frontispiece, *Gesicht* means *face* while in the final lithograph it signifies *vision*. Thus, both *The Burning Bush* and *Columbus Enchained* concentrate upon the spiritual development of woman, from her desire for, and dependence on, man to her angelic innocence and purity. Therefore, it is not surprising that in *The Pure Vision* the figure is illuminated by a torch; light, in both the drama and the graphic cycle, symbolizes the process of purification undergone by the woman.

But Kokoschka's drama and *Columbus Enchained* are not only thematically concerned with the spiritual development of woman: they also portray man's martyrdom as her means of spiritual liberation and share a common use of light symbolism.

In addition to the close relationship between *The Burning Bush* and *Columbus Enchained,* there are important parallels between the play and the paintings which Kokoschka executed at the time of his dramatic conception in 1911. When he returned to Vienna in that year, he lived with his parents, an experience which reawakened the feelings of childhood innocence and religious piety which were absent in the avant-garde intellectual circles of Berlin. In his new environment he began to view his painting in a different way:

> On my return to Vienna from Berlin, I went back to live with my parents. My mother had rented for me an empty workshop in a garden not far from the house. . . . It was a rare pleasure, after the turmoil of Berlin and every other place where I had painted, to work in such tranquillity. No longer confused by external activity, the eye could turn inward, illuminating my inner self. It was like a gift from God, allowing me to see everything in an entirely new light.[14]

Painting for himself rather than for commissions, Kokoschka turned from portraiture to smaller canvases, often with religious subjects, such as *Knight, Death, and Angel, The Flight into Egypt, Crucifixion, The Visitation,* and *The Annunciation,* all of which were executed in 1911.

That Kokoschka indeed saw everything "in a new light" is literally true. He turned to a more painterly approach to the canvas and paid less attention to singularly expressive details such as hands, and far more to the technical effects of light and color. As Hans Maria Wingler observed, "He had bought himself a prism with which he studied the colours of the spectrum. . . . The opaque colouring of Kokoschka's pictures in this period was the direct result of these experiments with his prism.[15] His concern with the experimental and expressive resources of light are also evident in the third scene of *The Burning Bush.* There three images are suddenly illuminated, one by one, on the darkened stage to suggest the three paths available to the Woman; Kokoschka also uses a spotlight at the end of the scene to dramatise the metamorphosis of the Woman.

In the works of this "opaque period," as it has been called, edges are flattened, transitions softened, and flesh tones given a soft, milky texture. In *Knight, Death, and Angel* and *The Flight into Egypt,* for example, the canvas is filled with networks of criss-crossing strokes in poster-like hues. Although the figures still have dark outlines, as in many of the earlier "black portraits," they are now enmeshed in a crystalline structure which is new to Kokoschka's work and gives a glimmering iridescence to the whole. Indeed, "the effectiveness of the iridescent surfaces is increased by their being contrasted with large dark areas so that they seem to shine forth from out of the darkness."[16]

In *The Burning Bush,* an analogous use of light and dark is achieved in the third scene when the Woman searches for the Man in the darkened forest. There, the black trees are the visual equivalents of the dark contours between the figures in Kokoschka's religious paintings, while the light reflected from the white ground creates something of the ghostly iridescence of *Knight, Death, and Angel.* Another use of light similar to that found in Kokoschka's paintings of this period is seen in the beginning of the first and second scenes, where moonlight filters through the windows of the Woman's room and patterns the floor with strange shapes and figures, creating a shadowy, prismatic effect as in the paintings. So striking are the visual parallels between the use of light in the play and in the paintings that Robert Breuer's impressions of the 1917 performance of *The Burning Bush* in Dresden read as though he were describing one of Kokoschka's 1911 paintings:

> Of *The Burning Bush*, I recall: the spaciousness of a forest, dense rows of pine trees; above, a rib-vaulting of branches, half-prison, half-cathedral; the surfacing and collapsing of a lost woman; human shadows, striding, seeking and meeting; lines and masses which intersect, pass one another and are lost.[17]

However, the relationship between Kokoschka's paintings of 1911 and *The Burning Bush* goes even further than a similar subject matter or comparable techniques of employing light. They also share common symbolic elements with the play. In *The Flight into Egypt* (Fig. 27) the bearded figure of Joseph leads Mary onward, the latter with one hand apprehensively before her, while he carries a burning candle with which to lead the way. Unlike most treatments of this subject, Joseph is not shown as an old man. Indeed, he looks more like a traditional representation of Christ than of Joseph. This unorthodox representation, together with the lighted candle, suggests a connection with the Man in Kokoschka's play, who likewise leads the Woman forward with a candle toward spiritual rebirth.

In *The Visitation* (Fig. 28), instead of portraying the traditional meeting between Mary and Elizabeth (Luke 1:40), Kokoschka paints a solitary woman sitting naked in a deserted landscape. The canvas is divided into three planes. In the foreground is the woman; in the middle ground, a large wild animal; and, in the background, a cityscape. Offering no apparent connection with the biblical reference in the title, the painting suggests, in the woman's melancholy expression as she gazes, with her hand on the side of her head, the essential conflict between spirit and body which is so central to Kokoschka's concern in *The Burning Bush*. Although her gaze is directed upward, her nakedness and the animal behind her suggest the desires of the body which tempt her as much as does the spiritual. As in the fifth illustration of *Columbus Enchained*, where the woman points toward the moonlight with one hand and toward the candle with the other, she is presented as a divided creature.

The painting with the closest symbolic connection to *The Burning Bush* is *The Annunciation* (Fig. 29). The canvas captures the moment of the Archangel Gabriel's coming "in unto" the Virgin Mary (Luke 1:28), revealing to her that she is to bear the Son of God. On the right, Mary, in her blue gown, is reclined with eyes shut and mouth tightly compressed, her left hand pressed to her womb, the fingers of her right hand tentatively groping towards the Angel. On the left is Gabriel, naked and with wide-open eyes chastely averted, one hand nearly touching her leg, while his left arm (expressively twisted into an S-shape) is close to her head. Beneath the left arm of Gabriel, in the background, is a burning building; on the left of the scene a fiery volcano erupts.

The background of the painting suggests a world of cataclysm and discord. The foreground, particularly in the face of Gabriel, who closely resembles the portrait of *The Pure Vision* in the final lithograph of *Columbus Enchained*, suggests the overcoming of conflict. Symbolized by fire, as in the play, the resolution leads to the moment of the woman's spiritual awakening: "Woman, you who trample the snake, your heart swells with the joy of motherhood."

Yet another example of the close relationship between *The Burning Bush* and Kokoschka's visual works of this period is furnished by the series of painted fans which he made for Alma Mahler between 1912 and 1914 (see Figs. 30, 49). Kokoschka himself referred to the relationship between these fans and his early writings in a letter dated March 10, 1968: "My fans are love letters in pictorial language, as are my early plays and essays."[18] There are also remarkable parallels between the fans and the plays, particularly in the fire and light symbolism with which Kokoschka charts the rise and fall of his relationship with his mistress:

> The image of the flame, which Kokoschka employs in his lecture ["On the Nature of Visions"], nearly has, in the fans, the function of a *topos* in literature. On each of the fans flames and fire are depicted. . . . From the lighting of the candle on the first to the fiery explosion on the last fan, the depiction of fire accompanies the portrayal of events, marking each phase and offering illumination to each incident.[19]

Of significant relationship to *The Burning Bush* is the first fan, painted in 1912 (Fig. 30). Its delicate pastel background, in shades of pink, yellow, and green, recalls the crystalline paintings of Kokoschka's "opaque period." The fan is divided into three sections, each separated by a decorative floral design, which was intended to reveal the "organic interweaving of man, animal, plants, and spirits . . . as in the *Book of Kells*,"[20] and which once more emphasizes the artist's tranquil state of mind upon his return from Berlin.

On the left portion of the fan, two boats are represented, one occupied by a man (bearing the artist's features), the other by a woman. The boats are floating in opposite directions, and both are threatened on all sides by the snapping jaws of red fish and sea monsters. As in *The Burning Bush*, where the Man and the Woman were represented in separate rooms or on opposite cliffs, or in the ninth lithograph of *Columbus Enchained* (see Fig. 23), where they were depicted as walking past one another, Kokoschka created an image of the tormented separation of the sexes. The righthand image on the fan shows the couple being carried off on the back of a flame-colored horse. In contrast to the previous image of separation, Kokoschka now depicts

the violent world of sexual attraction by the fiery, leaping animal, which suggests the vision of sexuality described in the third scene of *The Burning Bush:* "I see a metallic man fastened to a beast in heat."

In the central portion of the fan the man kneels before the woman (whose features are those of Alma Mahler), his hand upon his breast: the woman's right hand is upon his shoulder; with her other hand she lights the candle she is holding by touching his. In this image of the woman receiving light from the man, Kokoschka re-creates in pictorial terms a central image in the play, the equivalent of the stage directions in the first scene: "The Man kneels before the Woman and illuminates her face, she lights her candle on his and looks at him."

In Kokoschka's development from *Murderer Hope of Women* to *The Burning Bush,* there was a shift in emphasis from the violence of the former, toward the calm sense of resolution with which the latter play ends: "The glowing nightmares and burning daydreams of before have yielded to a peaceful calm."[21] This evolution is revealed in Kokoschka's contemporary work in the visual arts as well, which have been described as possessing "something of the mild gentleness of a recovery."[22] To illustrate clearly this dramatic break in Kokoschka's style between 1910 and 1911 only two representative works depicting the same subject, the poet and critic Karl Kraus, need be examined.

Kokoschka's drawing of Kraus which appeared in *Der Sturm* on May 9, 1910 (Fig. 31), is executed in nervous, twitching strokes. The profile is drawn by a thick black line and the face is dotted with sudden, jagged marks, giving the whole a pulsing rhythm which is accentuated by a flurry of lines and dots in the upper righthand corner. It is the graphic equivalent of the shapes etched into the canvas with the

Fig. 27. *The Flight into Egypt*, 1911, oil on canvas, 22 × 27 in. (55 × 68 cm.). Courtesy D. Angehrn, Thalwil.

Fig. 28. *The Visitation*, 1911, oil on canvas, 31 × 50 in. (80 × 127 cm.). Collection Österreichische Galerie, Vienna.

Fig. 29. *The Annunciation*, 1911, oil on canvas, 33 × 48½ in.
(83 × 123.5 cm.). Collection Museum am Ostwall, Dort-
mund. Photograph by Walter Kirchberger.

Fig. 30. *First Fan for Alma Mahler*, 1912, watercolor on swan-skin, 10 × 17 (25 × 42 cm.). Collection Museum für Kunst und Gewerbe, Hamburg. Photograph from *Oskar Kokoschka* [catalogue] (New York: Marlborough-Gerson Gallery, Inc., Oct.–Nov. 1966).

Fig. 31. *Karl Kraus*, from *Der Sturm*, 1910, pen and ink drawing, 11½ × 9 in. (29.2 × 24 cm.). Courtesy Count Reinhold Bethusy-Huc, Vienna, and The Stedelijk Museum, Amsterdam.

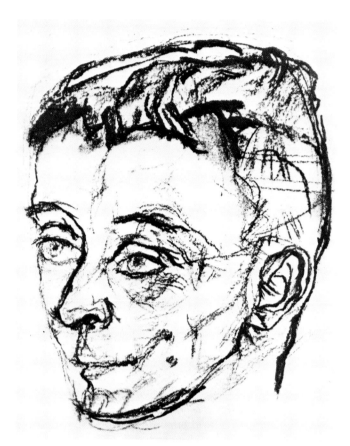

Fig. 32. *Karl Kraus*, 1912, chalk drawing, 17⅔ × 12 in. (45.2 × 30 cm.). Photograph from H. M. Wingler, *Oskar Kokoschka: The Work of the Painter*, translated by Frank S. C. Budgen, J. P. Hodin, and Ilse Schrier, in cooperation with Mrs. D. P. Hodin (Salzburg: Galerie Welz, 1958).

artist's fingernails in the Tietze portrait. But the most characteristic element is Kokoschka's treatment of Kraus's hands, whose fingers are grotesquely elongated and spiderlike, imparting a disturbing, nervous energy to the entire portrait.

In contrast to the Berlin portrait is the 1912 drawing of Kraus (Fig. 32), done after Kokoschka's return to Vienna. Less emphasis is placed upon the outline of the face and the strokes are lighter and softer, imparting to the face a calmness that was absent two years earlier. The face has a marblelike quality and seems to have been modeled as a whole rather than as a collection of details. In the later portrait, Kokoschka has chosen to portray only the face; the hands are no longer needed to emphasize the harsh, strident mood. In place of the dramatic tension in which the head is bowed and the hands seem to be involuntarily twitching, in the 1912 portrait Kokoschka concentrates on painterly technique. He no longer creates an image of a hypersensitive, tormented intellectual. Instead, there is a repose, even a childlike innocence to the face, making it look more youthful than in the earlier drawing. Although less dramatic as a description of a man's spiritual condition, the later portrait is more successful in plastic terms and conveys the same sense of peace and harmony to be found at the end of *The Burning Bush*, as well as in the other visual works of this period.

3. Creation Overturned
Job

Captain: You always dominated me. You could hypnotize me when I was wide awake, so that I neither saw nor heard, but simply obeyed. You could give me a raw potato and make me think it was a peach; you could make me take your ridiculous ideas for flashes of genius. You could corrupt me—yes, make me do the shabbiest things. You never had any real intelligence, yet, instead of being guided by me, you would take the reins into your hands.

August Strindberg
The Father

Job (Hiob), Kokoschka's third play, was written in 1917 while he was recuperating in Dresden. As a recruit in the cavalry of the Austro-Hungarian army in 1915, he had suffered near-fatal wounds to the lung and temple which required long convalescence.

Like the earlier plays, *Job* is focused on the relationship between the sexes. But there is a significant alteration in Kokoschka's treatment of this theme. What was previously examined from a serious or tragic perspective is now considered from a tragicomic point of view: "*Job* is a sleepy summer afternoon on the sun-drenched side of the house, on the garden bench between the shadows and the ripe peaches, a nap at two o'clock, disturbed by butterflies and bumblebees."[1]

Nevertheless, *Job* is not the frivolous satyr play that many of its critics have termed it. Kokoschka uses comic devices as a means of revealing on overturned world. Thus *Job* is a thin sheet of laughter covering an abyss of despair: "The morning crows and not the cock, the game shoots the hunter down—a weary man curses the carnival and now shuts shop."[2]

Unlike *The Burning Bush*, which was written when Kokoschka's tempestuous affair with Alma Mahler was at its height, *Job* manifests the feelings of cynicism and disillusionment which followed the breakup of the affair in 1914 and precipitated Kokoschka's decision to enlist

in the cavalry. Far from being a "sleepy summer afternoon," *Job* is a far more tragic play than *The Burning Bush*. In *The Burning Bush* the death of the Man has a symbolically redemptive function, while the grotesque death of Job serves only to demonstrate that love or spiritual contact between the sexes is impossible.

Kokoschka noted that he did not have "even a finger of wit." He said, however, that he regarded the wit and humor evident in *Job* as "different . . . that's pain! The pain after the first deception, after the first disillusion."[3]

Even though *Job* reflects Kokoschka's depressed emotional state in 1917, the origins of the play and the prototype for its characters are found in a play written ten years earlier, *Sphinx and Strawman (Sphinx und Strohmann)*. It exists in two versions, both of which consist of a single scene.[4] The first version was performed improvisationally at the School for Arts and Crafts in Vienna in 1907. *Sphinx I* was written in 1909 and performed on March 29 of that year at the Cabaret Fledermaus. On July 4 it was performed at the outdoor theater of the Kunstschau, together with *Murderer Hope of Women*.[5] A second, somewhat longer, version of *Sphinx and Strawman* was written in 1913 and published in *Dramen und Bilder (Plays and Paintings)* that same year.

67

The two early versions of the play that was ultimately to be called *Job* are indispensable to an understanding of the final version. Without them, it is impossible to trace Kokoschka's evolution as a dramatist or to ascertain what *Job,* particularly its visual elements, contributes to that development.

Sphinx and Strawman I, Kokoschka's first staged work, consists of a single three-and-a-half-page scene on the theme of sexual conflict. The play is subtitled a "Comedy for Automatons" and, even though performed by actors rather than marionettes, it reflects Kokoschka's youthful enthusiasm for the puppet theater: "When I was a child, a marionette theatre given me by my father represented the whole beauty of existence as far as I was concerned; it was surely responsible for my passion for the theatre."[6] Kokoschka's first dramatic endeavor might well be termed an "antiplay" or a "tragic farce," an attempt by the young "Scourge of the Bourgeoisie," who had made a bet with some fellow students that he could write a play that would make fun of the outworn conventions of realistic theater.[7] In the opening lines of the play the dramatic illusion is destroyed by the protagonist, Herr Firdusi, who says to the audience, "Why do you look at me so coolly? A thousand indifferent faces against one. Only a mere detail separates the hero from the audience."

Nevertheless, *Sphinx and Strawman* is more than a gratuitous piece of iconoclasm. It treats the fundamental motif of nearly all of Kokoschka's literary works—sexual conflict—by means of striking visual images and stage effects.

The play deals with the deception and betrayal of its central character, Herr Firdusi, a man with a gigantic head of straw. His name "Firdusi" is intended primarily as a play on the words *Führ(st) du sie!* meaning "lead her!"—ironically alluding to his helplessness in relation to his promiscuous wife, Lilly. This weakness is also suggested by the play's title, which humorously juxtaposes Firdusi, the Strawman, beside the omniscient Sphinx (half woman, half animal), his wife.[8]

The slender plot consists of Firdusi's being tricked into marrying his own sphinxlike wife Lilly, who is visually described as both a painted whore and a pious angel with folded hands. As the play begins, she has already deserted him for a "muscleman." This deception is achieved on stage through an extraordinary visual device. Since the play is about the power of a woman to "turn a man's head," Kokoschka transforms this figure of speech into a visual metaphor. Thus, by turning his head to gaze after Lilly, Firdusi becomes incapable of returning his head to its normal position. The stage directions, stating "Lilly thus remains unknown to Firdusi until the end of the play," clearly express Kokoschka's intention to communicate Firdusi's blind ignorance of the opposite sex.

Since he is physically unable to see Lilly, Firdusi proposes marriage to his own wife, who has all the while been flirting with Mr. Rubberman (Herr Kautschukmann), a demonically sensual contortionist with a top hat and lobster-red face. Although disconcerted by the identity of the names of his former wife and his newly acquired fiancée ("this name was my downfall once before"), Firdusi never suspects that he is marrying his own wife. At the end of the play, having realized his error, he dies from shock. Lilly, the wife, remains casual about her loss. "Beautiful as a show horse," she climbs over his dead body, saying: "Clear away his mortal remains. I will live on without him."

Kokoschka's first dramatic endeavor is built around a visual metaphor which is both a serious symbolic statement of Firdusi's blindness toward Lilly and a comic device through which numerous visual gags are created. Examples of the latter occur when Firdusi, his head twisted, walks backward to a chair on which he cannot properly sit down, then picks up a mirror which reflects the back of his head, and next sticks a rose into his back instead of his lapel.

Another visual innovation in this play, later retained in *Sphinx and Strawman II* and in *Job*, is Kokoschka's decision, no doubt borrowed from the cabaret, to paint characters onto rear backdrops to emphasize the grotesque, nonrealistic elements of this "Comedy for Automatons." Thus, the nine gentlemen who have been invited as wedding guests to Firdusi's marriage to his own wife are merely top hats and black suits painted on a rear curtain. They have nothing but holes for faces. When the time comes for each of them to speak, one at a time a face is pushed "automaton-like" through the required hole. They "screech out a sentence shrilly and vanish with a stench":

> *First Man:* rrrsss! It is really queer that the nature worshippers are mostly nobodies, and the geniuses weaklings. ftsch (*off*)

> *Second Man* (to the *Third Man*): cooooh . . . the refined feelings. The memories of puberty, when I failed my sex education class. I did not solve the Sphinx's riddle.

The result of this experimental staging is the integration of the painter's visual imagination and the playwright's appreciation of the possibilities of the theater creating a single image of a man as a dehumanized puppet. Similarly, Firdusi's own emptiness is depicted visually by his enormous, wobbling straw head and by the rubber handpuppet which he removes from his pocket and introduces to the Rubberman as "my son Adam, my hope."

At the end of the play all the sights and sounds—the inverted wedding ceremony with exchange of rings and photograph, the explosion, the nine faces popping through their holes and vanishing, the parrot shrieking, the shadow of Lilly and the Rubberman kissing, and Firdusi's realization of his error in marrying his own wife—converge to create a spectacle of complete chaos. Significantly, *Sphinx and Strawman*, because of its hysteria and nihilistic humor, was the first dramatic production of the Dadaists in 1917.

In the second version of *Sphinx and Strawman* (1913) the dramatic situation remains unchanged. Once again Firdusi has his head turned by his wife. She has already been unfaithful to him as the play begins and deceives him again with the Rubberman during the play. Nevertheless, there are important changes which reflect Kokoschka's development as a dramatist between 1907 and 1913, when *Sphinx and Strawman II* was written and published in *Plays and Paintings*. If the first version of the play in its "explosive" chaos could be seen as a comic analogue to *Murderer Hope of Women*, the second version, more highly conscious and philosophical about issues that are simply "detonated" in the earlier play, has parallels with *The Burning Bush*, which was written in the same year, 1913. This relationship between the two plays may be observed in a speech by Anima in *Sphinx and Strawman II* which would read like a parody of the desperate longing of the Woman in *The Burning Bush* to find self-fulfillment through the Man were it not for the sudden ironic twist at the conclusion of the speech:

> Oh, where is the man who is worthy of me, the man I dreamed of as a girl? Oh, no man like that proved himself worthy of me! I took a feature from one man, another from the next, to my lover I offered resigned lips, to my husband scorn and melancholy. I am forced to wander and wander, eternally, from one to the other. (*to Firdusi*) Hello handsome!

Although in the earlier version Kokoschka presented the conflict between man and woman as farce, in *Sphinx and Strawman II* he is more concerned with the philosophical implications of the conflict. As might be expected, the more philosophical orientation of the second version results in an expansion of the dialogue (*Sphinx II* is more than twice as long as the previous version) and in the abandonment of the marionettelike figures of the first version in favor of more articulate yet representative types. Firdusi, for example, refers to his condition as an abandoned spouse in a more discursive manner than before: "I had a wife, I treated her like a goddess and she left my bed. She said to our sad little chambermaid, 'help me on with my travelling cloak' and then disappeared with a healthy muscleman. I had created a human soul but the ground vanished from beneath its feet." In *Sphinx II* Firdusi commits suicide, whereas in *Sphinx I* he simply dies from the shock of having married his own wife.

Lilly is also transformed in *Sphinx II* into an allegorical representation of the "feminine soul, called Anima," a change which is visually reinforced both by the "light blue conventional angel's costume" that she wears and by her discourse: "Oh Lord, if only I could save a man's soul! They say that men suffer so from the mysteries of their delicate and cultivated eroticism." However, her dual role as spirit-whore is also retained, as suggested by her response to Mr. Rubberman which is made immediately after the speech quoted above, and ironically undercuts it: "You must be worthy, You have powerful muscles."

The Rubberman's role has also been expanded to fit the more philosophical implications of the later version. He now introduces himself as a doctor, sardonically prescribing a deadly poison as the cure for Firdusi's lovesickness. The wedding guests of the first version, whose nonsensical remarks were accompanied by foul noises and smells, now reappear as pseudo-Freudian intellectuals offering their professional opinions about what has taken place between Anima and Firdusi.

However, the most significant change among the characters is the addition of "Death," who is ironically described in the *dramatis personae* as a "normal, living person." His presence in the play emphasizes the strangeness of the other characters by contrast, and forces Firdusi to see himself clearly, thus reflecting the greater sophistication of the second version in probing a self-deception which the first version merely presents as farce. An example is the moment when Anima avows her love for Firdusi, who confuses his sexual desire with self-confidence and exclaims "My self-respect grows by leaps and bounds!" Suddenly Death appears in thunder and lightning to undermine Firdusi's false illusions. Similarly, at the end of the play, in response to Firdusi's dying words, "I have faith in the genius of mankind, Anima, amen," Death reappears amid thunder and lightning to expose Firdusi's erroneous belief: "strong faith is like blindness. It covers over unpleasant things, but those things never disappear."

Although the second version of *Sphinx and Strawman* is primarily an extension of the intellectual foundation of the play, it also extends some of its visual components. Firdusi now carries with him a pig's bladder on a string, symbolizing the emptiness of his "creation," Anima: "I had created a human soul. . . . Now my creation floats in the air like a pig's bladder—*Horror vacui!*"

Later, when for a moment Firdusi seems to realize his folly, he bursts the bladder, saying, "That used to be the soul. Oh, I'll never again disbelieve in fairy tales." The bladder, aside from representing Firdusi's sexual impotence, is an external representation of his puffed-up vacuousness as well as of the betrayal of Anima, his creation.

Another amplification of the visual element in the

second version of the play is evident in Kokoschka's treatment of Firdusi's suicide. Having had his head snapped back into place as a result of the Parrot's mimicry of the sounds of Anima's making love to Mr. Rubberman, Firdusi finally becomes aware of Anima's deceit. He asks himself, "Who am I?" and then shoots himself. But, instead of hearing the sound of a gunshot, the audience suddenly sees antlers spring from Firdusi's head. The answer to his question is thus given visually.

On April 14, 1917, *Sphinx and Strawman II* was performed as the first dramatic work shown at a Dada soirée in Zürich. Kokoschka himself took no part in the production, which was directed by Marcel Janco, who also designed special body masks for the performance. Hugo Ball was featured as Firdusi and Tristan Tzara as the Parrot. In his journal of the period, Ball describes the performance:

The play was performed in two adjoining rooms; the actors wore body masks. Mine was so big that I could read my script inside it quite comfortably. The head of the mask was electrically lighted; it must have looked strange in the darkened room, with the light coming out of the eyes. Emmy [Hennings, who played Anima] was the only one not wearing a mask. She appeared as half sylph, half angel, lilac and light blue. The seats went right up to the actors. Tzara was in the back room, and his job was to take care of the "thunder and lightning" as well as to say "Anima, sweet Anima!" parrot fashion. But he was taking care of the entrances and exits at the same time, thundered and lightninged in the wrong place, and gave the absolute impression that this was a special effect of the production, an intentional confusion of backgrounds. Finally, when Mr. Firdusi had to fall, everything got tangled up in the tightly stretched wires and lights. For a few minutes there was total darkness and confusion; then the gallery looked just the same as before.[9]

Despite some exploitation of the chaotic elements in the play for Dadaist ends, the production was generally faithful to Kokoschka's intentions. The Dadaists were interested in *Sphinx and Strawman* because of its antirealist production, its apparent spontaneity, its use of the grotesque, and its manipulation of the visual elements of the stage in a new way. In his use of body masks, Janco perhaps unconsciously adopted Kokoschka's suggestion that *Sphinx I* was a "Comedy for Automatons." In his journal, *Chronique Zurichoise*, Tzara himself noted the impact which the performance of *Sphinx and Strawman* had upon him and upon his conception of the Dadaist theater:

This performance decided the role of our theatre, which will entrust the stage direction to the subtle invention of the explosive wind, scenario in the audience, visible direction, grotesque props: the DADAIST theatre. Above all masks and revolver effects, the effigy of the director. Bravo! & Boom boom![10]

The third and final version of the play, by then titled *Job*, was first performed in Dresden on June 3, 1917. Kokoschka directed it, with Käthe Richter and Ernst Deutsch, both of whom also starred in *The Burning Bush*, in the leading roles (Fig. 33). In May 1919 *Job* was performed again, under Kokoschka's direction, at Max Reinhardt's intimate Kammerspiele theater in Berlin. The result was a riot comparable to that which attended the opening performance of *Murderer Hope of Women* in Vienna in 1909. In a review, "The Kokoschka Scandal," Heinz Herald wrote:

On Sunday, May 25th, two stage works by Oskar Kokoschka were performed. A half hour after the curtain fell for the last time, an excited and frightened crowd booed and cat-called, hissed and whistled in the finally darkened auditorium. On the other hand, others opposed this reaction with applause and shouting. Speeches were given, both for and against, which no one could understand.

People quarreled excitedly with one another; whether they actually came to blows I do not know."[11]

Kokoschka refers to the incident in his autobiography:

Reinhardt feared that his safety-curtain would not hold back the mob, and the police had to be called in to separate the warring factions outside the theatre. I gave the actor who played Job, Paul Graetz, a removable head mask. When all hell broke loose at the end of the performance, I came on stage, bowed to the audience, picked up the hollow skull of the dead Job, tapped on it and shouted, "Your skulls are just as empty!"[12]

Stripped to the essentials of its plot, *Job* is similar to the two versions of *Sphinx and Strawman*. Nevertheless, despite superficial resemblances, it is a radically different play:

Version I autonomously exploits a variety of artistic and cabaret-like elements. II takes the earlier version's incipient parody of traditional theater and drama a good deal further and satirically puts in question the problem posed as well. Version III comes to terms with the primal myth of man's creation and raises the theme to a tragicomedy of universal implications.[13]

The most important departure from the previous versions is apparent in the very title of the play and in the change in the name of its protagonist from Firdusi to Job, indicating the significance given to myth in the final version.[14] Kokoschka's *Job* is not a modernized version of the biblical Job story, as is Archibald Mac-Leish's *J. B.* Rather, Kokoschka incorporates the story of Job into his own recurrent and obsessive vision of the struggle between the sexes. His Job is not toyed with and tormented by God and Satan but by his desire for woman: "The soul of man or magic lantern. . . . Times were when it projected God and Devil into the world; these days it casts women on the wall!" Like other twentieth-century writers who use myth as a means of depicting man in an age devoid of myth,

Kokoschka used it as a fundamental structuring principle to reveal the sexual torment of modern man.[15]

The Prologue to the play is set in the Garden of Eden. A bored and drowsy God awakens the sleeping Adam with a kick in the ribs in order to create Eve. Adam immediately regrets the order, saying, "My God, if only He had left my rib in peace," indicating that in *Job* there is a connection between Kokoschka's highly personal application of the creation myth and his use of the Book of Job. In keeping with the importance of myth is the play's increased use of allegory and literary allusion. Firdusi, the Strawman of the earlier versions, has become a composite figure incorporating not only Job but Adam. The latter is suggested by Job's entrance in the first act in nightcap and dressing gown, recalling the sleeping Adam of the Prologue, a connection made even more explicit by the entrance of Adam himself in act 3. In addition, Kokoschka evokes another figure who is toyed with by God and the Devil: Goethe's Faust.

The characterization of Anima is also more allegorical than in the previous versions. The apparent dualism which governs her perplexing nature as both Job's sexual temptress and spiritual guide is finally resolved. Whereas earlier she answered Job's question about her identity with "Anima I am—your wife! Your soul I am," at the end of the play she reveals that "Anima, who settled the heavy cross on Job's shoulders, is truly—Eve."

The Rubberman is similarly represented in an allegorical manner. He now plays Mephistopheles to Job's Faust or the serpent in the Garden of Eden. The allusion to the character of Mephistopheles in Goethe's *Faust* is made explicit at the beginning of act 2, when Job, like Faust, attempts to commit suicide in a mood of despair but is suddenly restrained by the sight of a poodle. ("A faithful dog—the last solace to him in

Fig. 33. The last scene of *Job,* direction and stage design by Kokoschka, Dresden, 1917. Photograph from Hans Maria Wingler, ed., *Oskar Kokoschka: Schriften 1907–1955* (Munich: Langen/Müller, 1956).

Fig. 34. Parrot pointing to the head of Job, from the 1919 production of *Job,* direction and costumes by Kokoschka. Photograph from Hans Maria Wingler, ed., *Oskar Kokoschka: Schriften 1907–1955* (Munich: Langen/Müller, 1956).

whom humankind inspires hate.") Appropriately, the Mephistophelian Mr. Rubberman steps out of the poodle's skin and announces, quoting Goethe, that "I am the poodle's core!" In addition, minor characters such as Eros, the offspring of Job and Anima, and Adam, the gardener, who appears in the third act and leaves the stage with Anima (Eve) at the end of the play, are also allegorical representations.

This preoccupation with allegory, allusion, and myth in *Job* suggests that in this version of the play Kokoschka was attempting to create a self-conscious and wide-ranging literary work, with less emphasis on the purely visual. Further, *Job* is the longest of Kokoschka's plays so far considered, as well as the first to consist of more than a single act. It is also the first work which the author designated a "Drama," in contrast to the two versions of *Sphinx and Strawman,* which were called a "Comedy for Automatons" and a "Curiosity," respectively.

In keeping with these literary pretensions, greater significance is placed on language, as is indicated by the switch from the prose of the earlier versions to the poetry in *Job.* Unlike the plays previously considered, language functions independently of the visual elements as a means of creating tension and sounding the major themes of the play. An example of such use of language is the song hummed by the Chambermaid, a character absent from previous versions, which is used to announce the basic theme of sexual incompatibility and the image of the unsuspecting man trapped by the woman:

'Tis the balmy summer night—
Vanished and sighing from a deep crevasse.
It lubricates tongues, it puts the salt in tears—
The blond lock of hair weaves and spins its web behind the flickering flame—
Ensnares the heroes versed in dangers. . . .

However, the visual elements, which were previously so important in Kokoschka's plays, have not been subordinated. Rather, as suggested by Camill Hoffmann, who saw and reviewed the original Dresden production, in *Job* Kokoschka "creates a tense, fantastic theater without precedent. Words and visual art, no longer running parallel, are inextricably interwoven, indissolubly one."[16] Robert Breuer, reviewing the same performance, referred to the greater refinement of the visual images in the later version: "One only needs to compare the few pages of *Sphinx and Strawman* with what has grown out of them in the scenes now called *Job.* The process whereby an abstract conception has been given concrete form is manifest."[17] Therefore, despite the significance of its dialogue, *Job* is the most visually oriented of Kokoschka's plays: "More than in any other play Kokoschka has, in this comic, scintillating piece, also carried out pictorial effects."[18]

If the two versions of *Sphinx and Strawman* were dominated by the visual metaphor of a man's head being turned by a woman, in *Job* this image has been expanded in relation to the larger scope of the play and its incorporation of myth. In act 2, Job has his head turned as in *Sphinx and Strawman:* "They've twisted my head! They've twisted my head!" The only significant visual addition, although there is more wordplay regarding Job's condition, is in keeping with Mr. Rubberman's expanded role as the representative of demonic sensuality. Having professed to be a psychologist, he prescribes a quick cure for Job's malady of having head and heart at odds with one another:

The heart is still intact! I must interrupt the double circulation
(*Pulling out a surgeon's saw*)
so that the infection won't paralyze his heart. Head off, courage! If you live headless the trouble isn't half as bad!

In the third act the visual image is extended. Having had his head turned by a woman, Job now literally sprouts the horns of the cuckold (as in *Sphinx II*) while standing beneath a rose-colored window where the silhouetted figures of Anima and Rubberman are embracing. Job rushes back and forth in terror, and as he passes under the window, the two shadows toss down upon him cuffs, collars, jackets, and men's and women's underwear—so that his horns catch the discarded clothing of his wife and her lover. Brilliantly, the image of the cuckolded husband is transformed into something even more grotesque and tragicomic: Job has become their human clothesrack!

The visual images relating to Job's death scene further demonstrate the richness of the visual elements in *Job,* in contrast to the relative simplicity of its earlier versions. Instead of succumbing from shock or committing suicide, Job dies as a result of Anima's fall from an open window while she is making love to Mr. Rubberman. The stage directions that "Anima drops like a ripe apple down from the window, scantily clothed, to land with her buttocks on Job's head. He collapses under Anima's weight and dies" suggest an explicit connection between Anima's "fall," which causes Job's death, and the Fall of Man. The image of Anima's fall "like a ripe apple" is then reinforced when she returns to the stage, munching an apple, after Job's death.

The grotesque comedy is completed a few moments later, when Job's head falls off and rolls in front of Anima's feet. (For this purpose Kokoschka designed a large head mask for the Dresden production.) Viewed in the allegorical terms of the play, Job's decapitation represents not simply the ultimate triumph of Anima over Job, or of woman over man, but also the destruction of the spirit by the body, the loss of the head at the expense of the heart. Job, therefore, is a frustrated Faust figure, a creator whose creation (Anima) has deserted

him. The relationship between Job and Anima is both an illustration of the conflict between the sexes (as in the earlier versions of the play) and a war waged between body and mind. Like Eve, who was created from Adam's rib, a separate being who precipitated his fall, Anima is both a part of Job ("your soul I am") and Eve, the temptress who lures him to destruction.

That Job's decapitation is a visual representation of the body's conquest of a weakened spirit which had previously succumbed to a paralysis is symbolized by his inability to move his head after having twisted it to look at Anima. The play is filled with both gestures and textual references which support this interpretation:

> That treacherous woman has gone to my head—
>
> In short, I'm like a pumpkinhead that must with a mystic halo putrefy in a ditch.
>
> I no longer know where my head is! . . . *wanting to tear his head off his shoulders, pummeling with his fists against his forehead.*

Mr. Rubberman, who symbolizes the demonic sensuality which attracts Anima and leads to her "fall' and Job's death, also advocates the removal of Job's head. And even Anima refers to the possible loss of his head in act 1: "He who does not take care, who errs in judgment, may lose his head!" At the conclusion of the play Adam sums up the events that have transpired, not in terms of a sexual conflict but of the division between the head and the heart of Job. When asked by Anima if the decapitated Job is in fact dead, he replies: "No! Only his head and heart and other things are gone."

An examination of *Job* makes it clear not only that the earlier versions have been extended in terms of depth of meaning, language, and visual components but that visual elements have been freshly added to replace what were simply figures of speech in previous versions. The Parrot, whose main function heretofore had been that of mimicking and accentuating Job's despair by screeching "Anima, sweet Anima," becomes in the final version a representation of Job's own suppressed consciousness. At the beginning of the play the Parrot lands on Job's head and pulls at his hair, forcing him to realize his own emptiness: "Ouch, ouch, my head! It's disappeared, destroyed!" (Fig. 34). Similarly, in the third act the Parrot prevents Job from jumping off the protective wall of his house to avoid seeing Anima and her lover together.

The changed role of the Parrot as a representation of the awareness that Job seeks desperately to avoid is demonstrated by the omission of the expression "joy reigns supreme, conscience is dead," uttered by Mr. Rubberman as Firdusi lies dying at the end of *Sphinx and Strawman II*. Instead, in *Job*, a visual image, one of the most striking of the play, clearly reveals the Parrot's allegorical role as Job's spirit which literally disintegrates. As the stage directions for *Job* note, *"Parrot explodes and drifts as pinkish cloud up through the sky."*

Another example of a visual technique not present in either version of *Sphinx and Strawman* may be found in act 1 of *Job*, where Job is separated from Anima by a locked door and can only hear her singing from within. The result is that the audience is made aware of a division between the sexes—of Job's frustrated longing to get in and of Anima's inaccessibility—through an image which functions like the barred cage separating the Man and the Woman in *Murderer Hope of Women*, or the precipices and separate rooms with criss-crossing beams of light in *The Burning Bush*.

However, the image of the locked, and therefore enticing, room also operates in a way specific to *Job*. Job's unsuccessful attempt to break into Anima's room is a suggestion both of his sexual impotence and of the

degree to which he has become a slave to his desire for Anima at the expense of the spirit—which Job's first paralyzed and then decapitated head have symbolized. That the scene before Anima's door reflects this degeneration may be ascertained in the next scene, the beginning of act 2, in which Mr. Rubberman grotesquely parodies Job's animal desire by sniffing and drooling at Anima's keyhole, like the dog whose skin he has just shed. When the door finally opens and she appears, Job's attempts to control his desire are abandoned, and he fatally turns his head to look at her.

Immediately following Job's attempts to gain entry into Anima's room, the audience is confronted by another image which expresses his tortured sensuality. Frustrated by his sexual failure, Job rushes into the bathroom to be alone. Instead of enjoying solitude, he is forced to confront a mirror image of his own desire in the men's and women's underclothing hanging on clotheslines to dry. This sight causes him to attempt suicide, and he is only restrained by the sight of the apparently friendly dog.

Other lifelong enthusiasms which for the first time enter the world of Kokoschka's plays are the elements of Baroque spectacle and Viennese popular theater. These concerns emerge in his plays at the beginning of the third act of *Job*, when, having fallen asleep on a bench before his house, Job is awakened by ten girls who emerge from among the trees and rosebushes like "Rococo cupids from the flower bed, darting out from behind trees and bushes."[19]

What follows as the girls speak to him in his sleep are a series of comic pratfalls. One girl is insulted, another is kicked by the sleeping Job. These moments of comedy are an indication of Kokoschka's enthusiasm for the popular nineteenth-century Viennese theater of Raimund and Nestroy, with its mixture of fairytale and broad farce:

It was only in the theatre of Ferdinand Raimund and Johann Nestroy, the two last great poets of the Monarchy, that the social order, once accepted as divinely ordained, had not yet yielded to the *Zeitgeist*. These two, poets of humorous fairyland as well as of bitter farce, peopled the already magical world of the Baroque with figures of their own imagining, tragicomic characters who aspire to ever-greater heights, reaching even to the spirit Kingdom.[20]

Kokoschka does not use this scene, absent from previous versions, to provide an escape from Job's troubles. Rather, its purpose is to provide a lighter, more whimsical comment upon them. In this garden scene, Job is mocked, tickled, slapped, and kissed by the girls in a way that parallels the manipulation and abuse he suffers from Anima's dichotomous nature. He says, "Is this no demon towering in the sky who sets her heel upon me in the mud—but yet gentle angel who cools my head?"

Even this scene of apparently simple slapstick threatens to turn into tragedy. Driven to despair by the mockery of the girls, Job rushes into his house and brings out a bottle of poison, along with a skull and two bones, suggesting the bottle's contents and further emphasizing his connection with Adam, whose skull and bones are often depicted at the foot of the Cross in Renaissance art. But even his planned suicide fails when one of the girls reaches down from a tree and drums on the skull with the bones, causing Job to lose his temper and throw the bottle at her.

Unlike *Murderer Hope of Women* or *The Burning Bush*, *Job*, perhaps the most visually innovative of the three plays, does not have an abundance of effects involving color. Robert Breuer refers to the scene in act 1 as "a gray, commonplace room," and to the Parrot as "a strange fowl, a color patch which, tearing apart the grayness, cavorts about the room,"[21] suggesting that, with the exception of the Parrot, there is an absence of color in both text and scenery. Only the Parrot, which symbolizes the denied spirit, stands out from the gray drabness of the body. Thus, the sole exciting visual moment involving color in the play occurs when the Parrot explodes into a rose-colored cloud at Job's death.

Of greater importance than the use of color is the symbolic use of light. As in Kokoschka's two previous plays, *Job* begins at night. (Job is dressed for bed and wearing a nightcap.) But whereas *Murderer Hope of Women* ends with a cock crow, indicating the birth of a new day, and *The Burning Bush* ends with the main figures transfigured by a halo of inner light, *Job* concludes as it began, in darkness, suggesting a circular process instead of the familiar linear progression from darkness to light.

At the beginning of act 3, Job is asleep just before sunrise. As the sun appears he awakens, and the stage directions indicate that he "staggers into the light the better to see," reminiscent of a similar situation in *The Burning Bush*, where the Woman, "a flower in the darkness," moves from sleeping to waking, and from darkness into light, on her spiritual journey. But whereas the Woman's pilgrimage in *The Burning Bush* is taken seriously by the dramatist, in *Job* it is immediately undercut by one of the girls who says: "Uprooted plants wither in the sun no less than in the shade."

That Job has abandoned the light of spiritual awareness in favor of sleep, darkness, and blindness is confirmed by the girls singing him a lullaby as they leave. The use of light symbolism is given its most explicit form at the end of the play when Adam, Job's alter ego, switches off all the lights, plunging the stage into darkness, symbolizing Job's spiritual death: "The only good I still can do is blow out the light so that it needn't shine at all."

With Anima speaking the last words of the play

alone on the darkened stage, *Job* ends on the most pessimistic possible cadence, particularly apparent if contrasted with the conclusion of *The Burning Bush*, in which the physical light of the sun was extinguished in favor of a halo of spiritual illumination. *The Burning Bush*, written in 1912 and 1913, at the height of Kokoschka's love for Alma Mahler, depicts the physical death of the Man as a sacrifice to a higher, transcendent love between the Man and the Woman. In the later play, Job's grotesquely comic death leaves Anima alone and unredeemed in the darkness of her sensual being.

In the single black-and-white drawing entitled *Sphinx and Strawman*, which was published in *Der Sturm* in March 1911, Kokoschka did not reproduce the farcical elements of his early play in graphic form. Rather, in subject matter, the illustration is closer to the violence of the four illustrations for *Murderer Hope of Women* published in *Der Sturm* in 1910.

The drawing depicts a man and a woman confronting one another. The reclining woman is voluptuous and passive. The man is taut, angular, and aggressive. The man, who wears a mask, has one arm forcefully jerked above his head, while with the other he sprays a liquid substance at the woman's belly. The woman, one hand languidly raised to her head in the pose of a model, and naked to the waist, seems impervious to the violent, apparently sexual, assault of the man. Despite the grim intensity which distinguishes the illustration from the play of the same name, it captures the contrast between the indifferent, awesome, and erotic female animal and the violent but impotent desire of the passionate male.

Although the subject matter unites this drawing with the earlier *Murderer Hope of Woman* illustrations, in style it clearly belongs to the period of Kokoschka's il-lustrations for Albert Ehrenstein's novella *Tubutsch* of 1911. Like the *Tubutsch* drawings, the *Sphinx and Strawman* illustration is scratched out with a hard pen, making the figures appear to be slivers of broken glass. The drawing is lacking in the softer, modeled effect of the illustrations for *Columbus Enchained* (1913), which modulate the hard jagged edges into crystalline softness.

In the same year in which *Job* was written, 1917, Kokoschka produced fourteen lithographs illustrating the play in alternating black and red chalk.[22] Unlike the 1911 illustration, *Sphinx and Strawman*, these lithographs attempt to capture the tragicomic atmosphere of the drama:

These *Job* drawings were a side-line of my activity as the producer of my own play. In my youth I had witnessed in Vienna the last period of the famous popular "Hanswurst" comedy, with Girardi leading in Nestroy's plays, which ended a tradition of true people's art continuing in Vienna from the Middle Ages.[23]

With their thick, dark outlines and light areas of shading, the lithographs have a hectic and nervous look previously absent from Kokoschka's graphic work. The result is that the cartoonlike drawings convey in pictorial form precisely the grotesque, dissonant atmosphere of the agitated and fantastic theatricality of *Job*:

Over-large heads made the figures top-heavy, while their over-large hands and feet emphasized their expressive gesticulation. These *Job* drawings are very strongly reminiscent of certain Yiddish theatre scenes such as those of the Palestine Habima or the Moscow Yiddish State Theatre: they have the same grotesque picturesqueness, the same wide gestures, which are as expressive as any words, the same rhythmic movements and the same pathetic humour of people schooled in resignation.[24]

The first drawing, in red chalk, is an illustration of the Prologue to *Job*. However, Kokoschka chose not to depict the scene in the Prologue in which God wakes the sleeping Adam to create Eve, but rather the moment of Adam's acceptance of the apple from Eve's hand. Eve is portrayed naked and languorously reclining on her elbow, extending the apple upward to Adam while he reaches down to accept it, looking not at her, but beseechingly upward to Heaven. Behind them is the Tree of Knowledge, while the Parrot, who symbolizes Job's spirit in the play, flutters above. Although this illustration does not depict a particular moment from the Prologue, it clearly portrays its fundamental situation: the fall of man through his own weakness and the sensual temptation of woman. It is a situation to which Adam alludes in act 3 of *Job*, immediately following Job's death and the Parrot's explosion: "Once long ago in Paradise this same bird whispered a warning to me. Busy gathering apples, I failed to listen."

The second illustration, *Job, Chambermaid, and Parrot*, adheres more closely to the text of the play. It depicts the outsize figure of Job in dressing gown and slippers, the strain of his domestic situation manifested in deep circles under the eyes of his enormous head. He is pointing with one hand to the empty door through which Anima has just fled with her latest lover, and with the other to the huge Parrot with which she has left him to converse in her place.

Job before the Door of Anima carries his miseries further. Job is seen down on all fours, pleading before Anima, while she calmly pours a bucket of water over his head.

In the next illustration, *Job and the Poodle*, Kokoschka depicts the moment at the beginning of act 2 when Job plans to hurl himself out of the bathroom window but is stopped by the yapping of a large dog, which turns out to be the Rubberman. The only significant addition to the scene is the presence of a burning candle in the upper righthand corner of this red chalk drawing. Placed far to the right of Job and the dog is the candle, a familiar symbol for the spirit in Kokoschka's works. It ironically indicates Job's state of self-delusion, which is typified by his trust in the Poodle.

Job and the Rubberman portrays the Rubberman after the removal of his dog costume. He stands in top hat, fawning over Job with his hands on Job's shoulders, while the latter, a ridiculous stooping figure in a nightcap, grimaces at his touch. This drawing, executed in black chalk with heavy swirling lines, gives the overlarge figures, which stand out from the sketchy interior, a particularly comic theatricality.

Job, Anima, and the Rubberman (Fig. 35) adheres less literally to the text of the play. It comically depicts the Rubberman kneeling before a surprisingly haggard-looking and aged Anima. His hands are raised up to her in supplication while she looks past him into the distance, bored and indifferent, her arms folded. Job, just entering the room, is shocked at the sight of his beloved and her lover. He has raised his hands to his forehead with fingers splayed, clearly prefiguring the cockold's horns he will soon wear.

The seventh illustration shows Job in his garden, sadly examining a horribly grinning skull, while three naked girls seductively pose before him. This lithograph, *Job and the Young Ladies* (Fig. 36), is a variation on the scene in act 3 in which the sleeping Job is mocked and toyed with by ten girls. But Kokoschka does not give a simple pictorial equivalent of the scene. Rather, his visual adaptation captures the tragicomic mood of the original scene in which the tormented Job is driven to suicide by the girls' mockery.

The eighth drawing, *The Young Lady and the Ardent Young Man*, serves as an illustration to the remark made by the Second Young Lady in the play: "Indeed,

Fig. 35. *Job, Anima, and the Rubberman*, illustration to *Job*, 1917, lithograph in black chalk, 11¼ × 9¼ in. (28.8 × 23.5 cm.). Courtesy Verlag Galerie Welz, Salzburg.

Fig. 36. *Job and the Young Ladies*, from *Job*, 1917, lithograph in black chalk, 12½ × 9¼ in. (31.9 × 23.5 cm.). Courtesy Verlag Galerie Welz, Salzburg.

Fig. 37. *Cupid and the Pair at Table*, from *Job*, 1917, lithograph in black chalk, 6 × 8¾ in. (15.4 × 22.7 cm.). Courtesy Verlag Galerie Welz, Salzburg.

yes, when an ardent young man visits her, she goes to roost at once. She begs his pardon—does he have his red comb?" The drawing depicts a smiling woman lying supine on a couch, inviting the man at her side to join her. The man has a featureless round head that looks like a pumpkin, and is reminiscent of Job's line, "In short, what I am is a pumpkinhead." The man's head is topped by a red cock's comb, which serves to underline both the recurrent notion of Job's imagined potency and his reduction to a state of foolishness through his sexual desire for Anima.

The Witches' Curse, the next lithograph, is similarly a pictorial illustration of a snatch of dialogue from the play. Having been given a kiss by the Eighth Young Lady in the scene in his garden, Job spits and rubs it off, explaining "I have lumbago, the witches' dart." The illustration takes the verbal expression and metamorphoses it into a visual image in which a young, naked woman is riding on a broomstick with Job chasing after her, holding tentatively to the broomstick with one hand and to his hat and cane with the other. In both the eighth and ninth lithographs a figure of speech has been transformed into a work of graphic art, a procedure parallel to that by which Kokoschka created his most striking visual effects in *Job.*

The tenth illustration, *Cupid and the Pair at Table* (Fig. 37), comments more indirectly, but nonetheless forcefully, on the basic themes of the play. A man and a woman are seated at a table out of doors. The woman gazes upward and receives a flower from a young boy by her side who corresponds to Eros, the child of Job and Anima in the play. Beside this woman is a man who completes the scene of apparent domestic tranquility. However, in stark contrast to this peaceful couple, whose attentions are directed to the left, a defecating dog is depicted to the right of the man, while another dog sniffs eagerly at the feces. In no

other illustration has Kokoschka so devastatingly expressed his revulsion and cynicism toward love between the sexes. Although without explicit reference to the play, this illustration gives a vivid description of its central theme: the relationship of erotic love (personified by Anima's acceptance of the flower from the child, Eros) to the degradation of the spirit which must ultimately accompany it. As Firdusi remarks at the end of *Sphinx and Strawman II,* "Passion must have spirit as a filter; otherwise it floods over body and soul and dirties them both."

In *Job with Antlers* (Fig. 38) Kokoschka depicts the moment just before Job's death when Anima is about to land on Job's head after having fallen from the window. Job, reduced to the level of an animal, is now visualized as one and is portrayed on all fours, wearing an enormous pair of antlers. Beseechingly he looks up at the gigantic Parrot, who is now in an upright position looking scornfully down at Job in his subhuman degradation. The figures and the treatment of the scene reveal the depths to which Job, in his impotence and self-delusion, has sunk, as well as the symbolic significance of his death as a result of Anima's "fall" and her collusion with the satanic Rubberman. As Adam punningly eulogizes moments later over Job's dead body: "You've placed your wife too high in the heavens. Only now when she falls can you see through her and view her bottom."

In *Gentlemen Dressed in Mourning* (Fig. 39) Kokoschka portrays the interment of Job by Adam. Behind these two central figures are a number of top-hatted mourners talking among themselves. In the remote background there is a country church. In the play these mourners, merely figures with holes for faces, were painted on a backdrop so as to emphasize the absurd emptiness of their comments (see Fig. 33). However, in the lithograph the use of the stage backdrop is abandoned since its effect, due to the grotesque blending of live actors and painted figures, would be impossible to reproduce in a purely visual medium.

What is most striking about this drawing is that the figure of Adam, who throughout the play is Job's alter ego, is represented by a self-portrait of Kokoschka. The artist is tenderly placing the dead Job in his coffin, his arms encircling him and his eyes gazing sadly into the distance. By depicting himself in this way, Kokoschka suggests that the ridiculous Job is a self-parody of his unhappy experiences with Alma Mahler.

In the thirteenth lithograph, *Anima and a Gentleman,* Anima sits, naked from the waist up, on the lap of a man who does not appear in the play, urging him to have a bite of the half-eaten apple which she holds up to his open mouth. With his free arm, the man gesticulates wildly in the air. This illustration emphasizes once again the connection in the play between Anima and Eve, and also stresses the ambiguous position of the man who has the apple forced upon him, yet whose open mouth indicates willingness and complicity in his own fall.

In the fourteenth and final illustration, *Anima and Job* (Fig. 40), Kokoschka concludes his cycle of lithographs with a terrifying image of Anima's conquest. The drawing depicts Job immediately after his death against a background of faceless mourners in top hats who are lined up in a row as they were in the production of the play. In the foreground lies Job, his eyes bulging and his head still twisted; Anima kneels beside him with arms folded. She is dressed in a gown of filmy gossamer. But her angelic appearance is undermined by her sardonic smile and the position of her body, one foot firmly planted on Job's neck.

In its dramatic starkness and brutality, this last drawing recalls the ending of *Sphinx and Strawman I,* in which Lilly "climbs over the cadaver like a show

horse," while Anima's appearance recalls her angelic, "spiritualized" description in the stage directions of *Sphinx II,* "light blue conventional angel's costume, wings, hands folded." However, above all, the drawing captures the gloomy pessimism of the ending of *Job* in which the defeat of the weak and wayward spirit by the all-consuming body has been allegorically conveyed by Anima's final words, which she speaks alone on the unlit stage: "And Anima, who settled the heavy cross on Job's shoulders, is truly—Eve."

The disillusionment and bitterness which Kokoschka harbored as a result of the end of his love affair with Alma Mahler, his experience of war, and the wounds which impaired him physically are also apparent in many other graphic works dating from 1917. In the cycle of six lithographs ironically entitled *In Praise of Reason (Lob des hohen Verstandes),* Kokoschka reveals the depth of his own despair in images of madness, death, and suicide. In one drawing soldiers are hacking one another to death with crucifixes, and a winged reptile flies in the background. In another lithograph a top-hatted representative of the ruling classes is calmly drills a hole into the back of one of his subordinates. Hans Maria Wingler's comments on this drawing are not only applicable to the *Job* illustrations, which it closely resembles in style, but equally well to the atmosphere of Kokoschka's play: "The figures are puppet-like, ridiculous and terrifying; it is an absurd scene which the artist has executed in a frenzy of lines."[25]

The paintings which Kokoschka produced at, and around, the time *Job* was written also express the feelings of personal isolation, cynicism, and despair which he felt upon his arrival in Dresden in the third year of the First World War. But whereas *Job* and the graphic works that are contemporary with it represent an attempt to deal with himself and the world through satire, sarcastic comedy, or self-parody, the paintings of 1917 reflect the need for a less satirical and aggressive, and a more introspective, search for human contact and communication in a world in which he felt an outcast and in which, as his graphic works suggest, he had given up all hope. Stylistically, the paintings of this period, although shorn of the grotesque humor, are clearly related to the graphics in their nervous brushwork, abandonment of flowing lines, and breaking up of the composition into numerous component parts. Gone is the fluid line of *Columbus Enchained* which so exquisitely matched the lyricism of *The Burning Bush.* Instead, the tormented, whorled style of both paintings and graphics forms the visual equivalent of the agitated dramatic style of *Job.*

In his *Self-Portrait 1917* (Fig. 41), in which the artist is depicted pointing to his breast, Kokoschka seems less self-assured and more profoundly questioning than in his earlier self-portraits, most notably the *Self-Portrait 1913* or the *Self-Portrait with Alma Mahler,* also of 1913. The feeling of uncertainty is in part generated by the tilted positioning of the head, but it is also a result of the less even, more swirling application of *taches* of color, which are used to define the body's structure. The basic difference in the painter's attitude toward himself is particularly apparent in the shift from the warm pinks and blues of the earlier self-portraits to the colder green tones of *Self-Portrait 1917.*

Another painting of this period shows a pair of lovers seated before a verdant landscape. In *Lovers with Cat* (1917) (see Fig. 3) Kokoschka is less concerned with the delineation of character than with the representation of a basic human action—a man wooing a woman. The man portrayed is the playwright Walter Hasenclever. The actress Käthe Richter, who starred in the Dresden productions of both *The Burning Bush* and *Job,* is the woman.

The man is desperately, imploringly trying to win the woman's love. His entire body strains towards her, his arms try to encircle her. His upturned gaze and tightly closed mouth suggest his devotion to the task, as well as indicate his fear of being refused. Blotches of red and purple heighten the intensity of his masklike face. The woman, however, is not responsive to the man's appeal. Her cocked left elbow suddenly checks the left-to-right movement of the painting, which emanates from the straining man. This shift of movement is mirrored by the large cat on her lap, which turns on a smaller cat held by the man, thus heightening the tension of the battle of wills. These "cats," which seem to have been born from some fantastic cloudlike substance, further accentuate the nonrealistic, symbolic character of the work. In addition, the woman's glance is downward, away from the man, making her appear distant, solitary, and immune to his advances despite her temptingly bare right shoulder and low-cut dress.

The stylistic difference between Kokoschka's paintings and his graphics of this period is ascertained by comparing the painting *Lovers with Cat* with a preparatory sketch for it which also dates from 1917. The softer, more lyrical "woven" style of the highly textured painting stands in marked contrast to the thick, nervously broken lines of the drawing, which are reminiscent of the *Job* illustrations. Indeed, the difference between the man's pained grimace and the woman's voluptuous indifference is exaggerated and almost comic beside the more profoundly subtle play of emotions in the painting.

In many of the paintings of this period Kokoschka depicts the friends with whom he was staying at the military convalescent home near Dresden. Two of the most important of these paintings, *The Exiles* and *The*

Friends, are group portraits which show a small circle of people who, like Kokoschka, felt cut off from their fellow men because of the horrors of the war.

In *The Exiles* (Fig. 42) a man and a woman (Käthe Richter and Dr. Fritz Neuberger, to whom *Job* was dedicated) are depicted before a foreboding landscape with bare trees; the artist himself is shown on the far right, looking over Neuberger's shoulder. The figures of Richter and Neuberger seem visually linked through analogous gestures of their hands and arms. Each has one wrist drooping languidly over one knee, with the other hand propped against his (or her) side. But each figure also possesses a heavy, brooding gaze which does not connect but rather isolates it from its counterpart, suggesting that their apparent union is more a common isolation. The self-portrait in the righthand corner, which peers with hollow, anxious eyes, intentionally disrupts the equilibrium of the symmetrical figures of the man and the woman, adding to the overwhelming feeling of disorientation and uneasiness.

Unlike *Lovers with Cat,* where the *taches* of color are woven together to create a lyrical wholeness in delicate counterpoint with the uneasy longing of the man wooing the woman, Kokoschka's brushstrokes in *The Exiles* work against one another, adding to the general feeling of the outcasts' desolation. John Russell, writing about *The Friends,* which was executed in a similar style, refers to the "fat hooked brushstrokes . . . that darted and flickered across the picture surface like flames across the façade of a doomed building."[26]

Although all these paintings share the mood of despair and disillusionment that is implicit in Kokoschka's tragicomedy *Job,* it was only in 1920 that he painted a work which shares the play's grotesquely sad humor, a perspective which is normally expressed only in his graphic work and not in his paintings. In 1919, with the painting *The Woman in Blue* (Fig. 43), Ko-

koschka's technique of applying paint to the canvas had changed. Instead of nervous, slithering brushstrokes, he turned in 1920 to the juxtaposition of large masses of color applied with the palette knife "that lie against one another as if they had been dragged or pulled into place."[27]

Among the works executed in this new style is *The Slave Girl* (see Fig. 4). In the foreground is the kneeling slave, an enormous naked woman painted in the hottest possible reds. Behind her stands her master with the face of Kokoschka, timorously pulling aside a red curtain with one hand, while the other is held to his genitals. Even though she is kneeling, the woman dwarfs the man in size. Like the woman in *Lovers with Cat,* and the figure of Anima in the sixth *Job* illustration (see Fig. 35), she seems self-absorbed and indifferent towards the little clownish man with the sad eyes who has apparently come for her. No painting could present a closer analogy to *Job.* In Kokoschka's play, Job and Anima also have a master-slave relationship that has degenerated into a situation in which the master, Job, has become a slave to the object of his sexual desire, Anima. As Job says: his "dominion hangs in the air like a pig's bladder!" Analogously, in *The Slave Girl* the man is master to the woman in name only. It is he who is enslaved by his physical desire, which is so well expressed in Kokoschka's painting by the glowing reds which burn through the canvas. The master in the painting has literally been "reduced" by his desire, just as Job has literally had his head "turned" in the play. The woman in the painting, like Anima in the darkness at the end of *Job,* is doomed to be confined to the prison of her own sensuality, since her man, a grotesque little clown, is powerless to redeem her.

In 1923 Kokoschka was commissioned by the Dresden Artist's Union to design a plaque to be executed by the Meissen porcelain factory. The subject

Fig. 41. *Self-Portrait 1917*, oil on canvas, 31 × 24 in. (78 × 62 cm.). Collection Von der Heydt Museum, Wuppertal. Photograph by Foto Studio van Santvoort, Wuppertal.

Fig. 43. *The Women in Blue*, 1919, oil on canvas, 30 × 39 in. (75 × 100 cm.). Collection Württembergische Staatsgalerie, Stuttgart.

Fig. 42. *The Exiles*, 1916–17, oil on canvas, 37 × 57 in. (94 × 145 cm.). Collection Staatsgalerie moderner Kunst, Munich, Sofie and Emanuel Fohn Bequest.

which he chose, five years after the publication of *Job* and fifteen years after its genesis, indicates his obsession with the theme. As in *Sphinx and Strawman* and *Job,* the plaque illustrates the dual nature of woman and the eternal struggle between the sexes. On the obverse side is a self-portrait of the artist at work, accompanied by a smaller representation of the head of a woman. Beneath the figures is the word *Anima.* On the front, a man and woman wrestle violently, and underneath them is the anagram of Anima, *Mania.* As in *Job,* the woman is depicted as the soul of the artist, his creation, and his demonic nemesis. It is unlikely that, as Edith Hoffmann surmises, "this strange relapse into a stage the artist had left behind eight years earlier can be explained by his inexperience in a new technique."[28] Rather, the unusually violent style (for 1922) of Kokoschka's plaque must be attributed to the degree to which the struggle between the sexes was embedded in the psyche of the artist.

4. Autobiography and Myth
Orpheus and Eurydice

One sheds one's sickness in books—repeats and presents again one's emotions, to be master of them.

D. H. Lawrence,
"The Spirit of Place"

Orpheus and Eurydice (*Orpheus und Eurydike*), most of which was written during Kokoschka's convalescence in Dresden in 1917 and 1918, is his most mature and complex examination of the conflict between the sexes.[1] The play is also his most strongly autobiographical work. In it, as in *Job,* he uses myth as a means of maintaining the necessary distance from his subject, the tempestuous, ambivalent affair with Alma Mahler which lasted from 1912 until he enlisted in the Austro-Hungarian army at the end of 1914.

In September 1915, a few weeks after arriving at the Galician Front, Kokoschka was gravely wounded in the temple and lung and lost the use of his right arm. For weeks he lay in a field hospital before being transported back to Austria through the Ukraine and Poland in an open railway carriage. It was in the field hospital, in a state of semi-consciousness due to pain and the drugs necessary to ease it, that *Orpheus and Eurydice* was conceived:

> I had to wait many weeks for transport home, always in danger that the Front would be rolled back. I had lost all sense of time, and for some reason I felt spatially isolated as well, as if in a cell. There were flies everywhere. Sometimes I was overcome with memories of the past: I saw the woman from whom I had so painfully parted standing there before me. I felt myself succumbing to her power of attraction, as if I could never part from her. The head wound had impaired my power of locomotion and my vision, but the words of my imaginary conversations with her phantom impressed themselves so vividly on my mind that without having to write anything down I could progressively expand them in my imagination to create whole scenes. My play *Orpheus and Eurydice* grew out of the repeated hallucinations I experienced in the camp at Wladimir-Wolhynsk. I wrote it down from memory afterwards.[2]

From the single scene of *Murderer Hope of Women* to the three acts of *Job,* Kokoschka's plays increase in length and in complexity of plot, character, and dialogue. *Orpheus and Eurydice,* his fourth play, is three times longer than *Job;* its three-act structure is divided into scenes which are, for the most part, logically and causally connected. The three acts constitute an A-B-A sonatalike form of statement-departure-return, which moves from the house of Orpheus in act 1, to Orcus and the sea in act 2, before returning to Orpheus' home at the beginning of act 3. In addition, *Orpheus* has a multitude of characters (including the unseen but ever-present Hades, who is listed among the *dramatis personae*), a fully developed subplot involving the myth of Cupid and Psyche, and a highly rhythmic and metaphorical language which employs abstract nouns and archaic syntactic inversions to convey a classical effect.

89

The play is set in the remote mythic past. As the play begins, Eurydice welcomes home the anxiously awaited Orpheus. The atmosphere is one of idyllic peace and contentment unique in Kokoschka's dramatic work. Psyche, depicted as an impish little girl who lives with Eurydice and Orpheus, although not their child, enters carrying a little snake in her arms. Despite hints of impending sorrows, indicated by such symbols as the snake and the distant sound of a calf lowing for its mother, the tone of this opening scene is one of harmony and bliss.

The second scene begins with Psyche, whose task is to faithfully guard and serve Eurydice, asleep before Eurydice's door. There is a knock outside. It is three Furies, comically addressing one another in Viennese dialect, who are on a mission from Hades and who have come to take Eurydice to the Underworld. Psyche, who is still asleep, is able to block their entrance even in this state, but suddenly she sees her beloved Cupid flying toward her on his chariot drawn by doves and in her joy opens the front door. The Furies rush in, and Psyche, now half awake, tries to bar them from Eurydice's chamber. However, after covering her torch, one of the Furies suddenly illuminates it again behind Psyche's back so that Cupid, who is near, is blinded and his chariot overturned.

In the third scene the Furies have pressed forward into Eurydice's chamber, where they deliver their message: Eurydice is to live in Hades for seven years in order to forget Orpheus and bring him misfortune. She insists on spending a last night with her beloved, but Orpheus has overheard part of her conversation with the Furies, and their blissful state of union has already been destroyed. Orpheus and Eurydice sit down for a final meal but are no longer happy together. At the conclusion of the meal, a ring falls from her finger, symbolizing the destruction of their union, and the snake bites her on the heel. Eurydice is then borne off by the Furies.

The second act begins in Orcus, where Psyche spots Eurydice amidst the shadows. Psyche has advised Orpheus to descend into Orcus to outwit Hades and to satisfy his desperate longing to recapture Eurydice. Using his life as ransom, he offers himself in order to have Eurydice for a single summer. Through a fog of ghostly shadows Orpheus seeks his beloved, who looks like an angel in Orcus and is dressed in white, with Psyche carrying her veil. As the lovers meet, Psyche warns Orpheus not only to avoid looking at Eurydice, as in the Orpheus myth, but also to avoid mentioning her past spent with Hades, an invention of Kokoschka's:

> Orpheus, turn away!
> Fix her not with your eyes,
> Frighten her not with the past,
> And consciousness, which she has buried
> Will return to Eurydice!

With averted glance, Orpheus carries Eurydice out of the Underworld, while Psyche remains behind.

The second scene of act 2 begins with hope, as the pair leaves the icy, jagged landscape and descends into a temperate valley where they see a dove, apparently a good omen. But the difficulties foreseen by Psyche soon begin as Orpheus looks for the ring on Eurydice's hand. Trembling, Eurydice warns him that it is not yet too late to turn back. She follows him onto a black bark (belonging to Hades), which Orpheus sees as a means of escape, but their subsequent journey, ostensibly towards freedom, proves to be a descent of an even worse nature.[3] A leaden calm possesses the ship, above which hangs a black cloud. The three Furies, who are weaving a net of misery for Eurydice, crouch before the cabin which houses the lovers. The ship runs aground because a Fool among the sailors on board has been in charge of the rudder. The other sailors, who had been asleep, now notice the net left by the Furies; pulling it on board, they find that it contains a skull. In the mouth of the skull is the ring for which Orpheus searched in vain on Eurydice's finger. The Fool—a cross between the German Hanswurst and the Shakespearean fool—who has been engaged by the Furies in a series of comic pratfalls reminiscent of the Viennese popular theater, then throws the skull into the lovers' cabin.

Noticing the skull before him, Orpheus' unquenched desire to hear about Eurydice's past in Orcus is reawakened. He finds the gold ring, but its inscription has been scratched out, leaving only the Greek words *Allos Makar,* which Orpheus translates as "something else is happy!" or "is another happy?"[4] He wants to hurl both himself and Eurydice into the sea but instead forces her to disclose her past spent with Hades. She does, at first reluctantly and then with a vengeance, revealing how it was only Psyche's cleverness that enabled her to withstand Hades' advances for nearly seven years, after which her loyalty so impressed him that he agreed to let her return to Orpheus. Instead of returning, however, she became even more attracted to Hades and finally succumbed willingly to his desire:

> Thus shameless I stand,
> And I laugh, Hades!
> You have conquered me!

Having admitted her infidelity to Orpheus, Eurydice leaps from the ship to return to Sister Psyche amid the shades.

The third act returns to the location of act 1, the home of Orpheus. But it is now in ruins, and as Orpheus enters, in rags and with wasted features, he only gradually becomes aware that the crumbling place where he now stands was once his home. He comes on stage with a shovel and begins to dig a grave for himself. Amid the rubble he discovers his lyre, which is broken. He begins to play it, and as he does, his cacophonous lament arouses the peasantry, who appear out of the ruins to mock and hurl abuse at him. A terrible row ensues among the peasants and soldiers who have joined in. It evolves into a Dionysian orgy of violence and sexuality, in which a centaur finally appears in the distance among stampeding horses. Amid the frenzied din Orpheus continues to play his broken lyre, and the scene culminates in his being hanged by the hysterical mob.

The stage then shifts so that the tumult recedes into the background. As the noise subsides, Cupid and Psyche advance slowly to the foreground. Psyche loosens the bandages from Cupid's eyes, which were blinded by the actions of the Furies in act 1, and washes them, using water from a golden box.

As the final scene of act 3 begins, a column of fog rises from the pit which Orpheus has been digging amid the ruins of his house. The fog moves through a field of dead who perished in the bacchanal and stops before the beam from which Orpheus is hanging. From out of the fog a female voice is now heard, which Orpheus, having jumped to the ground, addresses as "Mother of Death." The voice reproaches Orpheus for violating the order of nature by longing for death instead of life. But Orpheus refuses the suggestion of renewed life and digs deeper into the earth with his shovel, preferring death to life.

The fog trembles and sinks back into the pit, only to emerge again, this time with the voice of Eurydice. The fog is now rose-colored and gradually reveals Eurydice's veiled form. The ensuing conversation between Orpheus and the Spirit of Eurydice is painful. As the intensity of their conversation increases, Eurydice begs for her freedom from Orpheus, while he continues to dig deeper into the hole. The Spirit of Eurydice finally emerges naked from beneath her veils, flames suddenly spurt from the apparently dead hearth of their former home, and, as the blaze increases, the head of Psyche gleams for an instant in the fire. Orpheus attempts to seize the Spirit of Eurydice. As he does so, the dead rise from the earth and begin a macabre Dance of Death, which Orpheus and the Spirit also join, as he hysterically confesses his hate for her and his refusal to set her free:

> With fiendish joy I confess:
> I hate you! . . .
> Look! This Hades wouldn't let you live!
> So rejoice! I won't let you die!
> Behind love, until death, lurks . . . hate!

This revelation is accompanied by a fit of uncontrollable laughter, and the Spirit, trying to stop the torrent of Orpheus' insane mirth, strangles him. The Spirit of Eurydice delivers her last lines, proclaiming her final freedom from Orpheus and asking the question, "Isn't it, rather, hate, this love?"

In the Epilogue which follows, Psyche is seen standing on the spot where the Spirit of Eurydice just vanished.[5] She carries ears of corn and flowers in her arms as well as Orpheus' lyre. Awakening from sleep, she stretches out her hands toward her departed lover, Cupid, but realizing that he is gone, she strews the flowers over the fields, awakening groups of young girls and boys, who gather the flowers into bouquets and declaim choruses of peace and happiness. Accompanied by these signs of hope, Psyche boards Hades' bark and sails slowly out of view.

Kokoschka's dramatic work is largely autobiographical, but none is more pervasively so than *Orpheus and Eurydice.* In a letter to Hans Maria Wingler dated November 1950, more than thirty years after the play had been published, Kokoschka wrote: "It still means a lot to me, this play, which, as I told you, I wrote not in ink but with the blood that gushed freely from my wounded lung, and which I couldn't write down because my hand was still useless from my head wound, but instead spoke, whispered deliriously, ecstatically, sobbed out, cajoled, howled feverishly at death's door. But will all this blossom into life on the stage?"[6] The play, however, is not simply a faithful reflection of the physical suffering which Kokoschka endured as a result of the war. It is a precise record of the playwright's relationship with Alma Mahler as seen through the eyes of one suffering not only physical but emotional agony. "As for what she whispered to me then and what I asked her—let *Orpheus and Eurydice,* up there on the stage, reveal it to everyone! Word for word I committed it to paper, from memory, in those days in Dresden."[7]

That these reflections are not simply the emotionally distorted views of the author toward his subject, that they represent the attitudes of both parties involved, is evident from Alma Mahler's autobiography, *And the Bridge Is Love,* in which she says that "the three years that followed [her meeting with Kokoschka] were one fierce battle of love. Never before had I tasted so much tension, so much hell, so much paradise. He and I were homogeneous to the last fibre of our being."[8] Further, upon receiving her copy of *Orpheus and Eurydice* from Kokoschka, she responded: "Yesterday Oskar Kokoschka sent me his new play *Orpheus.* Presumptuous as it is, it nevertheless has great significance. To think I once believed that my way lay through *him.* . . . Kokoschka's play hinges wholly on our experience together."[9]

In a play as richly ambiguous as *Orpheus and Eurydice,* the well-documented link between the drama and the author's personal life is a rewarding avenue of exploration. Although the conception of *Orpheus and Eurydice* dated from 1915, during the period when Kokoschka was wounded in the war, the genesis of the play goes back earlier, to 1913, when Kokoschka and Alma Mahler traveled together to Italy. In the Dolomites, not far from Tre Croci pass, they visited a valley where horses, cattle, and sheep came at their call and allowed themselves to be petted. This idyllic valley was called the Valle d'Orfeo. As a soldier in the First World War Kokoschka had occasion to revisit that memorable spot, but then it was enmeshed in barbed wire and torn by grenades and shells. As he later recalled in the autobiographical story *Jessica*, "the music of Orpheus' harp, which tamed the wild beasts, was something that had not been heard there for a long time."[10]

This anecdote not only explains why Kokoschka employed the myth of Orpheus in his play but also provides a key to the play's circular structure, in which the third act returns to the setting of act 1, now horribly in ruins. Just as Kokoschka's return to the valley during the war was made even more poignant by the termination of his love affair in the interim, so the destruction of Orpheus' home in the play is a reflection of his loss of Eurydice.

Another strongly autobiographical element in the play is the parallel between Orpheus' jealously about Eurydice's past with Hades and Kokoschka's obsessive concern with his mistress' relationship with her late husband, Gustav Mahler. Although it would be simplistic to identify Mahler with the all-powerful figure of Hades in the play, it would be unwise to overlook the obvious analogies between them.

Both Hades and Mahler loom as unseen powers which either exert a powerful attraction or pose a threat to the lovers even after death. Hades, whom Hans Maria Wingler describes as the principle of "external creative regeneration,"[11] and Mahler, the great composer, constitute implicit artistic threats both to Orpheus (whose lyre has been crushed in the ruins of his house) and to Kokoschka who was suffering both physical and spiritual anguish at the time of the play's conception in 1915.[12]

That Kokoschka chose to add to the familiar command that Orpheus should not look back at his beloved until safely out of the Underworld the prohibition that he may not remind her of her past life with Hades is significant. Kokoschka himself, in his private life with Alma Mahler, also had a morbid fear of being reminded of her dead husband, a fear strong enough to be instrumental in ending their relationship:

> Because I am superstitious, I had always insisted that nothing of the dead Gustav Mahler, not even his bust by Rodin, should be brought into our house. . . . In particular I had forbidden the introduction of Mahler's death mask, which we knew was in the post to her. . . . Perhaps this, more than anything else, brought on the crisis.[13]

Alma Mahler in her autobiography confirms Kokoschka's extreme jealousy toward his deceased rival.

> We thought and talked often and earnestly about our future, and Mahler's death mask, which had come by then, made a powerful *canto fermo* for the grave choral chant of these discussions. Wherever I lived after Mahler's death I would put on his desk his music and his pictures from childhood through the last years. One day Kokoschka suddenly got up, picked up Mahler's pictures one by one, and kissed Mahler's face. It was an act of "white magic"—he wanted to combat the dark, jealous urges within him. But I cannot say it helped.[14]

Art and life are even more closely interwoven in *Orpheus and Eurydice*. At the beginning of the fourth scene of act 2, which takes place at sea on Hades' bark, Eurydice announces that she has dreamed that she was pregnant with Orpheus' child. He answers by recounting his dream "that vengefully you plunged a needle into the heart of the unborn child." Indeed, it seems likely that Eurydice is pregnant—although with Hades' child, not Orpheus'. Nevertheless, this interchange corresponds to the fact that, while recuperating from his wounds in a hospital in Vienna, Kokoschka learned that Alma Mahler had aborted their child. Similarly, Orpheus' extreme jealously of Hades in the play ("are you thinking of him, when I am with you?"), his suspicion that their child has been fathered by Hades and not by himself, corresponds to Kokoschka's preternatural suspicion that any child he conceived with Alma Mahler would bear the features of his dead rival: "I feared that the child she was carrying might have the features of the dead man, of whom she spoke too often for my liking."[15]

A final hint of the presence of the dead composer, who haunted and provoked Kokoschka's jealousy, is found in Eurydice's final lines at the end of the third act. There, having gained her freedom at last by killing Orpheus, she refers to the "monotonous song of the earth," alluding to Mahler's song cycle *The Song of the Earth* and attesting to the partial identification between Hades as the object of Orpheus' jealousy and Mahler as the object of Kokoschka's.

For Kokoschka the writing of *Orpheus and Eurydice* was an attempt to find a path back to life from an existence which had been shattered physically, emotionally, and spiritually. The affair with Alma Mahler, which seemed to promise such transcendent joy, as seen in the mystic-religious conclusion of *The Burning Bush*, had instead brought him to a despair from which his attempted escape, by enlisting in the cavalry, led him to the brink of death. That *Orpheus and Eurydice* was indeed written at a point of extreme crisis in the author's life is confirmed by Kokoschka's statement about the origin of the play, made in an interview with Wolfgang Fischer in 1963:

> In my mind all this was beginning to coalesce into one whole, promising rescue. From all the pain and fear of death I was badly in need of a clean break. At the time only one question mattered to me: Who am I, what am I, what of me is still alive? . . . It was an attempt to rescue myself from my own chaos.[16]

Just how Kokoschka sought to rescue himself from his personal chaos is seen in his use of myth in the play.

Unlike the tragicomedy *Job*, where the biblical stories of the Creation of Man, the Temptation, the Fall, and the sufferings of Job were used to comment with oblique irony on the grotesque sufferings of Kokoschka's protagonist, in *Orpheus and Eurydice* Kokoschka's use of myth is more pervasive and direct. In addition to using the myth of Orpheus and Eurydice, he introduces the extended subplot involving the myth of Cupid and Psyche, which is based upon the story in Apuleius' *The Golden Ass*. He also employs references to the myth of Hades and Persephone and to the mythic story of the origin of the Centaurs, the most important source for which is Pindar's Second Pythian Ode.

Despite Kokoschka's greater reliance upon myths in *Orpheus and Eurydice,* his application of them remains individual and unconventional. His concern is not the mere modernization of the myth but its application to his own situation. Through myth what would otherwise have been pure autobiography is raised to the level of art: "To cover up the autobiographical traces, I have used Greek myth. There is something disagreeable in seeing immediately recognizable people (on the stage) and exposing their doings to the public eye. It was not my intention to stage a Greek myth."[17]

The legendary Orpheus is remembered in two particular ways; first, as the epitome of the faithful lover who tries to recover his dead wife Eurydice from the Underworld but who, from an excess of love, disobeys the command of Persephone (whom he has charmed by his music into granting Eurydice's return) not to look at his beloved until they have departed the realm of Hades, and so loses her forever; second, as a great singer and player of the lyre, a prototype of the artist and the beloved of Apollo, who not only charms Persephone but also enchants the animals, trees, and stones, as well as the shades who inhabit the Underworld. In this Apollonian context, Orpheus is killed by a group of frenzied worshippers of Dionysus, the Maenads, who resent Orpheus' indifference to their revels, stone him, and tear him to pieces. But even after his body is ripped apart, the lyre of Orpheus continues its plaintive melody, and his tongue continues to utter mournful sounds.

There is much that would attract Kokoschka to this particular myth, aside from the significant role which the Valle d'Orfeo played in his life. As disappointed lover and artist, Kokoschka found much with which to identify in Orpheus. (It is interesting that although the characteristic lyre does not appear in the play until the third act, in act 1 Orpheus lovingly *sketches* Eurydice's face.) Such affinities help to explain why Kokoschka stuck to the basic framework of the myth in the first two acts of *Orpheus and Eurydice.* The harmonious domestic scene followed by the fatal snake bite (borrowed from Ovid's *Metamorphoses*), the descent to Hades and its shades, and the discovery of Eurydice and their ascent to earth, culminating in disaster, are all scenes directly related to the mythic sources.

Only in the third act does Kokoschka abandon his sources and plunge into a world of Dionysian frenzy. There he is in a world closer to the "Greece" of Heinrich von Kleist's *Penthesilea,* a work Kokoschka illustrated in 1970, or to the "antiquity" of his own

Murderer Hope of Women than to the Greece to which Orpheus, favorite of Apollo, would belong.

However, the Apollonian perspective on the myth of Orpheus has been convincingly disputed by Karl Kerényi, who maintains that Orpheus, in his associations with music, the Underworld, and darkness ("Orpheus" means "veiled in obscurity") and in his martyrdom, is as much a representative of Dionysus as he is of Apollo: "This is not to say that the Orphean music was purely Apollonian. It was also Dionysian, as was the singer himself. . . . It is not enough to say that Orpheus is the mythic singer. He is the mythic initiator, the priest who in mythic prehistory ordained youths and men."[18] From Kerényi's perspective, Kokoschka's play, and especially the third act, with its Dionysian martyrdom, its preoccupation with death, and its refusal to see the lovers happily reunited at the end, is a return to the very essence of the myth. Indeed, Kerényi, in his discussion of the nineteenth-century versions of the myth, says that "the myth had been broken up, its elements intermingled with others: that is how since Offenbach things had stood with the universally known story of Orpheus and Eurydice. Its high seriousness was completely lost. It occurred to no one that it is in fact a death myth. . . . Kokoschka swims in the element of death."[19]

But fidelity to his mythic sources was clearly not Kokoschka's main purpose in writing *Orpheus and Eurydice.* Although Orpheus remains the prototype of the faithful lover, the essence of the myth is tragic, as Kerényi demonstrated, and attests to the impossibility of happiness in love between the sexes. Thus, this fundamental irreconcilability, a theme which is always present in Kokoschka's literary work, explains his use of the myth: "What is the tie that binds man and woman together? Our own imagination! What fools it makes of us! What more did you have, did I have, than what fancy conjures up in dreams, which belong to all women, all men, as night belongs to day?"

Orpheus has been in love not with Eurydice but with the product of his own imagination, in which he has believed too strongly and which ultimately brings about his destruction: "You've breathed in the flame, it's burning you up. Centaur! Now you are ashes!" It is, therefore, not so much incompatability that separates the two lovers as Orpheus' own weakness, uncertainty, and jealousy, made clear in the play through Eurydice's often repeated plea, "The ground is swaying under me. . . . all that I crave is stability from you." Like Job and the male protagonists in the two earlier plays, Orpheus is represented as the bearer of the spirit who fails to provide the necessary light. Both Job and Orpheus are also artist figures who have failed in their creative missions: Job's failure is symbolized by the pig's bladder which he carries around with him; Orpheus' broken lyre, which is capable only of dissonant music, symbolizes his ruin. Nevertheless, there are significant differences between the failures of Job and Orpheus, which are readily apparent in the accounts of their deaths. Job's death, resulting from Anima's "fall," is grotesquely comic, in keeping with the satirical tone of the earlier play. Orpheus' "deaths" in act 3, by contrast, coincide with the purpose of a play written as self-purgation, "an attempt to rescue myself from my own chaos."[20]

Orpheus' first death at the hands of the frenzied mob has allusions to the death of Christ. His second death, by strangulation, is reminiscent of the Pietà formed at the conclusion of *The Burning Bush*, although lacking the triumph of love over death which is so dominant in the mystic ending to Kokoschka's earlier, more optimistic, play. Yet in both cases Orpheus' death points to the scene of final transcendence and hope in the Epilogue.

Eurydice is an ambivalent and ambiguous figure in the play, as are the women in Kokoschka's earlier plays, most notably Anima in *Job*. At times Eurydice is submissive and clings to Orpheus. At other times she is lustful and openly defiant. On the one hand, she is the bride of Orpheus, and on the other, she is the bride of Hades. She also is identified with the figure of the "Mother" (by means of the fog from which they both are formed), who tries to persuade Orpheus to return to life, not death: "What treachery it is to turn upon the mother who has proffered you the tasty dish of life." When Orpheus is strangled by the Spirit of Eurydice at the end of act 3, his dying words further suggest this identification: "Mother! How does it go again? Thou shalt not kill . . . not kill."

Such contradictions in Eurydice's role in the play are resolved only if her dual function as both Orpheus' lover and Hades' bride is understood. In this latter role she stands for Persephone, abducted by Hades to the Underworld to serve as his queen. Sought by her mother Demeter (goddess of the fruit of the earth, especially corn), Persephone was persuaded to return to Olympus, but as she had eaten pomegranate seeds in the Underworld she could not return entirely, but had to spend part of every year underground. The season connected with Persephone's return is early autumn, and the myth itself was used by the Greeks to explain the annual cycle of death and rebirth of the crops.

This myth of death and regeneration is of great significance in understanding Eurydice's character in Kokoschka's play, however personal his interpretation of the myth. Although Orpheus' lover in life, Eurydice is inexorably drawn toward Hades, to whom she must return, as in the myth. In Kokoschka's personal application of the Persephone myth, Eurydice is taken by the Furies, who act as emissaries from Hades. She is sought in the Underworld by Orpheus and Psyche (the latter is analogous to the figure of Demeter in the original myth) and is returned to earth. But this return is only partial and temporary. When pressed by Orpheus to account for her past life with Hades, she flees back to the Underworld.

When Eurydice returns to the earth in act 3, it is as a purified spirit begging to be set free from the last remains of her earthly bondage to Orpheus. She says, "Now at last let go of me. Spare me if only at the end!" But Orpheus, his erotic desire whetted by the memory of what was and cannot be again ("ah, for an aftertaste of the goblet that provoked my thirst"), clings to her with the tenacity of an animal and will not release her from his desire, which would defile what it cannot have: "You sicken instantly from the blood you lust after." It is, therefore, only when Orpheus has been killed that her final transcendence over his physical desire can occur.

The apotheosis of the Spirit of Eurydice is, then, the final step preparatory to the full liberation of the feminine spirit (Psyche) which is achieved in the Epilogue. That it is Eurydice, the female, and not Orpheus, the male, who provides this impetus is surprising, but is not inconsistent with Kokoschka's fundamental way of thinking. In an autobiographical piece, "Vom Erleben" ("From Experience"), Kokoschka, ostensibly in reference to *Murderer Hope of Women,* made the following statement which, as Wingler has noted, is more apposite to the case of *Orpheus and Eurydice:* "I had taken a swipe at the thoughtlessness of our male-oriented society, advancing the fundamental notion that man is mortal and woman immortal and that only murder will reverse the basic condition of modern life."[21]

The ultimate triumph of the spirit, suggested in the killing of Orpheus by the Spirit of Eurydice, is only fully realized in the Epilogue when the latter is transformed into Psyche, "the loving soul itself."[22] It is consistent with Kokoschka's application of myth in *Orpheus and Eurydice* that when she awakens in the Epilogue, Psyche bears the ears of corn and bundles of flowers which are the hallmark of the "Earth Mother" herself, Demeter. The fact that Eurydice-Persephone should finally be identified with Psyche-Demeter is consistent with Kokoschka's mythological sources; even more important, the *coup de théâtre* has been foreshadowed dramatically.

From the beginning of the play, Psyche is referred to as Eurydice's child, sister, servant, guardian, and companion. When Eurydice jumps overboard at the end of act 2, she flees not only to Hades but to Psyche as well: "In the house of the shadows I escape to you, my sister Psyche." Therefore this association between the two at the end of the play, when Eurydice, finally liberated, becomes pure spirit, that is, Psyche, is not an arbitrary one but has been carefully prepared. But how and why this sudden transformation takes place can only be understood by examining Kokoschka's use of the myth of Cupid and Psyche as a necessary counterweight to the myth of Orpheus and Eurydice. While the latter myth is used primarily to demonstrate the impossibility of earthly love and the decay of physical desire into hate, the former myth is used to depict the process by which the soul frees itself from physical enslavement (Psyche's love for Cupid) and is finally elevated into the realm of pure spirit.

In *The Golden Ass,* Psyche is a girl so beautiful that she makes even Venus jealous of her. The goddess sends her son Cupid to make Psyche fall in love with an outcast of no rank, but instead Cupid himself falls in love with her. He places her in a palace and secretly visits her only at night, forbidding her to attempt to see her lover. Psyche's sisters jealously tell her that her unseen lover is a monster who wishes to devour her.

Finally Psyche decides to disobey her lover's command and looks at him while he is sleeping. Shaken by the sight of his extraordinary beauty, she accidentally lets a drop of oil fall from her lamp upon the sleeping god, waking him. Angry at her disobedience, Cupid leaves. Alone and full of remorse, Psyche searches for her lover all over the earth, and is forced by Venus to do various superhuman tasks as penance for her transgression. The last of these is to go down to Hades and fetch a casket of beautiful things from the Queen of the Underworld, Proserpina (Persephone). This she does, but on her way back to earth, she opens the forbidden casket out of curiosity and finds within it not divine beauty, but death. However, at Cupid's entreaty, Jupiter takes pity on her and forgives her, consenting to her proper marriage with Cupid, her divine husband.

The dominant myths which Kokoschka employed in *Orpheus and Eurydice* have essential elements in common. Most important, both concern the search for a lost lover and a journey to the Underworld which contains a prohibition: Orpheus must not look back at Eurydice, and Psyche must not open the casket. Although both prohibitions are violated, the Orpheus myth ends tragically, while Psyche's disobedience is ultimately forgiven by Jupiter and her transcendence of the human sphere is permitted (by marriage to a god). From this brief comparison, it is clear why Kokoschka saw the two myths as complementary, and why he used the myth of Cupid and Psyche not only as a contrast to the tragic conclusion of his own version of the Orpheus myth but also to suggest, in the ultimate union of Eurydice and Psyche, a transcendence of the tragedy itself.

Most illuminating for the understanding of Kokoschka's application of the myth of Cupid and Psyche is that his play ends not with a wedding celebration among the gods, as does his source (which would have jarred with the essentially tragic conclusion of act 3),

but with Psyche's awakening to the loss of Cupid, and her resigned acceptance of it: "When Cupid softly stole away Psyche awoke in tears." The ears of corn, flowers and choral songs suggest an atmosphere of renewed hope and fecundity, despite the tears with which Psyche mourns the absence of her departed lover: "Hope, seed that spurts from the night, is it ready yet for harvest?"

But this hope for the future clearly does not lie within the framework of renewed physical love, since the relationship between Orpheus and Eurydice and that between Cupid and Psyche have both concluded with death or separation. Nor does Kokoschka suggest the possibility of love after death, as does Ovid's version of the Orpheus myth. Instead, the hope perceived at the end of the play suggests the transcendence of physical desire by spiritual awareness, a theme inherent in the myth of Cupid and Psyche, which Robert Graves has termed "a neat philosophical allegory of the progress of the rational soul towards intellectual love."[23] Within the play's autobiographical context it is clear that the Epilogue represents the hope of Kokoschka the artist calling himself, not without sadness, back to work and renewed life after the death of his love for Alma Mahler.

Another significant use of myth in *Orpheus and Eurydice* is in Kokoschka's frequent reference to the Centaur, a horse from the waist down and a man from the waist up. Although there are many Greek myths dealing with these beasts, most notably in their fight with the Lapiths and the Centaur Nessus' fight with Heracles following his attempted rape of Deianira, they are almost always used to symbolize bestiality, lust, and barbarism. In *Orpheus and Eurydice* Kokoschka does not refer to any of the specific myths involving Centaurs but rather to the myth by which they were created, that of Ixion, as found in Pindar's Second Pythian Ode.

In Pindar's ode, Ixion, the first man to shed the blood of a kinsman, is purified and forgiven by Zeus, but while dwelling in the company of the gods on Olympus he attempts to rape Zeus's wife, Hera. Zeus deceived Ixion with a cloud image of his bride, and the result of Ixion's union with the cloud (Nephele) is the bestial Centaurus, who mates with mares near Mount Pelion and fathers the race of Centaurs.

In Kokoschka's play, the fate of Ixion is deliberately connected with the race of monsters which were sired by the product of his deluded desire, the Centaurs. There is a reference to this myth even in the idyllic opening scene of act 1, foreshadowing the eventual dissolution of the love between Orpheus and Eurydice:

> *Eurydice:* When you see me smile,
> It's over the goddess
> With whom a Centaur fell in love,
> And upon whose cloudy shape
> He forces an embrace.

In the first scene of act 3, in the midst of the *Walpurgis-nacht* of violence and sexuality which reflects Kokoschka's experiences in the war, there is not only an allusion to a Centaur, but a Centaur is spied in the distance by one of the peasant women, clearly symbolizing the bestial level to which humanity has sunk:

> Look, the white mare leaps,
> Unbridled, over the stallions.
> With her belly she sweeps the ground.
> She is pursued by a monster,
> Half man, half horse,
> Its haunches lathered with sweat.

In the third scene of act 3 Orpheus himself is fully identified with the Ixion-Centaur figure he has become. He first attempts to seize, and then is strangled by, the Spirit of Eurydice, who appears as a cloud and is given corporeal form as the image of Orpheus' own desire.

Because of the play's sheer length and the greater importance given to discourse in this drama, there is no central stage image in *Orpheus and Eurydice* as there was in *Murderer Hope of Women*, where the entire play could be interpreted through the metamorphosis of a single image. In addition, here Kokoschka relies more heavily on traditional literary symbolism such as the ring, which symbolizes the union of Orpheus and Eurydice in act 1 and whose disappearance and later recovery with altered inscription suggests the disintegration of their relationship. Nevertheless, in *Orpheus and Eurydice* the visual elements are by no means ignored, despite the greater role played by purely literary devices. As one critic noted in 1922, "There is almost a plot, a well-knit story, but it is whirled in fever, torn in weeping. . . . a drama of inner radiances, a tragedy of visions."[24]

One important stage image in *Orpheus and Eurydice* is Kokoschka's use of earth and Orcus to suggest the polarity between the sexes. In previous plays such images were evident in the use of bodies separated by the bars of a cage, in the use of separate but adjoining rooms and opposite precipices, and in the protagonist's inability to enter his wife's locked bedroom. In *Orpheus and Eurydice* an analogous situation is apparent in Orpheus' attempt to locate Eurydice in the Underworld after she has been taken from him by the Furies. In the opening scene of act 2 Orpheus descends into Orcus in search of his wife, but instead of welcoming him she quite literally is unaware of his existence: "Who is Orpheus? Orpheus is a shapeless form." In this context, the traditional prohibition that the lovers must not look at one another as they leave the Underworld gains new poignancy as an image of their incompatability.

Another important stage image is found in the play's opening scene. Although his earlier plays had been called "verbally supported pantomimes,"[25] the first scene of *Orpheus and Eurydice* is one of nonverbal action, of pure pantomime, which is unique in Kokoschka's dramatic work. Eurydice sits in a shady arbor of their garden as Orpheus arrives, but in moving from the dazzling light of the street into the darkened arbor he is momentarily blinded. He accidentally kicks over a sewing basket on the ground beside Eurydice, and a child's ball rolls out. Orpheus then throws the ball into Eurydice's lap and kisses her playfully as the play proper begins.

Before a single word has been spoken on stage, the course of the dramatic action has been defined through purely visual means. It is therefore significant that Orpheus is blinded and stumbles upon entering this realm, for this action prefigures his ultimate failure to bring Eurydice back with him out of the darkness of Orcus and to restore her to the light. Indeed, Orpheus' blindness also figuratively suggests his inability to understand either the regenerative power symbolized by Hades or the fact that Eurydice belongs to the darkness of the Underworld rather than to him. By having Orpheus enter the darkened arbor from the dazzling sunlight of the street, Kokoschka has already foreshadowed his unsuccessful journey from earthly light into the Underworld in search of Eurydice.

That the child's ball symbolizes a human fetus is suggested by the fact that when the ball is retrieved by Orpheus it is thrown back into Eurydice's lap. Orpheus' accidental kicking of the ball out of the basket, therefore, suggests Kokoschka's own feeling of responsibility for Alma Mahler's abortion of their child, as well as the essential barrenness of the union between Orpheus and Eurydice, whose expected child is, after all, fathered by Hades, not Orpheus: "You! I am dead and my child is not your doing."

Although not a stage image, another example of Kokoschka's rich use of visual technique in *Orpheus and Eurydice* is the description of lover's passage out of the Underworld in the second scene of act 2:

> Under pendant veils and on through the many icy lava-folds debouching on their path but gradually receding so that, between the cliffs of snow, one catches a glimpse of a lovely seashore below. Melting snow. Fir branches shed masses of snow onto the thawing path. As they draw nearer the valley, the day becomes warmer. On Orpheus' arm Eurydice is dragged like a burden from the icy mass. A flight of doves is seen through a rift in the mistbank, revealing the sea.

This description is so obviously conceived by the eye and the imagination of Kokoschka the painter that a critic of Kokoschka's plays, Otto Kamm, has viewed it as extraneous to the dramatic action: "This can only be an evocation of mood for the reader and a purely optical representation. . . . In any case, these images are irrelevant to the unfolding of the dramatic action and without influence upon it."[26]

But to read this passage as pure description is to miss its symbolic purpose and to overlook the intimate connection between Kokoschka the artist and Kokoschka the visual dramatist. As Orpheus and Eurydice leave the Underworld they move from a forbidding landscape, a frozen wasteland, into a valley. The haze lifts and as they descend the temperature grows warmer. Surely this warmth is intended to suggest the thawing of emotions as well, so that the lovers seem about to regain the happiness that was theirs in the first act. This warming to one another after the years of separation while Eurydice was in Orcus is symbolized particularly by the flight of the dove, which cuts through the fog and reveals the sea in the distance. The dove is not only a herald of peace but is also the symbol of Cupid; it signals the return of desire and love in Orpheus and Eurydice.

The trenchant irony of this apparent return to

peace and harmony is only made clear in the following scenes, after the lovers have boarded the bark of Hades in their attempted escape. Sitting in the ship's cabin, they remain oblivious to the myriad indications that their apparent safety is illusory. Therefore, the description of the passage out of Orcus is dramatically of the utmost significance; without it the ironic distance between the lovers' fragile hopes and their present helpless situation would be lacking.

An additional example of a stage image in *Orpheus and Eurydice* is the bark of Hades, upon which the lovers hope to reach safety but which is in fact a visual metaphor of their doomed love. They remain within the province of Hades by resting in his bark, and there are various signs along their journey to show the impossibility of their renewing their love. Among them are the ominous leaden calm which makes it impossible for the ship move, the black cloud hovering overhead; the glowing moon in the sky; the infernal heat; the Furies, who are crouching on deck weaving a net of doom for the lovers; and the vain pleading of the sailors to Cupid (whose dove is now significantly absent) to bring them a good wind: "Cupid! We fold our hands and pray for a favorable wind. O, if only we could fly like your doves." All these elements suggest that the boat is controlled by Hades and that the apparent thaw was but the prelude to the final destruction of their love.

In addition, the vessel which carries the lovers is steered by a Fool—not without significance in the light of Eurydice's plea to Orpheus at the beginning of the play, "All that I crave is stability from you." Like the Fool, who is asleep at the helm and whose negligence is responsible for the shipwreck which follows, Orpheus in act 3 acknowledges his own lethargy. "I have been asleep," he says. Later in the act he makes the comparison between himself and the Fool even more explicit: "What fools we are! To claim that one stands uniquely apart from the crowd, what self-deception!" That the Fool represents a comic analogue to Orpheus has been noted by Lia Secci: "The fool is an instrument of destiny; he reveals the grotesque side of the tragedy which befalls Orpheus."[27]

In keeping with the bark's nature as the visual symbol of their doomed love, it is fitting that, with the Fool at the rudder, it should hit a reef and run aground. But if the Fool is responsible for the shipwreck, it is clear that the wreck is also a symbolic statement about the doomed love which is its cargo:

The Fool, who has all along forsaken the helm:

Surely it's the fault of that lot in the cabin
That we haven't kept clear of the reef.
There are two this bark doesn't carry gladly:
This woman and our master!

Of course the true captain of the ship is the unseen Hades, whose name literally means "the unseen." He keeps the boat drifting in a leaden calm while the lovers are together in the cabin below. Only when Eurydice confesses her past and returns to the Underworld by leaping overboard does Hades allow the wind to blow the ship forward.

Just as in *Job*, where many figures of speech about "headlessness" were used to suggest the mind's subservience to the body and to foreshadow Job's actual decapitation at the end of the play, so the many references to the Fool's hollow head may be applicable also to Orpheus:

First Fury to the other Furies:

Any minute now our taunting
Game with Hollowhead can begin.
to the Fool:
Bend over, Hollowhead,
Together with your balance you lose
Your gravity, nothing holds you down
Anymore, you shall fly!

Thus the skull which is discovered in the net woven by the Furies is not only a symbol of the presence of the God of the Dead, Hades, on board the ship; it is also a comment upon Orpheus' own "headlessness," his lack of self-awareness, as the Fool's remarks make clear:

Let's place it on the master's neck,
Him with the pale wife!
Asleep inside when all the while
They put us in this terrible danger.

The Fool suggests that they place the empty skull upon the neck of Orpheus, indicating that one empty skull is as good as another. However, unlike *Job*, where the figures of speech regarding Job's "headlessness" culminate in the visual image of the head's decapitation by the body (Anima), Kokoschka's tragic conception in *Orpheus and Eurydice* precludes any such grotesquely comic visual enactment of a figure of speech.

At the beginning of the third act Orpheus, having failed to bring back Eurydice from the Underworld, returns unknowingly to his home, his state of spiritual decrepitude conveyed in visual terms. Not only is Orpheus represented as a physical wreck, "ragged, with worn-out, wizened features," but his emotional state is mirrored by a stage image of decay: "Over his head is suspended the last remaining part of the wall. On the verge of collapse, it is overgrown with creepers which will soon level it to the ground." This image is even more powerful because the audience is immediately reminded of the idyllic opening scene of the play in the same location, and because Orpheus himself is not as yet aware that the heap of rubble is the site of his house. The *anagnorisis* occurs as Orpheus scoops a handful of ashes from the ruined hearth, a symbol of his broken union with Eurydice, and recognizes that the house is his.

Amid the rubble, Orpheus discovers his broken lyre, an apt symbol of the spiritual discord which reigns within him. He plays on the unharmonious instrument. As he does so, he summons from the ruins of his home the drunken peasants and soldiers. Literally given life by the dissonant music, they engage in acts of bestial sexuality and violence which culminate in the appearance of the Centaur and a wild Dionysian dance.

The tumult of the first scene has receded far into the background as Cupid and Psyche come forward at the beginning of the second scene, but the audience is made aware of the precise connection between the overturned world of the previous scene and the present one by means of another stage image: "an uprooted tree hangs, its root mass up, topsy turvy in the sky." The uprooted tree is an image of the overturning of the natural order by Orpheus' dissonant music, which is described as being "against nature." The ritual purification by which Psyche heals Cupid is accomplished by means of the metamorphosis of a figure of speech into a visual image, a technique already familiar from *Job*. The maxim that Love Is Blind, illustrated by the blinding of Cupid in act 1, is now superseded by the washing and healing of the god's eyes with water collected from the tears of the dead in Orcus, victims of the arrows of hate shot from Cupid's bow of love. This purification of physical love by its spiritual counterpart is also an integral part of Kokoschka's mythic source and points to the moment of Psyche's final awakening in the Epilogue:

The idea that the human soul is not passively cleansed and purified, but actively imposes the same purification upon the loving Eros [Cupid], is prefigured in the folk tale and achieves its full meaning in the myth of Psyche. Here it is not Psyche alone who is transformed; her destiny is indissolubly intertwined with that of Eros, her partner. We have then a myth of the relation between man and woman.[28]

The long and complex third scene of act 3 presents perhaps the play's most significant visual image. Having rebuffed the efforts first of his "Mother" and then of the Spirit of Eurydice to induce him back to life, Orpheus digs deeper toward Hades and the Underworld he rules. But suddenly, from the hearth of his former home, which he has uncovered in his digging, flames begin to shoot out in all directions: a visual analogy for the act of sexual intercourse. The fire symbolizes the culmination of Orpheus' passion for the now naked figure of Eurydice, who, having shed the cloudlike form in which she first appeared, stands unveiled before him. In these terms the plunging shovel functions as a phallic symbol and the hearth as a vaginal symbol. The spurting flames represent the ejaculated semen.

But these flames have yet another and equally significant meaning, made clear in the stage directions of the play, in which the fire symbolizes not sexual passion but the creative possibilities inherent in the figure of Hades, from whom it has indeed originated. This aspect of the fire's significance is suggested by the stage directions: "The glow appears to fructify itself, multiplying all over, begetting new fire." Thus the procreative flames compare with the cleansing fire allusion in the final chorus of *The Burning Bush*, which both consumes and transcends the world of physical desire at the end of that play:

Space takes shape like water, air and earth.
Fire burns it forever and consumed it.[29]

That the fire has a purgative and sexual significance and also represents the possibility of creative regeneration for Orpheus is made clear by the appearance of the head of Psyche, "gleaming celestially," amidst the flames and raising the lyre of Orpheus from the glowing embers. But when presented with this possibility of self-renewal as an artist, Orpheus reaches

for the illusory image of his desire—the woman, instead of his art:

Ah, is your face hiding amid the swirling flames?
This way! I want to leap, with you in my arms,
Out of this tinderbox, rescue us from the yawning
Abyss blazing all round us.

Similarly, Kokoschka also felt the impossibility of artistic creation without possession of the woman he loved. In a letter to Alma Mahler he wrote, "I must have you for my wife soon, or else my great talent will perish miserably."[30]

Orpheus' choice for the physical over the spiritual is unmistakably expressed in visual terms when he grabs Eurydice and begins to dance with her, joined by the dead bodies strewn around them in a grim Dance of Death. Like Ixion, who was offered the privilege of living among the gods on Mount Olympus but who spurned Zeus' favor by attempting to rape Hera, Orpheus ignores the possibility of redemptive union with Hades in favor of his Nephele, Eurydice.

Whereas the third act culminates in the visual image of the summoning up of the dead from the earth, the Epilogue opens with a strikingly antithetical image, that of the newly awakened Psyche strewing flowers over the field and thereby raising from the earth slumbering groups of girls and boys who gather them into bunches, symbolizing new life and hope. In the Epilogue the liberated feminine spirit achieves its apotheosis in the transformation of Eurydice into Psyche, who awakens alone without Cupid. As Psyche boards the bark of Hades, she constitutes a complete visual synthesis of all the major characters in the play, uniting the Spirit of Eurydice (from whom she has been metamorphosed), Hades (by boarding his bark), and Orpheus (whose lyre she holds).[31] She thus represents a configuration of the spirit which has surmounted past physical torment and promises, in the union of the feminine spirit and the poet's lyre, the renewed creativity which Kokoschka himself so desperately desired after awakening from the unhappy dream of his own love.

As in *Job,* Kokoschka's use of stage images in *Orpheus and Eurydice* far outweighs his use of color symbolism. There are, however, two significant instances in the third act where color is employed for symbolic effect. The first is Eurydice's reappearance to Orpheus as he is digging in act 3. Her voice is heard first from a column of smoke, "which is now rose-tinted." Kokoschka has chosen to express Eurydice's spiritual regeneration in the same visual terms used in *Job,* where, after Job's death, the Parrot, similarly a representative of the spirit, explodes into the sky as a pinkish cloud. The second instance of color symbolically used in the play is demonstrated by the "small blue opening" through which the head of Psyche momentarily appears amid the procreative flames of Hades' fire at the end of the third act. Psyche's head, "gleaming celestially" within this blue opening, suggests by means of color the possibility of spiritual redemption which the fire of Hades symbolizes. It is also important that the only notation regarding the costumes of the actors is that Eurydice wear a "flowing violet robe," suggesting a symbolic connection with the color blue and with Psyche herself.

The significance which the symbolic use of light and dark has in *Orpheus and Eurydice* is apparent from the opening moments of the play, when Orpheus rushes from the brilliant sunlight of the street into the shady darkness of the arbor. This pantomime foreshadows Orpheus' ultimately unsuccessful journey into Orcus in act 2, but it also expresses the basic polarity between the lovers in terms of light and darkness, the world above and the Underworld, a dichotomy present throughout the entire play.

In this dual conception Orpheus is the representative of light and Eurydice of darkness, with Eurydice dependent on Orpheus' love for her own illumination, reminiscent of the Woman's dependence on the Man in the opening scenes of *The Burning Bush:*

> I can never be utterly lost once a life
> Reposes here; brought out from the
> Equivocal darkness. Born of our love's urgency—
> Like light, love rekindles itself ever anew.

Unsustained by the light of their love, Eurydice allows the Furies to carry her off to Orcus, where the sexual polarity is expressed through their mutual responses to the darkness of the Underworld. While Eurydice exclaims "what harmonies—what hope," Orpheus' helpless response is "Eurydice! Orpheus is bereft of hope to the point of dying."

Having tried to persuade Eurydice to follow him out of Orcus by reference to light ("Eurydice, dip your hand into the light"), Orpheus apparently convinces her of the possibility that their love can still be preserved. Once again his plea is expressed in such terms:

> The day's middle part opens to allow us through.
> Nothing forces us apart.
> Like a spider whose prey has got away,
> Night squirms underneath us and slinks off.

However, their hope of escaping from the powers of darkness is undercut in the succeeding scenes, in which Kokoschka uses the visual resources of the stage to reveal the omnipresent darkness which Hades represents. Scenes 3 and 4 of act 2 take place upon the black bark of Hades, at night, with an ominous black cloud hovering above.

Following Eurydice's return to Hades at the conclusion of act 2, Kokoschka's light and dark symbolism are suddenly reversed. Having lost Eurydice forever,

Orpheus now no longer appears as the representative of light. Instead, he craves darkness and death in a mad rush toward self-annihilation, which is visually conveyed by his digging deeper into the ground:

You ask me what I have done? I have tasted
Every morsel of life, happiness and sorrow,
And know all there is to know about it.
There is no fresh light you can shed for me,
I'll never see anything new.

By contrast, Eurydice, associated with darkness in acts 1 and 2, has been redeemed by her union with Hades in the redemptive darkness of the Underworld, and is now depicted as the emissary of spiritual light (symbolized by the rosy column in which she reappears); she awaits only her release from Orpheus' desire to attain final transcendence. In their dialogue in act 3, so strongly reminiscent of the language of *Murderer Hope of Women* in its clipped, fragmented form and solar-lunar symbolism, it is now Eurydice who seeks renewed life and is identified with the light of the rising sun, while Orpheus, desirous of death, is now identified with the moon, night, and darkness:

Eurydice's voice:
He is nearing the sun, which shines upon him,
Governing the earth's fecundity through him.
Orpheus:
I'll get him, I'll dig him out
He must. . . . I'll make him. . . . There we are: night.
Get away with you, sun; I say, it is night.

As the third act concludes, the newly won release of the Spirit of Eurydice is achieved through the death of Orpheus and is symbolized visually by the "tearing apart" of the darkness on stage.

As the progress of the feminine spirit, as personified by Eurydice, is marked by a movement from external light into the darkness of the self (symbolized by her union with Psyche in Orcus), and finally from darkness (through fire) into the light of spiritual awareness, so the progress of her alter ego, Psyche, moves along a similar path from sleep to wakefulness and from night into day. Although Psyche, whose duty it is to serve Eurydice on earth, announces "don't go to sleep, it is still day!" in the opening scene of the play, she herself is found asleep before the door to Eurydice's room as the second scene begins, and is therefore responsible for the Furies' gaining access to her mistress and, indirectly, for the tragedy which ensues. However, at the end of the play, in the triumphant Epilogue, the light of day finally does dispel the darkness:

May eternal light guide their way— . . .
Awake! The sun already pours its
Unending radiance over the sleeping night.

In 1917 and 1918, while completing work on *Orpheus and Eurydice*, Kokoschka (Fig. 44) made a series of etchings for a planned illustrated edition which, however, was never published.[32] Unlike the *Job* illustrations, which were executed with apparent carelessness in scribbled strokes, reflecting in graphic terms the grotesque, frenzied atmosphere of the play, the etchings to *Orpheus and Eurydice*, although roughly contemporary with the *Job* illustrations, reveal Kokoschka's extraordinary range within the graphic medium. The variety is best exemplified in the portrait studies which were done during this period and are most consummately displayed in the ten studies which express the changing moods of a single model, entitled *Variations on a Theme*, executed in 1920.

The first etching, *Eurydice Waiting for Orpheus in the Garden* (Fig. 45), depicts the harmonious atmosphere of the opening scene of the play. In the foreground Eurydice stands alone at the bottom of a path in her garden, eyes cast timidly down, hands clasped before her. Her

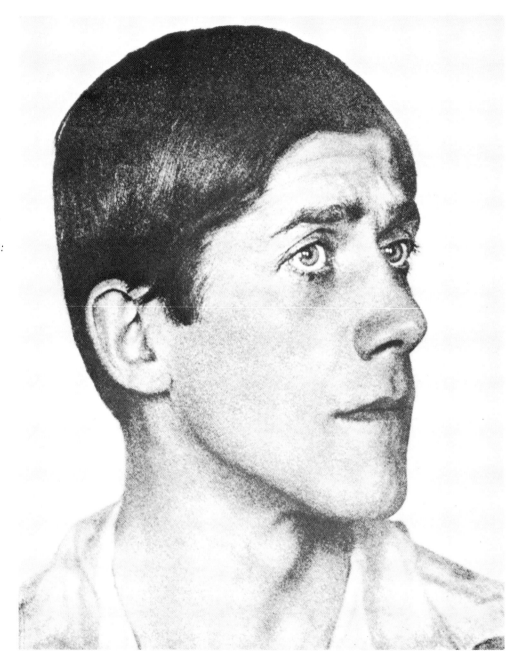

Fig. 44. Kokoschka, 1918. Photograph by Hugo Erfurth. Reproduced from J. P. Hodin, *Kokoschka: The Artist and His Time* (Greenwich, Conn.: New York Graphic Society, 1966).

Fig. 46. *Eurydice Collapses While Leaving the Underworld,* from *Orpheus and Eurydice,* 1918, dry-point etching, 6⅓ × 4½ in. (15.9 × 11.6 cm.). Photograph from Hans Maria Wingler and F. Welz, eds., *Oskar Kokoschka: Das druckgraphische Werk* (Salzburg: Galerie Welz, 1975).

Fig. 45. *Eurydice Waiting for Orpheus in the Garden,* illustration to *Orpheus and Eurydice,* 1918, dry-point etching, 5¾ × 4 in. (14.9 × 10.2 cm.). Photograph from Hans Maria Wingler and F. Welz, eds., *Oskar Kokoschka: Das druckgraphische Werk* (Salzburg: Galerie Welz, 1975).

Fig. 47. *Psyche Removes Cupid's Blindfold,* from *Orpheus and Eurydice,* 1918, dry-point etching, 9 × 15 in. (24 × 38 cm.). Photograph from Hans Maria Wingler and F. Welz, eds., *Oskar Kokoschka: Das drückgraphische* Werk (Salzburg: Galerie Welz, 1975).

slight, girlish figure is in calm repose as she awaits Orpheus, who is visible in the background on the left. In the upper righthand corner this scene of domestic tranquility is further heightened by the appearance of a dove, symbolizing both peace and the presence of the god of love, Cupid.

Orpheus Greeting Eurydice, the second etching, although stylistically similar to the previous work, is different in tone. The peaceful scene of the first etching is now parodied in the stylized positions of the lovers. Instead of being shy and submissive, Eurydice is now depicted as proud and aloof. Her eyes are still closed, but now with a calculated indifference before the smaller figure of her helplessly beseeching lover Orpheus. By means of ironic humor Kokoschka suggests the impossibility of maintaining the perfect love portrayed in the first etching.

In *The Three Furies,* the third etching, Kokoschka depicts the Furies of the play in all their animal grotesqueness. In the foreground a Fury with huge head, pig's snout, and hooves holds a spool and is in the act of weaving, reminiscent of the net of unhappiness the Furies weave for Eurydice in the third scene of act 2. Another Fury, also half-animal, half-human, crawls about on all fours, its face a hideous leer, its hindquarters facing the viewer. In style, the illustration is full of swirling, frenzied lines, the intentional disorder of its execution adding to the atmosphere of the whole.

The fourth etching is an untitled illustration of Eurydice wrapped in a white funeral garment, with the three grotesque Furies on one side of her and Orpheus on the other. In the background stands Hades' bark. This etching represents the third scene of act 1, in which the Furies come to bear Eurydice away to the Underworld, although it takes place outside rather than in Eurydice's room as in the play. In the illustration Eurydice seems undecided whether to stay or to go, while the

Furies point at her to underscore their claim. Orpheus, in water up to his ankles, points to the bark, trying to persuade her not to go. The drawing is executed with twitching, nervous strokes, providing something of the grotesque atmosphere of the *Job* illustrations.

The fifth illustration, *In Orcus,* with its heavier outlines, is even more clearly related to the style of the drawings for *Job.* It depicts Orpheus in the Underworld, as in the first scene of act 2. Holding what appears to be a lamp, he searches for Eurydice among the shades. In the distance, and evidently as oblivious to his appearance as she is in the play, Eurydice reclines on her elbow, smiling, while another figure lies before her. The illustration clearly reveals what is so apparent in the play: the contrast between Orpheus' tortuous search for his beloved and Eurydice's delight and contentment in Orcus.

The sixth etching, *Eurydice Collapses While Leaving the Underworld* (Fig. 46), continues the swirling, agitated graphic style of the previous illustrations. The etching depicts Eurydice on her knees before Orpheus, with her head turned toward her right shoulder, her helplessness conveyed by her left hand dangling limply by her side as the other hand reaches toward Orpheus. Orpheus stands over her, helping her to rise, with eyes lowered. His head is averted slightly to avoid her gaze, which would cause her disappearance. The most striking aspect of the etching is the extensive use of dark tones, which differentiates it from the previous drawings and increases the feeling of solemnity and sadness. This somberness is apparent in the face of Orpheus, who seems much older now and whose expression seems to suggest, even as he rescues her from Orcus, his knowledge of the impossibility of recapturing their past love. The illustration adheres closely to the stage directions at the end of the first scene of act 2: "Orpheus wavers, but, following

Psyche's advice, averts his gaze. Eurydice falls to her knees."

Orpheus Leads Eurydice Through the Forest, the next etching, is not intended as an illustration of any scene in the play. Rather, it depicts, in dramatic terms, the disintegration of the lovers' relationship. Orpheus and Eurydice bear no resemblance to the figures in the earlier etchings. Eurydice's body is withered and dry, her head resembling a skull; Orpheus is portrayed as heavy and flabby, his face a bulbous, papier-mâché mask. The figures are hideous in themselves, and there is no longer any contact between them. Comparing this etching with the first one, it is clear that Kokoschka's purpose has been to chart the horrifying metamorphosis from light and love in the opening illustration to the darkness and decay of the fourth and fifth illustrations.

The final etching, *Psyche Removes Cupid's Blindfold* (Fig. 47), represents a radical shift in focus. Despite the title, the central concern is still the two main characters of the play, Orpheus and Eurydice. In the foreground Orpheus, with an elongated chin (reminiscent of the artist's own features), is on one knee, his arms outstretched before the Spirit of Eurydice, who stands naked above him, her hands raised to her eyes as though she were under the spell of a sudden illumination, the column of smoke from which she has just appeared trailing off behind her. To the right of the two figures are the charred ruins of Orpheus' house. To their left, off in the background, the figure of Psyche removes the bandage from the eyes of Cupid, as suggested by the title. The etching is a composite of key elements from the third act in somewhat altered form. Certainly the removal of the bandage from Cupid's eyes occurs in scene 2 of act 3, but in the scene which follows the purified Eurydice pleads with Orpheus to be allowed her freedom, whereas in the etching it is Orpheus whose attitude is one of supplication as he kneels before

Eurydice with open arms. The key to this reversal is found in the visual identification of the artist with Orpheus in this drawing, suggesting his hope of redemption through submission to the feminine spirit, just as Cupid is healed by Psyche in the background. In the play this identification was only partial, since Orpheus refused to yield and had to be killed before the necessary transcendence of the Spirit of Eurydice could occur. By economizing within the graphic medium, Kokoschka links the purification of Eurydice with himself. In the play there is only an allusion to this is development in the Epilogue, when Psyche plays Orpheus' lyre as she boards the bark of Hades, indicating that the artist himself has been involved in the process of Psyche's awakening. In this final etching Kokoschka depicts the process of redemption, suggesting a final release from those bonds of physical desire which led to the horrifying transformation of the lovers in the first etching to the walking corpses of the fifth.

During 1917 and 1918, while working on the play, Kokoschka also executed an oil painting entitled *Orpheus and Eurydice* (Fig. 48). It indicates how obsessively this theme, so intimately bound up with his personal life, entered into every facet of his artistic endeavor: drama, graphics, and painting. Sitting in front, to the left and right of a recessed entrance, are a man and woman with their legs crossed. A winged figure above the man, not visible to either figure, sails downward and off the picture plane to the left. The woman sits with her body facing that of the man except for her left hand, which directs the viewer toward the recess, and her face, which is turned in the opposite direction with an expression of the utmost sadness. The man sits with his body facing the viewer, his face turned toward his companion with anxious longing and concern, holding one hand beside his cheek while he plucks distractedly at the strings of a lyre beside him with the other.

What is depicted on the canvas is not an illustration of a specific scene from the drama, but a comparison with the play illuminates the situation described. Kokoschka's painting conforms stylistically to the basic tone of the play in the scene of act 2, where the couple find themselves at the cavernous passage out of the Underworld (suggested by the recess in the background of the painting), and Eurydice in particular is faced with the necessity of leaving Hades. In the play she is figuratively pulled in several directions; in the painting this is literally the case. Her hand moves backward toward the recess, her face looks sadly into the distance, and only her body is turned toward Orpheus. The appearance of the plummeting winged figure, presumably Cupid, is also not irreconcilable with the play, since it is the appearance of the dove, a symbol for Cupid, which is mistakenly taken to represent a good omen for the lovers in the play. The appearance of Cupid, sailing in a downward arc in the painting, is a clear suggestion that the lovers (who are unaware of his presence) are doomed.

As in the paintings *Lovers with Cat* and *The Slave Girl*, whose subject matter was the relationship between the sexes, the woman in *Orpheus and Eurydice* is an isolated and withdrawn figure whose heavy-lidded eyes seem to gaze within, while the man is the failed bearer of the spirit who ignores his art in favor of his sexual desire, as Orpheus' inattentiveness to the lyre in the painting suggests. This concern with the physical is suggested as well by his expression of ardent longing and devotion, which is wholly in contrast to Eurydice's preoccupied gaze, and by the fact that the man is naked while she is dressed in a loose-fitting garment.

The separation between man and woman, otherwise communicated by the couple's lack of interaction, is further suggested by the heavy black line which runs through the center of the painting and forms part of the opening in the background. If the recess is indeed intended to depict the domain of Hades, then the painting forms the precise visual equivalent of the play—depicting the lovers, who are separated by the black line which seems to cut the painting in half, as both figuratively and literally divided by the presence of Hades.

Kokoschka's most successful means of communicating the conflict in the relationship between man and woman in the purely painterly way is his decision to have the couple in the painting sit with crossed legs. The tangle of feet and legs pointing in different directions suggests the irreconcilability between the sexes and echoes in pictorial terms the wild dance of love-hate performed by Orpheus and Eurydice at the end of the play.

Along with making the comparison with those visual works which were executed at the same time as the writing of *Orpheus and Eurydice* and which were, in fact, inspired by it, we must also remember that the play was conceived in many of its particulars during Kokoschka's time in hospital following his injuries in 1915. The most salient connection between the visions which possessed Kokoschka's imagination after his wounding, and which were eventually transformed into *Orpheus and Eurydice*, and the corresponding visual works of 1914 and 1915 is to be found in the last of the six painted fans (Fig. 49) which Kokoschka presented to Alma Mahler just a few days before his enlistment. These fans were "love letters in pictorial language" from the artist.[33]

In the first segment of this last fan, a woman in a war-ravaged landscape distributes food to two children from a bowl. Beneath her feet is a skull and crossbones. In the next segment, the atmosphere of war is continued with the depiction of a burning building before which a dead baby lies curled, its head in its

Fig. 49. *Sixth Fan for Alma Mahler*, 1914, watercolor on swan-skin, 10 × 17 in. (25 × 42 cm.). Collection Museum für Kunst und Gewerbe, Hamburg. Photograph from *Oskar Kokoschka* [catalogue] (New York: Marlborough-Gerson Gallery, Inc., Oct.–Nov. 1966).

Fig. 48. *Orpheus and Eurydice*, 1917–18, oil on canvas, 28 × 20 in. (70 × 50 cm.). Private collection, New York. Photograph from *Oskar Kokoschka* [catalogue] (New York: Marlborough-Gerson Gallery, Inc., Oct.–Nov. 1966).

111

hands. The following portion shows a cannoneer with gaping mouth who is firing a cannon which belches smoke, while beneath him is a soldier with a bayonet in his side, a weirdly prophetic vision of Kokoschka's own bayoneting. Above him is a group of soldiers carrying bayonets, surrounded by the blue smoke given off by the cannon. The next segment of the fan shows two warriors on horseback slashing at one another with swords; beneath them, kneeling figures, one ravaged by the war and in tatters and one swathed in pink from the waist down and naked from the waist up, stare at one another eye to eye, oblivious to the tumult which surrounds them. The penultimate segment of the fan is intended to correspond in shape with the second one. Once again a small baby is depicted, but it is now sleeping peacefully; above the child a woman is seen amidst a starry field of blue, her hands clasped in prayer, looking upward to heaven. In the final segment, which corresponds to the first in that it has a skull and crossbones at the bottom, three women in mourning carry a cross into a graveyard; the last woman is drying her eyes and is dressed in pink, while above her head a rosy dawn begins to drive back the dark night.

Certainly many of the themes and motifs which were later employed in *Orpheus and Eurydice* are already manifest in this fan. Both the horrors of war (in the first half of the fan) and the possibility of their being overcome by means of the feminine spirit (in the second half of the fan) are evident. (Similarly, the images of desolation, death, and brutal violence in the fan are mirrored in the opening scene of act 3 in the play, when Orpheus returns to his ruined home and summons up similar images, now based on Kokoschka's firsthand experience.) The two figures facing each other in the middle of the fan, one in tatters and one in pink, suggest the meeting between Orpheus and the Spirit of Eurydice, for whom Kokoschka also employs the color pink in the play.

Even more suggestive of the world of *Orpheus and Eurydice* are the pictorial means by which Kokoschka reveals the eventual transcendence of the grim violence of war portrayed in the first half of the fan. In the penultimate segment the divine figure of the feminine spirit appears amid the color blue, precisely as Psyche does at the end of the third act of the play. Her transcendence of the earthly state is suggested by the stars and by her enraptured glance, as well as by the child at her feet, who is clothed in pink instead of in the flame-colored browns in which it appears in the first part of the fan.

As the feminine figure enveloped in blue closely corresponds to Psyche, so the weeping woman of the final segment of the fan is analogous to the figure of the Spirit of Eurydice in the play, who is likewise represented by the color pink and heralds the dawn of the new day, which arrives with the apotheosis of Psyche. While omitting the theme of conflict between the sexes, Kokoschka nevertheless portrays, both on the fan and in the play, the ultimate triumph of the feminine spirit over the bestial in man.

In his monumental (181 × 220 cm.) painting *The Tempest (Die Windsbraut)* (see Fig. 5), also executed in 1914, Kokoschka comes closest to embodying the atmosphere and style of *Orpheus and Eurydice* in pictorial form. Originally entitled *The Large Boat*, the canvas shows a pair of lovers, with the familiar features of the artist and Alma Mahler, lying in an enormous shell which is adrift in a wild, tempest-driven sea. Most remarkable about this work is the magnificent energy with which it is suffused. The combination of the icy blues and greens of the relentless waves, with splashes of white, adds to the feeling of surrounding chaos and the boat's precariousness. The dashes of red and yellow likewise remain untamed, like residual embers from an extinguished fire.

Within the shell, the lovers lie helpless and passive amidst the frightful waves. The woman, the iridescent flesh of her torso reminiscent of the opaline-colored religious paintings of 1911, is asleep. She lies curled on her side, facing the man, completely oblivious to the tempest without. In contrast, the man, his body looking as though the outer layer of skin has been stripped away to leave muscles and sinews visible, lies awake. He stares up helplessly, with his hands folded together in resignation.

Clearly, this painting is a symbolic statement by Kokoschka regarding his relationship to his mistress, which was irretrievably damaged at the time of the painting's execution. The mood is strikingly similar to that of the second act of *Orpheus and Eurydice,* when the doomed lovers board the bark of Hades, which is destined to be shipwrecked and plagued by the Furies, who sit weaving their fate. That *The Tempest* is in fact an image of impending disaster and not, as it has been called, "a hymn, a song of love and of glory in life"[34] is made clear in Kokoschka's description of the completion of the painting in his studio: "my large canvas, which shows me and my erstwhile beloved woman in a wreck on the sea of life, was finished."[35]

Like Eurydice in Kokoschka's play, who, while in Orcus, exclaims "what harmonies—what hope," the woman, who lies peacefully sleeping amid what Paul Westheim has called the painting's "circling, subterranean streams,"[36] is ultimately separated from the anxious man with whom she is apparently united. This essential division is expressed visually in the painting by the placement of the two figures, who lie together and seem literally to be one below the waist. But their torsos and particularly their faces are executed in contrasting styles, suggesting the polarity between them.

Kokoschka's 1909 double portrait of the Tietzes also used contrast in the execution of the face and hands of the man and woman to suggest incipient conflict. The later painting depicts not only the shipwreck of doomed love but the division between the sexes, in which the woman is seen as a part of the destructive but ultimately regenerative powers in nature. Thus the presence of the ascendant moon at the top of the canvas is in Kokoschka's work a symbol for the power of woman to which the anxious suffering man remains eternally unreconciled, precisely as in *Orpheus and Eurydice.*

Kokoschka wrote the play *Orpheus and Eurydice* as a means of liberating his own spirit and returning to art, just as Psyche, lyre in hand, bids goodbye to Cupid at the end of the Epilogue and is therefore liberated. However, Kokoschka remained so attached to the image of his beloved Alma Mahler that in 1919 he commissioned a dressmaker in Stuttgart to make a life-size replica of her, down to the most precise and intimate details.[37] He even hired a woman as a lady's maid for the doll and bought the most expensive Parisian clothes and underwear with which to regale her. In describing the sense of anticipation with which he greeted the doll's arrival and his eventual disappointment in it, Kokoschka alludes, surely not by accident, to the myth with which his love was so intimately bound: "The packing-case was brought into the house by two men. In a state of feverish anticipation, like Orpheus calling Eurydice back from the Underworld, I freed the effigy of Alma Mahler from its packing. As I lifted it into the light of day, the image of her I had preserved in my memory stirred into life.[38] Later, however, after a wild party in which the doll was beheaded and doused with red wine, resulting in Kokoschka's interrogation by the police about the headless, bloodstained "corpse" seen in his garden, "the dustcart came in the light of dawn, and carried away the dream of Eurydice's return. The doll was an image of a spent love, that no Pygmalion could bring to life."[39]

However disappointing the arrival of the life-size doll proved to be, it served to liberate Kokoschka's artistic imagination: "Now, the cloth and sawdust effigy, in which I vainly sought to trace the features of Alma Mahler, was transfigured in a sudden flash of inspiration into a painting—*The Woman in Blue*."[40] *The Woman in Blue* (see Fig. 43) represents a decisive breakthrough in Kokoschka's development as a painter. The abandonment of the tortured, writhing brushstrokes of the 1917 through 1918 period in favor of a style based on large color patches signals the success of Kokoschka's attempt to liberate himself from the chaos surrounding him at the conclusion of his affair with Alma Mahler.

Thirty-three years after writing *Orpheus and Eurydice*, in a tripartite ceiling painting completed in 1950, *The Prometheus-Saga*, Kokoschka returned to the themes which preoccupied him in the play, although in significantly altered form. In his depiction of the myth of Prometheus, he differs widely from such romantic predecessors as Goethe, Shelley, and Byron, for whom Prometheus was the archetypal romantic rebel-hero. Instead, at sixty-six the artist viewed Prometheus as an eternal symbol of man's overreaching intellect: "In Prometheus man should recognize himself in danger of transgressing the laws which his own nature has imposed."[41]

The righthand canvas depicts Prometheus as a usurper of power who is justly punished by being chained to a rock by Zeus. The middle section reveals the results of this usurpation. A figure with a lyre (Apollo or Orpheus?) turns away from a hillside, representing the world of everyday reality, and toward four thunderous Horsemen of the Apocalypse who suggest the Last Judgment, a punishment meted out to Prome-

thean man: "Man, bowed down by the curse of mortality, is yet held subject to the Mother's sway by Moira, who persecutes the insolent."[42]

In the lefthand panel of the triptych, Kokoschka initially intended to portray Cupid surprised by Psyche, illustrating the moment when Psyche's long and difficult path towards self-fulfillment really begins. This work, intending to symbolize the possible future regeneration of man, was abandoned as a part of the *Prometheus-Saga* but was completed in 1955 as a separate canvas.

The work which Kokoschka eventually substituted for *Cupid and Psyche* is one which is also linked with *Orpheus and Eurydice*, yet it reveals how strongly the perspective of the artist had changed since the writing of his earlier play. The canvas depicts Persephone, sickle at hand, in the company of Demeter as she is released from the Underworld by Hades—who is no longer unseen but is depicted with the features of Kokoschka. In the lefthand panel of his triptych, Kokoschka perceives the possibility of renewed hope in the union of Persephone and Demeter, who return to the world after being cleansed by the regenerative fires of Hades. As in *Orpheus and Eurydice*, it is the feminine spirit which renews mankind after the presumptuous masculine intellect, symbolized by Prometheus, has destroyed it. How far Kokoschka, by depicting Hades with his own features, developed since the writing of *Orpheus and Eurydice* is evident. In the earlier play Kokoschka's alter ego was clearly Orpheus, the failed artist whose lyre was crushed. Now, however, Kokoschka identifies himself with the regenerative power of the true artist, whom he sees as the sole possibility of releasing the feminine spirit, formerly depicted as Eurydice-Psyche, now Persephone-Demeter, from the Promethean intellect threatening its destruction.

In *Orpheus and Eurydice* the dramatist employed

classical myth as the means of freeing himself from the torment of a disastrous love affair. Thirty-three years later (years which included World War II, in which Kokoschka found himself a persecuted exile), he used the same myths to indicate how Promethean Western civilization, otherwise doomed to extinction, might yet be saved through purifying contact with the regenerative powers of the creative spirit.

5. The Spark of Light
Comenius

If the doors of perception were cleansed every thing would appear to man as it is, Infinite.
For man has closed himself up, till he sees all things thro' narrow chinks of his cavern.

William Blake
The Marriage of Heaven and Hell

Comenius, Kokoschka's fifth and final play, was completed in 1972, fifty-four years after his last work for the stage. Having poured into *Orpheus and Eurydice* all the love, jealousy, and anguish he felt for Alma Mahler, the thematic core of all four of his plays—the sexual conflict between man and woman—had been exhausted and the emotional intensity which had driven him to write for the stage was finally spent. Thus, when he chose to write yet another drama at the age of eighty-six (Fig. 50), subject matter and dramatic form were quite different from those employed in the four plays written between 1907 and 1919.[1] Whatever the differences separating them, the previous four plays are nonetheless related in their subject matter and to some extent in form. Most clearly of all, they are unified by their common approach to the stage, which is decidedly visual in nature.

In *Comenius*, however, Kokoschka not only dispenses with the theme of the relation between the sexes, which had hitherto been central to his purpose, but also checks the tendency to rely upon myth which was evident in *Job* and *Orpheus and Eurydice*. Instead, in *Comenius* he is concerned with the history of the Thirty Years' War in general and with the life of the Czech educational reformer, theologian, and last bishop of the Moravian church John Amos Comenius

(Jan Amos Komenský) (1592–1670) in particular.[2] The form is quite different as well, since *Comenius* puts the emphasis on causally and chronologically connected actions and logical discourse. This four-act play not only is longer than the others but also relies more heavily on dialogue to convey its meaning and, consequently, plays down the purely visual elements.[3] Although the confessional *Orpheus and Eurydice* approaches this condition with its use of literary devices and symbolism, its fundamental orientation remains visual. In *Comenius*, however, with the important exception of the remarkable fourth act, the action is developed primarily through the medium of language rather than visual elements.

Kokoschka's debt to Comenius is of the most highly personal kind, nothing less than the most valuable gift a painter can receive—the gift of sight. The Czech reformer taught him

> that the world is a miracle which is constantly taking place before our eyes. It is because as a pupil of Amos Comenius I share this preception that I can explain to myself how my painting could produce such a great effect. . . . His method would, first of all, have led to tolerance and understanding among people, which is, however, only possible if one sees the world and sees into it.[4]

Fig. 50. Kokoschka, 1974. Photograph by Fritz Kempe. Courtesy Mrs. Olda Kokoschka and Fritz Kempe.

Kokoschka's fascination with Comenius dates from his earliest remembrances. As a child he was given by his father, as his first book, Comenius' *Orbis Pictus:*

My first book has influenced my entire life: it was the *Orbis Pictus* of the seventeenth century bishop of the Moravian Brethren, Jan Amos Comenius. In this book he set out in pictures, for the young, everything that he knew to exist. You could read the explanation of each picture in four languages. I kept to the pictures at first, for this was the real world that lay in wait for me. . . . Comenius was a humanist, and from the *Orbis Pictus* I learned not only what the world is, but how it should be in order to become fit for human beings to live in.[5]

In 1912 Kokoschka delivered the lecture, "On the Nature of Visions," in Vienna. Its shaping influence was Comenius' notion that life is based on receptivity toward visionary experience:

The consciousness of visions is not a mode of perceiving and understanding existing objects. It is a condition in which we experience the visions themselves.

In visions consciousness itself can never be grasped. It is a flux of impressions and images which once called forth give power to the mind.

But the consciousness of visions has a life of its own, accepting but also rejecting the images which appear to it.[6]

Five years later, Kokoschka followed this lecture with an essay, published in 1920, *On the Awareness of Visions,* which bears the subtitle, "Foreword to *Orbis Pictus.*" In this essay he expands his theory of the primacy of sense perception to suggest that adults should attempt to see the world with the freshness and immediacy of children: "Yes! Perception with the eyes of children shall be our spiritual power."[7] The essay concludes with words which echo the title of that book which had exerted such an influence upon him, the *Orbis Pictus:* "Now I will open the Book of the World

for you. And there are no words in it, only beautiful pictures."[8]

In the same year, 1920, Kokoschka wrote another essay whose opening sentence fully acknowledges his own debt to Comenius: "Bishop Amos Comenius wrote a book, the *Orbis Pictus,* which even today I would like to see put into the hands of every child when the time is ripe—when the young and receptive hearts reveal themselves to their teachers, and open themselves to the world."[9]

However, the influence of Comenius on Kokoschka's life is not only found in his philosophical essays. In 1919 he was named a professor at the Dresden Academy of Art. Instead of teaching art, Kokoschka tried to instruct his pupils in the spirit of the Czech pedagogue: to be open to experience, to the visual, in short, to the art of seeing.

I took my example from the humanist Jan Amos Comenius. In the course of his years of exile amid the troubles of the seventeenth century, he had tried in vain to persuade the parliaments of the Great Powers to introduce a system of education designed to improve the human understanding. Now I set out in my turn to open my pupils' eyes.[10]

In 1933, having returned to Vienna, Kokoschka tried to put the educational theories of Comenius into practice on an even grander scale. Offered the position of director of the School for Arts and Crafts, where he himself had been a student, he based his acceptance on the proviso that Comenius' theories be initiated over the entire territory of Austria. Not surprisingly, his proposal was turned down and the offer withdrawn.

The educational ideas of Comenius which made such an enthusiast of Kokoschka are found in Chapter 20 of Comenius' *Didactica Magna.*[11] There Comenius wrote the following, which forms the core of Kokoschka's own pedagogical and artistic credo:

From this a golden rule for teachers may be derived. Everything should, as far as is possible, be placed before the senses. Everything visible should be brought before the organ of sight, everything audible before that of hearing. . . . Since the senses are the most trusty servants of the memory, this method of sensuous perception, if universally applied, will lead to the permanent retention of knowledge that has once been acquired. . . . We find, accordingly, that children can easily memorize Scriptural and secular stories from pictures. Indeed, he who has once seen a rhinoceros (even in a picture) . . . can picture the animal to himself and retain the event in his memory with greater ease than if it had been described to him six hundred times.[12]

In 1934, living in Comenius' homeland, Kokoschka was again offered a chance to help put Comenius' ideals of educational reform into practice. Invited to paint a portrait of the president of Czechoslovakia, Thomas G. Masaryk, Kokoschka found his subject an equally ardent admirer of Comenius. In the three to four weeks during which Kokoschka worked with Masaryk, the two talked at length about Comenius' philosophy of education, and Kokoschka urged Masaryk to use his power as president to establish in Prague Comenius' dream of an international school, where children from all over the world would be educated on humanitarian and democratic principles, without regard for race, nationality, or religion.[13]

The completed portrait of Masaryk (1936) (Fig. 51) revealed the importance which the ideas of Comenius had assumed for Kokoschka at the time. To the left of the seated figure of Masaryk, in the center of the painting (a view of Prague is in the background on his right), is an even larger portrait of Comenius, who holds in his hands a huge chart, suggesting the figure of Moses with the Tablets of the Law. The chart bears the inscription *J. Amos Komensky—Via Lucis* and shows the organs of the five senses, "the sources of awareness, the gates of

perception of the human experience."[14] In addition, Comenius' enormous right hand rests on the president's right arm, as though reminding him of his presence. In the background of the painting, is the burning of Jan Hus, to symbolize, as Kokoschka put it, "the days when prejudices become stronger than all reason, when all sense is perverted into nonsense."[15] Before Masaryk could act upon the ideals of Comenius he died, and shortly thereafter the Nazis entered Prague. Like Comenius, whose dreams were frustrated by the events of the Thirty Years' War, Masaryk's and Kokoschka's hopes of establishing the ideals of Comenius in his homeland were to remain unfulfilled.

Immediately following the completion of the Masaryk portrait in 1936, Kokoschka began a play about Comenius. He continued to work on it even after his sudden flight from Prague to London in 1938. Only a fragment of the various drafts and versions which he produced between 1936 and 1938 has been preserved,[16] the fourth act (corresponding roughly to act 4 of the final version), which describes a fictional meeting between Comenius and Rembrandt van Rijn at the latter's home in Amsterdam.

As in the final version of the play, Kokoschka dispenses with historical accuracy for the sake of expressiveness. Rembrandt, who painted *The Night Watch* at the age of thirty-six in 1642, is shown in the play trying to complete his unfinished masterpiece at the end of his life. A similar rearrangement of historical fact is seen in the meeting between Rembrandt and Comenius, for which there is no historical evidence. However, Kokoschka's scenario is at least theoretically possible, since Comenius settled in Amsterdam at the end of a life of wanderings and died there in 1670, a year after Rembrandt's death. In both versions of the play, however, Kokoschka alters the facts so that it is Comenius and not Rembrandt who dies at the play's end.

Fig. 51. *Portrait of Thomas G. Masaryk*, 1936, oil on canvas, 35 × 50 in. (90 × 128 cm.). Collection Museum of Art, Carnegie Institute, Pittsburgh.

Fig. 53. Rembrandt van Rijn, *The Nightwatch* (detail), 1643, oil on canvas. Collection The Rijksmuseum, Amsterdam.

Fig. 52. Rembrandt and Comenius, from the televised production of *Comenius,* 1974. Photographs from *Oskar Kokoschka* [catalogue] (Hamburg: B.A.T. Haus, Feb.–May 1975).

Although closely related to the 1972 version in many details, and with several speeches in common, Kokoschka's fragmentary version suffers as a work of art because of its blatantly polemical protest against the evils of anti-Semitism and Nazism. At the end of the fragment the guardsmen of *The Night Watch* suddenly spring to life as "modern stormtroopers in uniform," shouting "burn down the synagogues! kill the Jews! the Jews nailed Christ to the cross!" Meanwhile the little Jewish girl, Hanna,[17] vanishes from sight to become the famous girl in Rembrandt's painting, who is suffused with light amid the darkness of the guardsmen. Indeed, she miraculously disappears "under the boots of the black militia, as if spiritualized, as if conceived in a dream."

Despite this potentially brilliant use of the stage, the whole scene is obviously too contrived and heavy-handed to be effective. In addition, the impact of the meeting between Rembrandt and Comenius is all but lost because of the emphasis on political protest. For this reason, when Hanna tells the audience of Comenius' death in the street, there can be little feeling evoked, since Comenius has captured little of the audience's attention during the act.

Kokoschka himself said that he abandoned his "play about Hitler" for nearly forty years because it was "too German," and that "I threw it all away because it wasn't true any longer."[18] In fact, the chief problem with the play and the reason why it probably could never have been finished is not so much that the attacks on Nazism and anti-Semitism were no longer historically relevant but because the political and didactic orientation which Kokoschka so desperately wished to achieve could not be incorporated successfully into the play as he had originally conceived it.

At this point in Kokoschka's career the medium of the literary or political essay was a more suitable vehicle for his ideas regarding Comenius and the evils of Nazism than either the drama or allegorical painting. Indeed, the political ideas that seem tendentious and ponderous in his artistic works of this period are often presented with eloquence and insight in essay form. In "As I See Myself," an essay written in 1936, at the time of his portrait of Masaryk and the *Comenius* fragment, Kokoschka, with a simple directness lacking in either the painting or the dramatic fragment, affirms the influence which Comenius exerted on his work, as well as the contemporary relevance of Comenius' ideas:

> Before I could read, Komenský's *Orbis Pictus* came into my hands. So I started early, basing my judgment on what my eyes saw instead of pricking up my ears and believing the empty phrases of adults. My love for Komenský as a child taught me later to love his life, the forty-year escape from his homeland because emperor, pope, and parliament constantly refused him the thing he asked, and the thing which he saw as the only way to peace among nations: the organization of elementary schools as protective bodies against tyranny, education of the people to an understanding by the use of the five senses, and the supervision of these elementary schools by an international board of superintendence which would keep out politics because young people are not ready for it. . . .
>
> Now I agitate for Komenský's main principle: the assurance of peace by the international elementary school; but despite the three-hundred-year-old tradition of this claim, I can find no institution in any country which wants to be the mouthpiece of those ideas, and which I would entrust with the protection of the children from the sins of their fathers.[19]

Similarly, Kokoschka's essay "Comenius, the English Revolution, and Our Present Plight" (1941) offers an intellectually more satisfying analogy between the situation in the seventeen century— Comenius' failure to convince the English of the necessity for the creation of a Pansophic College in London in 1641—and the rise of totalitarian regimes in the twentieth century than does the fragmentary drama:

> The greatness of Comenius' ideas becomes more striking when one thinks of how much more peaceful the development from feudalism toward the next stage of society—industrialism—might have been if the people of England had been allowed to reorganize themselves. Three centuries later the world still suffers misery and chaos because Comenius, the man with the message of universal brotherhood in knowledge and love, failed. Instead a Cromwell is followed by a Wallenstein, a Frederick, a Bismarck, a Kaiser Wilhelm and even a Hitler. . . . Turning to our situation in 1941, mass education seems sometimes to have been a failure. But Comenius' plan has not yet been realized. The resolve of the democratic peoples that this crusade against Fascism shall not again fade out in victory parades, but that it shall be succeeded by a long-lasting peace, can perhaps best be furthered by focusing attention on the problem of how to free the individual by removing the primary cause of his bondage, that is, education for national ends.[20]

Both the Masaryk portrait and the fragmentary *Comenius* reveal that a new, didactic impulse had entered Kokoschka's art in the mid-1930s. This change is related to the political climate in Europe, where he was branded a "degenerate artist" by the Nazis. Indeed, nine of his paintings were ridiculed at a touring exhibition of "degenerate art," and 417 of his works were confiscated from museums and private collections in Germany in 1937.[21] But his tendency toward didactic art was also a result of his renewed enthusiasm for Comenius. As he said, "According to Komensky pictures are more suited to teaching than words; consequently a modern symbolical portrait shall serve our educational purpose. One in the old style would glorify imperialism or 'domination' in general."[22] At a time of grave political crisis Kokoschka felt that to continue painting as though nothing outside himself mattered

was a luxury he could not afford. So he turned to the example of Comenius and began to paint pictures with a didactic message.

Referring to the Masaryk portrait, Edith Hoffmann emphasizes that the influence of Comenius was the basis of a new approach to portraiture:

> It becomes clear that Kokoschka in his conception of the portrait, was guided by Comenius in a double sense: he wanted his picture to be symbolical, to tell a story and teach a lesson. . . . his visual impressions . . . were made to serve a higher purpose: if they had formerly been used to express his emotions, they became now instruments for the expression of an intellectual system, of a moral conviction. The portrait of T. G. Masaryk was but the first milestone on this new road chosen by Kokoschka.[23]

But even as sympathetic an observer of Kokoschka's development as Hoffmann was forced to admit that the Masaryk portrait "had become an abstraction of what Kokoschka saw in Masaryk rather than a portrait" and that "in the end he only succeeded in creating what looks like Masaryk's ghost."[24] Nevertheless, this "new road" was to continue to dominate Kokoschka's conception of art during the war years and led to such allegorical paintings as *The Red Egg, Anschluss—Alice in Wonderland*, and *Lorelei*.

It is difficult to imagine a greater departure from the early "black portraits," in which Kokoschka attempted to strip away the exterior of his subject to reveal the inner self. Instead of delving into the lower strata of his subjects by means of concrete detail, Kokoschka's paintings in the thirties and forties strive for monumentality, tending toward the impersonal and the abstract. Even the self-portrait commissioned in 1937, *Self-Portrait of a "Degenerate" Artist*, suggests the political terms in which Kokoschka now viewed, or was forced to view, himself.

The political and didactic turn which Kokoschka's

art took at this time occurred almost against his own will. In a conversation with Edith Hoffmann he explained how, cramped in his London flat during the war, he was starved for something to see: "When spring comes I feel how it stirs in me as in a migrant bird, and I become quite nervous: I must leave town and paint something real." Yet upon his return to war-stricken London from the countryside, the very landscapes which had brought him such relief were transformed into political allegories: "My heart aches, but I cannot help it. I cannot just paint landscapes without taking any notice of all that happens."[25]

However indispensable these paintings of political protest were to Kokoschka's sense of personal integrity at a period when the freedom of the human spirit was threatened, as an artist whose life has been devoted primarily to the delineation of psychological rather than political perceptions he was obliged ultimately to reject them. Such paintings "no longer interest me in the slightest. . . . they were painted in hate—and I can only create out of love," he said.[26]

In the years after World War II Kokoschka moved increasingly away from direct involvement in politics. But the pedagogic impulse which had been instilled by Comenius, and which had found unsatisfactory expression in his allegorical paintings of the war years, remained as vital as ever. Indeed, his steadfast belief was that "the only way out of the catastrophe into which modern civilization has plunged us is: to see, to learn to perceive, instead of being a fatalistic looker-on."[27] Thus the possibility of human development through education remained his ideal.

Guided by this belief that man must truly learn to *see* before he can begin to create, Kokoschka opened his international "School of Seeing" in Salzburg in 1953. The purpose of the school was not to offer merely instruction in painting but in how to see:

In the summer of 1953 I opened my international School of Seeing, with twenty-four students. In my prospectus I made no promise of turning them into artists, but only of opening their eyes to what art is for. . . . There are thousands of possible ways of arousing surprise and getting students to see. And so, not with words, but through practical examples, I tried to educate these young people to discover their own sense of sight, atrophied by a second-hand education in an ordinary school. Anyone can learn, just as I had learned through the educational method of Jan Amos Comenius in his *Orbis Pictus*.[28]

When Kokoschka returned to the idea of writing a play about Comenius in 1972, his frame of reference had changed considerably from what it had been at the time of his first efforts in the years 1936 to 1938. The final *Comenius* is not a political play full of references to Nazi Germany, a *pièce à thèse* in support of Comenius' didactic methods, an allegory, or a profession of faith in the possibility of human development through educational reform. Instead, the final version was intended to explain his fundamental belief in the miracle of spiritual illumination, "the inner light."[29]

Suddenly in one hundred years a spark, a spark, and that's all humanity is worth. The history of the human spirit is a number of sudden sparks—the number of sparks of sudden enlightenment which are forgotten immediately afterward, of course, and that's the human spirit. . . . A cow hasn't got that spark.[30]

The world which Kokoschka constructed in *Comenius* is one in which "all is a madhouse . . . all of the characters are mad—mad with power, mad in love, etc. . . . even Comenius is mad, since he believes in education, reform, progress. . . . So never believe in progress, believe in the spark."[31]

Acts 1 through 3 describe the world of the "madhouse" during the Thirty Years' War, in which nearly all the major characters are possessed by an *idée fixe*.

Act 4, set in Rembrandt's studio in Amsterdam, describes the creation of the spark of artistic enlightenment. The first three acts rely almost entirely on dialogue rather than on visual effects, but act 4 relies predominantly on visual effects.

The play opens in the Hofburg in Vienna, where the Habsburg Archduke Ferdinand of Styria, who has been condemned to death, is being shaved by his barber, Shylock. At the last moment, instead of being executed, he witnesses a *coup d'état,* and after a narrow escape from the assault of a rebel faction, he is saved and becomes the new Emperor Ferdinand II.[32]

Following his miraculous rescue, Ferdinand immediately prepares for war against the Protestants in Bohemia, in violation of the Letter of Majesty guaranteeing religious freedom signed by the previous emperor, Mathias, and supported financially with money which he has extorted from the Jews through Shylock.

The "Prague Defenestration," in which two deputy governors and a royal scribe were thrown from the windows of Hradschin Castle by the Protestants (without being seriously injured, however) provides Ferdinand with a welcome excuse for the overt persecution of religious minorities and the subjugation of Bohemia. A Hitler-like proclamation declares, "One Reich, one master, one God! One world at peace!"[33] The act concludes with Drabik, a follower of Comenius, being tortured and nearly burned alive at the stake, his screams accompanied by cries of joy from the watching masses and the singing of hymns by a choir of children. The act demonstrates the madness of those who are possessed by hunger for power. In addition, the bestial in man is shown in the treatment of Drabik, which foreshadows the exile from Bohemia of Comenius and his Moravian followers in act 2.

The second act opens in Fulnek, a town on the Moravian-Silesian border where Comenius was teacher and minister between 1618 and 1621.[34] The exact date is given in the text as 1628, the year Comenius was forced to flee from his native Bohemia and seek refuge abroad. Comenius arrives at the hut of a wax chandler with a blind Jewish Girl whom he has adopted on his travels and has renamed Christl in order to save her from the pogroms. He announces his plan to begin his *Didactica Magna* and to form

> one humane, maternal school for all nations, as long as they are children, as long as their hearts can be cultivated and their spirits are young, in order to understand that the world can be a paradise, instead of a labyrinth in which we have ensnared ourselves.

Some children from the village arrive at the hut. Comenius entertains them with a fable about a meeting between a little girl and a queen bee. This allegorical story describes the history of Bohemia, doomed to be torn by conflict because the girl has forgotten the magical advice of the queen bee as to how the new state should be founded and governed.

Before Comenius' narration of the fable, he has described to the blind Christl the games that the village children are playing. They are celebrating the death of winter and the rebirth of spring by throwing an effigy of "old man winter" into the water, where hollowed-out eggs with tiny candles inside are floating, symbolizing the renewal of life. The potentially superb visual qualities of the scene are but inadequately conveyed through the medium of language. They might have been more successfully exploited by means of stage images, an example of the essentially nonvisual way in which the first three acts of *Comenius* are written. Nevertheless, Comenius' description is important to an interpretation of the play, since the children's games prefigure the final scene of the play, which also takes place in the spring and uses light to suggest rebirth.

Comenius' arrest has now been demanded by Ferdinand: "This teacher, who brainwashes the people of Bohemia, must be found." And as he continues his flight from Bohemia, another sort of madness is depicted in the amorous intrigue which involves Zerotin (the protector of Comenius and his sect), his wife, and Trcka, a Bohemian nobleman. All three are victims of their own blindness or *idée fixe*. Zerotin is deceived by his blind trust in his wife, who almost makes love to Trcka before his dazed eyes, and he nearly reneges in his love for Comenius because of his fidelity to the emperor. The madness of his wife is in her blind love for Trcka, who uses her to further his own political ambitions and then betrays her. Even Trcka, the unscrupulous manipulator, is blinded by his own lust for power in a corrupt world he has helped to create and in which "neither Emperor nor Pope—only money rules our country." As in act 1, where the bestial in man was revealed in Ferdinand's ascent to power, the leitmotif makes its appearance: "Truly, the ravaging beasts of prey are your models, you men."

In the final scene of act 2 Comenius greets his surviving followers, who are starving and in rags, on the Hungarian border on his way toward Leszno, Poland. Although he preserves his essential credo "to learn to see people and things with open eyes," his followers' doubts have increased as a result of their tribulations. "You not only want to reform religion, but nature as well; like the alchemists you want to breed a homunculus in a test tube,"[35] they say. The act concludes with Comenius' faith suffering yet another blow: he hears that his protector, Prince Rakoczy, has died of the plague and that Christl, who had been left in Rakoczy's care, is now homeless and, in all likelihood, doomed.

Continuing on his forced pilgrimage through Europe, Comenius receives an invitation from Chancellor Oxenstierna of Sweden to reform the Swedish educational system according to his own ideas.[36] Although Queen Christine offers him five hundred thalers annually to implement his plan, Comenius courageously sacrifices the opportunity for comfort and success and incurs royal displeasure when he decides to leave Sweden to attend the conference at Thorn in 1645, called to reconcile all churches. There he sought to plead the cause of the Moravian Brethren, which he feared might be ignored without his presence.

After dismissing Comenius in disgrace, Queen Christine welcomes the Spanish ambassador, who tempts her to visit Rome by offering her a statue of a naked woman as a gift, even though such a trip would mean ignoring her responsibilities as head of state. Although she finally refuses, she is obviously more interested in the handsome ambassador than in the aged bishop, who continues on his lonely way.

If the first three acts of *Comenius* give us a vast panorama of Europe ravaged by the events precipitating and resulting from the Thirty Years' War, act 4 is narrower in its focus and presents the dramatic core of the play. While acts 1 through 3 depict man primarily as a beast, the fourth act reveals his human characteristics. As in the fragment written between 1936 and 1938, the final version is set in Amsterdam on a spring afternoon in Rembrandt's studio. Rembrandt is portrayed as an old man living in dire poverty with his mistress, Hendrikje Stoffels, trying unsuccessfully to complete the enormous canvas of *The Night Watch*[37] (Fig. 52). As the act begins he is more intent on catching flies and drinking schnapps than painting. He seems more like another clown in the madhouse of *Comenius* than a genius. Hendrikje is angry but loving and compassionate toward her lazy profligate.

During one of their quarrels, Comenius enters the studio to have his portrait painted. He is strangely silent and says little to Rembrandt and Hendrikje except to marvel at her good-natured simplicity. He seems exhausted by his wanderings and even dozes off at one point while Rembrandt is speaking to him. He is invited to stay and share their simple meal. He does, but, suddenly becoming excited, he pushes his plate aside and voices the bitterness and resentment of a life of failure to reform men:

> The rapacity in which people resemble wild animals, and the ignorance in which they resemble a flock of sheep rushing after the wether into the abyss, have become worse during the Reformation. The war will never end. Nations treat their people like cattle at the slaughterhouse. The world is a hell. I believe man will become extinct in the same way as the giants and dinosaurs of prehistoric times if he does not listen to reason.

After this outburst of rage and disappointment at the blindness of humanity from an educator whose mission was to enable man to see, Rembrandt tries to soothe Comenius. Soon a little Jewish girl, Hannah, arrives, asking to see Rembrandt. Comenius insists that this is the girl whom he has been seeking for so long, the blind girl in Bohemia whom he named Christl to rescue her from persecution.[38] Although she does not acknowledge Comenius' claim and formally addresses him as a "strange gentleman," she tells him that "we will meet by and by, I with wings on the soles of my feet, as in a fairytale." Following this remark Comenius leaves the studio and is almost immediately stopped by a patrol of soldiers. After receiving negative answers to inquiries about his passport and his money, they arrest him and lead him away. Following a protest to the soldiers, Rembrandt slams the door of his studio, where it is now quite dark. It begins to storm outside and the studio is filled with smoke. Three times the child's voice in the darkened room calls Rembrandt's name. The third time the voice "rises jubilantly to the highest key," and the empty space in *The*

Night Watch begins to brighten until the entire painting is illuminated.

It is now morning, and in the empty patch on the canvas appears the figure of Hannah, the little girl in white, who seems to bear no relation to the soldiers in Rembrandt's painting. Once more the girl's voice is heard announcing that Comenius has died outside on the street and that she is portrayed on Rembrandt's painting "as a testimony to his [Comenius'] compassion, for all to see what it means to be human." Hendrikje enters, extinguishing the remains of the tallow candle, marveling at the miracle that Rembrandt has created: "You have painted the picture in the dark. To me it's a miracle, and I'm not ashamed to say so."

In contrast to the preceding three acts, in which visual elements play an extremely minor role, the fourth act of *Comenius* cannot be adequately understood without a careful examination of its dominant stage image and its use of light and dark.[39] The stage image which overlooks the action of act 4 is Rembrandt's *The Night Watch*. The painting functions as a visual image, rather than as a mere stage prop or literary symbol, in two ways. First, the subject is itself a symbolic representation of the play's major theme, namely, the conflict between the spiritual and bestial in man. The former is the path pursued by the lonely Czech humanist who intends to enable man to see; the latter is illustrated by the pursuit of power, lust, and greed which nearly all the other characters (Ferdinand, Trcka, Zerotin's wife, Queen Christine) share. In the painting this conflict is suggested visually by the little girl in white bedecked by flowers, surrounded by the smug, self-satisfied guardsmen. As the character of Rembrandt points out early in the act, these apparent defenders of human rights are actually suppressors of freedom: "look at this hero, Jan Gockelhahn, Captain of the Cloveniersdoelen, who wears the claw of the cock of liberty as a mark of distinction. Let no one dare call our civil rights a dim light in front of him, lest he burn down the houses of those who complain."

This interpretation of *The Night Watch* as a satiric indictment of the prosperous Dutch middle class is conveyed with even greater determination elsewhere by Kokoschka. He said that

> as early as *The Night Watch* the burghers have become mere puppets; instead of real rapiers they carry ornamental dress-swords. Rembrandt's contemporaries had painted the civic guard companies in a traditional, official arrangement, in order of rank, meritorious service and income. One can almost sense the painter's cynical grin. *The Night Watch* presents an entirely new kind of composition, expressing the hollowness of the progressive bourgeois order in a sort of carnival tableau.[40]

In addition to its subject matter, Rembrandt's *The Night Watch* is an important visual image in another way, suggesting the artist's power to produce visions of miraculous insight. Although Comenius says "I am searching for the child," the child, who should be viewed as an allegorical representation of inner light, comes not to him but to the artist, as her opening words reveal. "If only I could go in and see Rembrandt, quickly," she says. Her role as embodiment of the creative spark is also made clear by her insistence upon speaking to Rembrandt alone: "I will only tell you in private, when the strange gentleman has gone. It is a secret for your ears alone!" Although the girl tells Comenius that they will meet again, it is only the artist who is visited by the miracle of vision in this life:

> Rembrandt! Do you hear me? How the princess, Jehovah's pure virgin, locked up until this very day in her castle, puts forward her request to He, whose miraculously gentle spirit will become the breath of all things.

> *Her voice rises jubilantly to the highest key*

Even if the failure of Comenius' attempts to teach humanity to see is mitigated by the fact that his compassion is commemorated by the portrait of Hannah in *The Night Watch,* he has nonetheless failed, and his failure must be regarded as a statement of Kokoschka's own feelings of disillusionment with the possibility of human improvement through education. Indeed, in 1973, shortly after the play's completion, Kokoschka said: "Never believe in education. . . . that's why I make fun of Comenius."[41]

Comenius himself realizes the futility of trying to instruct mankind at the end of the play. Having dozed off while Rembrandt was speaking, he awakens to the realization that only the artist, the man who sees within, can bring forth the light he himself has tried, but failed, to create in others: "More fortunate painter's soul, you dig up pearls and gold from the dust of your wretched studio; you carry someone on wings, in a dream up to the Via Lucis. . . . If only the world were a vision of light and shade, purely our imagination!" Comenius, the pedagogue, has searched for a child his entire life, educating people to see as children. Thus he says, "I can't sleep, I've had wild dreams of peace, my whole life long. I'm searching for a child still." By contrast, Rembrandt, the artist-visionary, carries the child within himself.

The painting of *The Night Watch* is therefore crucial to an understanding of *Comenius.* Its subject matter echoes the basic conflict of the play between love of humanity and love of power, and its miraculous completion at the end of the play emphasizes the artist's visionary insight, which enables him to create a spark of light in the midst of darkness.

Kokoschka's own remarks about the Dutch painter serve to confirm this dual interpretation. In a speech made in 1956 in Amsterdam, commemorating the 350th anniversary of Rembrandt's birth, Kokoschka spoke

not about Rembrandt as artist but as humanist. He saw
him as a figure who, like Comenius, stood for compassion and love of one's fellow man in time of war:

> It was the greatest achievement of this genius that he
> eternalized the word mankind—humanity, fraternity—and
> now we are extremely grateful that we can see this work
> today, after this terrible period (similar to that which he
> experienced). . . . And then we have only to walk over to
> the exhibition to realize suddenly that both West and East
> contribute to our understanding of this message, this true
> gospel, as only an artist can preach it; it makes us see—
> the gospel of love for one's fellow man.[42]

In addition, Kokoschka saw Rembrandt as more
than a fine craftsman or humanist: he saw him as a
creator of inner light (as opposed to mere chiaroscuro),
particularly in his later works. This helps to explain the
motivation for Kokoschka's shifting of *The Night Watch*
to the end of Rembrandt's career in *Comenius*. Referring
to a favorite late painting by Rembrandt, *The Conspiracy
of Claudius Civilis* (1661–62), Kokoschka wrote:

> The whole composition is bathed in light. We are startled
> by the unexpected brilliance. We have no trust in our
> neighbours round the table, or in the everyday surround-
> ings to which we cling like shipwrecked men. In this
> painting the light has nothing to do with the color white,
> or indeed with any color at all; it is no longer the light of
> day—which illuminates objects, and which the human ret-
> ina detects—but an awesome, inner, spiritual light.[43]

The light symbolism in the fourth act of Kokoschka's play is striking as well. Opening in the afternoon, with daylight on the wane, a stage direction
specifies that the *"Night Watch* glimmers dimly on the
easel, touched by the sultry light."* As the act continues, it grows darker and darker in Rembrandt's studio
until the painting is enveloped in darkness as well:

Hendrikje, strike a light, it's getting dark!
. . . Rembrandt in increasing darkness . . .

Comenius

*. . . Comenius looks at the painting closely, which now grows
extremely dark.*

Not only is light literally absent onstage, but also there
are frequent allusions to the absence of spiritual light,
most notably by Rembrandt:

> Such a darkness, the world nowadays, I tell you. Hope
> only rarely steals in like a light. . . . A ray of light is
> wanting. I cannot finish the painting. . . . what a fortu-
> nate hour now that you, who plan to teach mankind to
> see and to understand, come to me, who lacks inspira-
> tion. A spiritual light! Here!

When Hannah arrives toward the end of the play,
it has grown so dark on stage that Rembrandt taps
after her like a blind man begging. "Come out of the
darkness," he says. Although she is dressed in white,
the stage directions make it clear that she is only indistinctly visible. After Comenius is led away by the police, Rembrandt busies himself about the canvas in a
dark room. He himself is no longer visible. Only his
grumbling voice is heard, accompanied by sounds of
thunder and lightning and by sights such as smoke,
which suggest an internal as well as an external cataclysm. It is at this moment—the moment of inspiration—that Hannah is heard calling him. The third time
she calls for Rembrandt is to announce his own spiritual awakening from darkness into light: "At the
springtime celebration someone will awake whose ser-
vitude is at an end!" Gradually the previously empty
patch on the canvas and then the rest of the painting
begin to grow lighter, revealing Hannah, veiled and
bedecked by garlands of flowers, as the mysterious girl
in *The Night Watch* (Fig. 53). It is now morning, and the
light in the studio heightens the movement of darkness
into light which has taken place within Rembrandt
himself.[44] Thus the pedagogue's failed ambition to educate men to see, symbolized by his vain search for his

129

adopted daughter Christl, is commemorated in the sudden flash, the divine spark of insight possessed by the creative artist, who discovers the girl and eternalizes her in a work of art.

Although there are differences between *Comenius* and Kokoschka's earlier plays, such as the lack of sexual conflict and the replacement of myth by history, a close inspection of the fourth act suggests that this play has much in common with Kokoschka's earlier dramas. Indeed, *Comenius* may rightfully be considered as a fitting climax to his dramatic work.

Not only *Comenius,* but all of Kokoschka's plays, with the exception of *Murderer Hope of Women,* are about the process of "seeing" or spiritual perception,[45] and in all four plays there is an allegorical figure personifying the human spirit itself: the virgin in *The Burning Bush,* the Parrot in *Job,* Psyche in *Orpheus and Eurydice,* and Hannah in *Comenius.*

The virgin who appears at the end of the third scene of *The Burning Bush* symbolizes the spiritual regeneration of the Woman, from whom she is metamorphosed as is Psyche from Eurydice at the end of *Orpheus and Eurydice.* As in *Comenius,* this moment of rebirth is visually suggested in the sudden movement from a stage that is dark to one bathed in light.

Job, of course, is a play about the absence of vision, suggested by Job's permanently twisted head which does not allow him to see correctly. It ends with the stage in complete darkness. However, the Parrot, who explodes into a rosy cloud at the moment of Job's death, is that play's allegorical representation of the spirit which Job has denied because of his sexual fascination with Anima.

The allegorical representatives of the spirit in Kokoschka's last two plays, Psyche and Hannah, are even more closely related than are the others. It is significant that both are females, since for Kokoschka "Man is mortal and Woman immortal,"[46] and are children as well, since for Kokoschka, as for Wordsworth, the child is indeed "father of the man." As man grows older he loses the ability to see into the heart of things: "The adult of normal intelligence has neither the spiritual means, nor the powers of observation to enable him to have an insight into the unity and continuity of life."[47]

Just as Hannah appears at the end of *Comenius* in the spring, a time of rebirth and regeneration, dressed in white and bedecked with flowers, so Psyche, in the Epilogue to *Orpheus and Eurydice,* celebrates the fecundity of new life and hope by carrying sheaves of corn, roses, and lilies. And as Psyche herself awakens and rouses new life in the fields around her, so Hannah symbolizes the birth of creative inspiration in the artist Rembrandt.

Both figures are also possessed of miraculous powers of sight. Even while asleep, Psyche "sees" Cupid's fall from his chariot. She finally cleanses and removes the bandages from his blinded eyes, while Hannah, also gifted with second sight, opens the eyes of Rembrandt and enables him to create a spark of light amid the darkness.

But in spite of this important link between *Comenius* and Kokoschka's previous dramatic works, there is an unmistakable difference in the tone of this last play. In the earlier plays Kokoschka was writing only about himself: the sexual conflicts which are at the core of these dramas were his own. As he said, "I am the hero of my [early] plays."[48] Of course, *Comenius* too is highly autobiographical. The dialogue between Comenius and Rembrandt, between the pedagogue and the artist, is fundamental to Kokoschka, a man who played both parts. But there is something unmistakably new that is sounded in Hannah's last words: "On your painting I stand as a witness of his [Comenius'] compassion, for all to see what it means to be human."

Kokoschka said that the word *Barmherzigkeit* ("compassion"), whose etymology and meaning greatly fascinated him, could be called "the *signum* for the whole play . . . never the brain, the ear, cleverness, pride. . . . everything else [but *Barmherzigkeit*] is futile." It is this quality of compassion which Comenius, Rembrandt, and especially Hendrikje possess and which Kokoschka wished to explore in his final play.

The plea for human compassion sounded throughout *Comenius*, but especially in the final act, is also felt in the single sketch for act 4[49] executed in 1942, and in such visual works contemporary with the play as the graphic illustrations to Euripides' *The Trojan Women* (1972) and the design for a colored mosaic of the Crucifixion, *Ecce Homines* (1974).[50] The illustration of act 4, *Comenius in Rembrandt's Studio* (Fig. 54), depicts Comenius and Rembrandt seated at a table facing the viewer, as Hendrikje approaches in profile to the left with a bottle of schnapps on a tray in honor of the guest. In the background on the left is a curtained bed; in the center is a dark door with a barred window. To the right of the figures stands the large canvas of *The Night Watch,* with the empty space in which Hannah will appear at the end of the play. Comenius, depicted as a tall figure with pilgrim's staff, is in contrast to the squat, slovenly Rembrandt with his turban. The most arresting feature of this sketch is the large bright candle standing between Comenius and Rembrandt on the table. It gives off much light and contrasts with the ominous darkness of the barred door behind them, symbolizing the contrast between darkness and light, the inhuman world without and *Barmherzigkeit* within, which is so central in the final version of the play.

The graphics for both *The Trojan Women* and the *Ecce Homines* (Figs. 55, 56) mosaic are further explorations of the theme of man's inhumanity to man and of the call for compassion. In the former Kokoschka deals with the horrors of war and its victims, as he does in *Comenius;* in the Crucifixion he depicts the dying Christ on the cross and beside him a luridly smiling Roman solider, whose face is a clownlike mask and who laconically raises a sponge dipped in vinegar to the mouth of Christ. Both figures in the mosaic are the same size, and therefore suggest the two possibilities— bestial and human—which are open to mankind, also suggested in the unusual plural form of the title, *Ecce Homines.*[51]

During the filming of *Comenius* in 1974, Kokoschka succinctly expressed the view of life which underlies both the play and the visual works contemporary with it: "The same old story—people are beasts, and I stick to that. With some education they are softened a little—for a short while. To me these bestial wars among people are actually the rule; if there is a glimpse of sun here and there, it is mere accident."[52]

In *Comenius,* the final dramatic effort of a long life which had witnessed much human suffering and been affected by two world wars, Kokoschka gives ample testimony to the bestial in man. But he also pays eloquent tribute to that spark of light which for an instant makes man divine and separates him forever from the beasts. How appropriate that the final ray of sunlight in the last of Kokoschka's plays should be communicated by means of a stage image which is itself a painting (*The Night Watch*) and which reaffirms the abiding connection between Kokoschka the playwright and Kokoschka the visual artist.

Fig. 54. *Comenius in Rembrandt's Studio,* 1942 (signed in 1957), pen and ink drawing, 11 × 15¾ in. (27 × 40.3 cm.). Courtesy of the artist.

Fig. 55. *Ecce Homo,* sketch for *Ecce Homines* mosaic, St. Nikolai Church, Hamburg, 1972, chalk on paper, 86 × 98 in. (219 × 250 cm.). Photograph from *Oskar Kokoschka* [catalogue] (Hamburg: B.A.T. Haus, Feb.–May 1975).

Fig. 56. Kokoschka before *Ecce Homines* mosaic, St. Nikolai Church, Hamburg, 1974. Photograph from *Oskar Kokoschka* [catalogue] (Hamburg: B.A.T. Haus, Feb.–May 1975).

Conclusion

In his long and productive career as an artist, spanning more than seventy years and two world wars, Kokoschka continually developed and matured, refusing to repeat himself. This process is reflected in his development as a playwright, from the primitive "screaming images" of *Murderer Hope of Women* to the civilized and monumental historical panorama of *Comenius.*

In spite of the obvious differences between Kokoschka's early and late works both on canvas and for the stage, there are similarities and parallels which connect his total *oeuvre* in ways that perhaps are not immediately apparent and often are overlooked today. For example, his illustrations to Kleist's drama *Penthesilea,* executed in 1970, are reminiscent of his lifelong obsession with the war of the sexes. It has even been suggested that a performance of Kleist's play as a schoolboy may well have served as the inspiration for *Murderer Hope of Women.*[1]

Perhaps an even more decisive connection between Kokoschka's early and late work is his concern with light. For him the use of light is never merely one of the formal resources of the painter or the playwright. Rather, it is the key to visionary, as well as visual, experience. Indeed, his belief in the creative power of human perception is best exemplified by his "School of Seeing," where he tried to teach his students not to paint, but to *see.* In all his dramatic works, light has a similar dual function, combining sight and insight—from the spectral illuminations of *The Burning Bush* to Rembrandt's flash of creative inspiration at the conclusion of *Comenius.*

Because of the unity which is basic to all of Kokoschka's work, it is ironic that he should be remembered best for the "black portraits" and landscapes of his early career, rather than for the works of his mature years. Although his technique grew more polished and sophisticated with age, his range wider and his subjects more profound and dignified, there is little, with the exception of some late graphic cycles, which approaches the intensity of his early portraits, those which ripped the civilized mask from the sitter and revealed a self hidden from all but the "Eye of God," as the young artist was called. Perhaps such works could only have been created by an artist whose spirit was both consciously and subconsciously in revolt against the world around him, rather than by an older, more philosophical painter of epics such as *Herodotus* or *Thermopylae.*

The evaluation of Kokoschka's contribution to the theater yields much the same result as the evaluation of his painting. It is the early plays, in which the dramatist transformed his private obsessions into searing stage images, that are the most unforgettable. In the later plays, *Orpheus and Eurydice* and *Comenius,* Kokoschka is a more highly skilled craftsman with words but a less successful visual dramatist. Many of the visual features of the later works are embedded in literary discourse, resulting in a less highly charged visual spectacle than in the early plays, where Kokoschka can rightly be called not merely an Expressionist but an Explosionist, whose startling visual images undermine complacency. In their capacity to shock and lay bare elemental conflicts, these plays, therefore, are comparable in achievement to the early portraits.

In the early dramas, so completely a product of the playwright's eye, Kokoschka anticipated the most radical experiments of contemporary theater: the reliance on scenic imagery, color, and light rather than on language; and the importance of myth, ritual, and dreams rather than causally connected actions and logical discourse. Thus, when Martin Esslin in 1961 stated that "the Theatre of the Absurd . . . tends toward a radical devaluation of language, toward a poetry that is to emerge from the concrete and objectified images of the stage itself,"[2] he was describing what Kokoschka had achieved some fifty years earlier. Even Antonin Artaud's *The Theatre and Its Double,* hailed by many critics since its publication in 1938 as offering a revolutionary conception of the theater, often reads as a theoretical justification of what Kokoschka practiced in his incantatory, archetypal depictions of the struggles between the sexes:

> The theatre restores to us all our dormant conflicts and all their powers, and gives these powers names we hail as symbols—and behold! Before our eyes is fought a battle of symbols. . . .

> The theatre will never find itself again except by furnishing the spectator with the truthful precipitate of dreams. . . .

> The domain of the theatre is not psychological but plastic and physical.[3]

The plays of Oskar Kokoschka, therefore, far from being merely the curious by-products of a great painter, are significant contributions to the history of the modern stage. His reliance upon visual expression offers eloquent confirmation of the mutual illumination of the arts, the language of images.

Appendix A
Versions and Translations of Kokoschka's Plays

A definitive four-volume edition of Kokoschka's literary work (*Das Schriftliche Werk*) is available in German, edited by Heinz Spielmann and published by Hans Christians (Hamburg). In addition to the first volume (*Dichtungen und Dramen*), which has been my chief source for the plays discussed in this book, a second volume (*Erzählungen*) is devoted to Kokoschka's stories, a third to his lectures and essays on art (*Vorträge, Aufsätze, Essays zur Kunst*), and a fourth to his political writings (*Politische Äusserungen*).

Prior to Spielmann's edition, completed in 1976, the texts of *Murderer Hope of Women* (final version), *Sphinx and Strawman II*, *The Burning Bush*, *Job*, and *Orpheus and Eurydice* were available (along with the fourth act of Kokoschka's original *Comenius* drama) only in Hans Maria Wingler's edition of *Schriften 1907–1955*, published in 1956 by Langen/Müller (Munich), also containing a selection of Kokoschka's stories, essays, and letters. A shortened version (*Oskar Kokoschka: Schriften*), also edited by Wingler, was published in paperback by S. Fischer Verlag (Fischer-Bucherei, Volume 616) in 1964.

Versions

Murderer Hope of Women (Mörder Hoffnung der Frauen)

Mörder, Hoffnung der Frauen, written in 1907; published in *Der Sturm* (Berlin and Vienna) on July 14, 1910 (No. 20), reprinted in *Dichtungen und Dramen*.

Hoffnung der Frauen, published in *Dramen und Bilder*, Leipzig, 1913. *Mörder Hoffnung der Frauen*, limited edition of 100 copies, Berlin, 1916.

Mörder Hoffnung der Frauen, Schauspiel, published in *Der jüngste Tag*, Vol. 41, Leipzig, 1917; reprinted in *Vier Dramen*, Berlin, 1919, *Schriften 1909–1955*, and *Dichtungen und Dramen*.

The Burning Bush (Der brennende Dornbusch)

Published as *Schauspiel* in *Dramen und Bilder*, Leipzig, 1913, pp. 37–62.

Der brennende Dornbusch, Schauspiel, published in *Der jüngste Tag*, Berlin, 1919; reprinted in *Schriften 1909–1955* and *Dichtungen und Dramen*.

Sphinx and Strawman (Sphinx und Strohmann); Job (Hiob)

Sphinx und Strohmann: Komödie für Automaten, written in 1907, performed in 1909; published in *Wort in der Zeit* (Graz), 2 (1956), pp. 145–48.

Sphinx und Strohmann: Ein Curiosum, published in *Dramen und Bilder*, Leipzig, 1913, pp. 23–36; reprinted in *Schriften 1907–1955* and *Dichtungen und Dramen*.

Hiob, Ein Drama, published by Cassirer, Berlin, 1917; reprinted in *Vier Dramen*, *Schriften 1907–1955*, and *Dichtungen und Dramen*.

Orpheus and Eurydice (Orpheus und Eurydike)

Orpheus und Eurydike, Schauspiel, published in *Vier Dramen*, Berlin, 1919, reprinted in *Schriften 1907–1955* and *Dichtungen und Dramen*.

Comenius

First version written in Prague and London between 1936 and 1938. Shortly afterward, Kokoschka translated sections of the manuscript into English. Only the fourth act of the Prague version published, as a fragment, by Hans Maria Wingler in *Schriften 1907–1955*, pp. 309–34. During the summer and winter of 1972 Kokoschka rewrote *Comenius;* first published in *Dichtungen und Dramen.*

English Translations

Murderer Hope of Women

Murderer the Women's Hope, trans. Michael Hamburger, in *An Anthology of German Expressionist Drama*, ed. Walter H. Sokel (New York: Anchor, 1963), pp. 17–21.

Murderer Hope of Womenkind, trans. J. M. Ritchie, in *Seven Expressionist Plays* (London: Calder and Boyars, 1968), pp. 25–32.

Sphinx and Strawman

Sphinx and Strawman, trans. Victor H. Miesel, in *Voices of German Expressionism*, ed. Victor H. Miesel (Englewood Cliffs, N.J.: Prentice-Hall, 1970), pp. 119–25.

Job

Job, trans. Walter H. and Jacqueline Sokel, in *An Anthology of German Expressionist Drama* (New York: Anchor, 1963), pp. 159–71.

Job, trans. Michael Benedikt, in *German Drama between the Wars*, ed. George E. Wellwarth (New York: Dutton, 1964), pp. 1–18.

Appendix B

Murderer the Women's Hope

1907

*Translated by Michael Hamburger**

PERSONS

MAN
WOMAN
CHORUS: MEN *and* WOMEN

Night sky. Tower with large red iron grille as door; torches the only light; black ground, rising to the tower in such a way that all the figures appear in relief.

THE MAN *in blue armor, white face, kerchief covering a wound, with a crowd of men—savage in appearance, gray-and-red kerchiefs, white-black-and-brown clothes, signs on their clothes, bare legs, long-handled torches, bells, din—creeping up with handles of torches extended and lights; wearily, reluctantly try to hold back the adventurer, pull his horse to the ground; he walks on, they open up the circle around him, crying out in a slow crescendo.*

MEN. We were the flaming wheel around him,

We were the flaming wheel around you, assailant of locked fortresses!

Hesitantly follow him again in chain formation; he, with the torch bearer in front of him, heads the procession.

MEN. Lead us, pale one!

While they are about to pull his horse to the ground, women with their leader ascend steps on the left.

WOMAN, *red clothes, loose yellow hair, tall.*

*From *An Anthology of German Expressionist Drama,* ed. Walter H. Sokel (New York: Anchor, 1963), pp. 17–21.

WOMAN, *loud.* With my breath I fan the yellow disc of the sun, my eye collects the jubilation of the men, their stammering lust prowls around me like a beast.

FEMALE ATTENDANTS *separate themselves from her, only now catch sight of the stranger.*

FIRST FEMALE ATTENDANT. His breath attaches itself to the virgin!

FIRST MAN *to the others.* Our master is like the moon that rises in the East.

SECOND GIRL, *quiet, her face averted.* When will she be enfolded joyfully?

Listening, alert, the CHORUS *walks round the whole stage, dispersed in groups;* THE MAN *and the* WOMAN *meet in front of the gate.*

(Pause.)

WOMAN *observes him spellbound, then to herself.* Who is the stranger that has looked on me?

GIRLS *press to the fore.*

FIRST GIRL *recognizes him, cries out.* His sister died of love.

SECOND GIRL. O the singing of Time, flowers never seen.

THE MAN, *astonished; his procession halts.* Am I real? What did the shadows say?

Raising his face to her.

Did you look at me, did I look at you?

WOMAN, *filled with fear and longing.* Who is the pallid man? Hold him back.

FIRST GIRL, *with a piercing scream, runs back.* Do you let him in? It is he who strangles my little sister praying in the temple.

FIRST MAN *to the girl.* We saw him stride through the fire, his feet unharmed.

SECOND MAN. He tortured animals to death, killed neighing mares by the pressure of his thighs.

THIRD MAN. Birds that ran before us he made blind, stifled red fishes in the sand.

THE MAN *angry, heated.* Who is she that like an animal proudly grazes amidst her kin?

FIRST MAN. She divines what none has understood.

SECOND MAN. She perceives what none has seen or heard.

THIRD MAN. They say shy birds approach her and let themselves be seized.

GIRLS *in time with the men.*

FIRST GIRL. Lady, let us flee. Extinguish the flares of the leader.

SECOND GIRL. Mistress, escape!

THIRD GIRL. He shall not be our guest or breathe our air. Let him not lodge with us, he frightens me.

MEN, *hesitant, walk on,* WOMEN *crowd together anxiously. The* WOMAN *goes up to* THE MAN, *prowling, cautious.*

FIRST GIRL. He has no luck.

FIRST MAN. She has no shame.

WOMAN.Why do you bind me, man, with your gaze? Ravening light, you confound my flame! Devouring life overpowers me. O take away my terrible hope—and may torment overpower you.

THE MAN, *enraged.* My men, now brand her with my sign, hot iron into her red flesh.

MEN *carry out his order. First the* CHORUS, *with their lights, struggle with her, then the* OLD MAN *with the iron; he rips open her dress and brands her.*

WOMAN, *crying out in terrible pain.* Beat back those men, the devouring corpses.

She leaps at him with a knife and strikes a wound in his side. THE MAN *falls.*

MEN. Free this man possessed, strike down the devil. Alas for us innocents, bury the conqueror. We do not know him.

THE MAN, *in convulsions, singing with a bleeding, visible wound.* Senseless craving from horror to horror, unappeasable rotation in the void. Birth pangs without birth, hurtling down of the sun, quaking of space. The end of those who praised me. Oh, your unmerciful word.

MEN. We do not know him; spare us. Come, you singing girls, let us celebrate our nuptials on his bed of affliction.

GIRLS. He frightens us; you we loved even before you came.

Three masked men on the wall lower a coffin on ropes; the wounded man, hardly stirring now, is placed inside the tower. WOMEN *retire with the* MEN. *The* OLD MAN *rises and locks the door, all is dark, a torch, quiet, blue light above in the cage.*

WOMAN, *moaning and revengeful.* He cannot live, nor die; how white he is!

She creeps round the cage like a panther. She crawls up to the cage inquisitively, grips the bars lasciviously, inscribes a large white cross on the tower, cries out.

Open the gate; I must be with him.

Shakes the bars in despair.

MEN *and* WOMEN, *enjoying themselves in the shadows, confused.* We have lost the key—we shall find it—have you got it?—haven't you seen it?—we are not guilty of your plight, we do not know you—

They go back again. A cock crows, a pale light rises in the background.

WOMAN *slides her arm through the bars and prods his wound, hissing maliciously, like an adder.* Pale one, do you recoil? Do you know fear? Are you only asleep? Are you awake? Can you hear me?

THE MAN, *inside, breathing heavily, raises his head with difficulty; later, moves one hand; then slowly rises, singing higher and higher, soaring.*

Wind that wanders, time repeating time, solitude, repose and hunger confuse me.

Worlds that circle past, no air, it grows long as evening.

WOMAN, *incipient fear.* So much light is flowing from the gap, so much strength from the gate, pale as a corpse he's turned.

Once more creeps up the steps, her body trembling, triumphant once more and crying out with a high voice.

THE MAN *has slowly risen, leans against the grille, slowly grows.*

WOMAN *weakening, furious.* A wild beast I tame in this cage; is it with hunger your song barks?

THE MAN. Am I the real one, you the dead ensnared? Why are you turning pale?

Crowing of cocks.

WOMAN, *trembling.* Do you insult me, corpse?

THE MAN, *powerfully.* Stars and moon! Woman! In dream or awake, I saw a singing creature brightly shine. Breathing, dark things become clear to me. Who nourishes me?

WOMAN *covers him entirely with her body; separated by the grille, to which she clings high up in the air like a monkey.*

THE MAN. Who suckles me with blood? I devour your melting flesh.

WOMAN. I will not let you live, you vampire, piecemeal you feed on me, weaken me, woe to you, I shall kill you—you fetter me—you I caught and caged—and you are holding me—let go of me. Your love imprisons me—grips me as with iron chains—throttles me—let go—help! I lost the key that kept you prisoner.

Lets go the grille, writhes on the steps like a dying animal, her thighs and muscles convulsed.

THE MAN *stands upright now, pulls open the gate, touches the woman—who rears up stiffly, dead white—with his fingers. She feels that her end is near, highest tension, released in a slowly diminishing scream; she collapses and, as she falls, tears away the torch from the hands of the rising leader. The torch goes out and covers everything in a shower of sparks. He stands on the highest step; men and women who attempt to flee from him run into his way, screaming.*

CHORUS. The devil! Tame him, save yourselves, save yourselves if you can—all is lost!

He walks straight towards them. Kills them like mosquitoes and leaves red behind. From very far away, crowing of cocks.

Appendix C

Sphinx and Strawman, a Curiosity

1913

*Translated by Victor H. Miesel**

THE CAST

MR. FIRDUSI,† *a gigantic, revolving straw head with arms and legs. He carries a pig's bladder on a string.*

MR. RUBBERMAN, *an accomplished contortionist.*

FEMALE SOUL, *called "Anima."*

DEATH, *a normal, living person.*

PARROT

FIRDUSI, *his gigantic head rocking back and forth on his legs; talks to the parrot.* Who are you? What is your name?

PARROT. The female soul, Anima, sweet Anima.

FIRDUSI *turns away.* I had a wife, I treated her like a goddess and she left my bed. She said to our sad little chambermaid, "help me on with my travelling cloak" and then disappeared with a healthy muscleman. I had created a human soul but the ground vanished from beneath its feet. Now my creation floats in the air like a pig's bladder—*Horror vacui!* What kind of God steals words out of my own mouth in order to make me believe that they are his words of wisdom? Just like a sponge drinks up vinegar only to give it all back without swallowing a drop.

PARROT. Anima, sweet Anima!

FIRDUSI. At first she was a woman. Then I found myself dining with a ghoul, in the ecstasies of love with a ghost

and then I solved the mystery of certain vocal phenomena. A nightmare entered my skull, it strangled my consciousness. Vitality, essentiality, reality help! That poor Adonis! She will feed on his mind until he begins to speak with my voice. She is a woman who lost her virginity for a soul and now she wanders from one man into another, she spins and wraps herself into a cocoon, she devours men's brains and she only leaves their empty skulls, as a magnificent butterfly, in order to lay her egg. Anima, Anima, the nucleus from one, protoplasm from the other, and we all recognize ourselves in the result. Resurrection from life. I want to die.

Death, who looks like an ordinary person, appears in thunder and lightning. He gestures threateningly, but with a smile and then disappears without doing anything.

FIRDUSI *to the public.* When I grab my handkerchief you all start to cry, how touching. But why do you look at me now so coolly, one hundred indifferent people against a single desperate person? Only a nuance separates the hero from the audience. Do you believe in a bluff?

I am only exploiting your intelligence and your nerves and our mutual romantic interest in ghosts.

RUBBERMAN *enters and touches Firdusi's leg.* Hey there, I'm a doctor. You say you want to die! Let's talk awhile, you know, to exchange impressions is not to explain insights but to interchange outlooks. You don't die as easily as you're born. However, I have something for you in case your last little hour should give you any trouble. I know a woman . . .

*From *Voices of German Expressionism,* ed. Victor H. Miesel (Englewood Cliffs, N.J.: Prentice-Hall, 1970), pp. 119–25.
†The name of a tenth-century Persian poet who wrote the national epic of Persia and the title of a poem from Goethe's *Westöstlicher Diwan.*

Anima peeks in the door.

who is slowly murdering her husband in such a way that no court in the world could prove a thing. "Fear of adultery" is a poison which works with absolute certainty. And how can I serve you?

FIRDUSI. Thanks—thanks.

Lost in thought.

I don't think—things have gone that far—yet— But you are a doctor, and you don't try to stop crime?

RUBBERMAN. Oh, I'm interested in experimentation. I'm no practicing doctor, just a modest priest of science.

ANIMA *half aloud.* A man, magnificence and modesty combined, anything spectacular like that fascinates me.

FIRDUSI *embarrassed, he puts a rubber figure on his finger and lets it nod back and forth.* May I introduce my child, Emanuel, my hope—Mr. Rubberman!

RUBBERMAN. Be a credit to your father Mr. Emanuel, my dear sir. *To Firdusi.* But to be frank with you, if you want your offspring to be legitimate—legal—you have to declare at least who its most important producers were.

FIRDUSI. *He becomes confused and pulls the figure from his finger.* Oh my dear sir don't talk so loosely, my child is still pure. But you're right, Emanuel's progress might be hurt by not having a mother.

PARROT. Anima, sweet Anima.

ANIMA *in a light blue conventional angel's costume, wings, hands folded, she approaches the men.* Oh Lord, if I could only save a man's soul! They say that men suffer so from the mysteries of their delicate and cultivated eroticism. *Pointing to Rubberman.* You must be worthy, you have powerful muscles.

Rubberman, pleased, shows off his thigh muscles. She looks down at her own feet coquettishly, one placed a little ahead of the other.

Horrors! Don't you think that one of my footsies is shorter than the other?

RUBBERMAN *gallantly.* Perspective is an optical swindle invented by art experts.

ANIMA *acts reassured.* And that's why I'll have to limp for the rest of my life!

She lifts her dress and gives Firdusi, who has not paid any attention to her, a light kick in the pants with her graceful leg.

FIRDUSI *grumbling.* Women should only be looked down upon. *He turns his head slowly without moving his body. Anima, moving step by step, keeps out of his line of sight until Firdusi's head has turned completely round; in spite of great effort he is then unable to get his head back where it belongs. Thus right to the end Firdusi never sees Anima.*

FIRDUSI *whining.* If you are kind and considerate in love, those raging Amazons feel themselves cheated, but if you are rough and domineering your own sensibility is violated. *Backing up to the door like a crab, he rings for the butler.* Johann, bring a mirror, a red rose and the photograph, also the cockatoo, bring them into the Rose room.

The servant brings the rose and the mirror. Firdusi, going backwards as before, storms to the armchair, sits down backwards. He puts the rose first in his back, then on his necktie, puts the mirror to his rump and then to his face.

ANIMA *in new, exquisitely luxurious clothes, singing with a book in her hand.* Oh, where is the man who is worthy of me, the man I dreamed of as a girl? Oh, no man like that proved himself worthy of me! I took a feature from one man, another from the next, to my lover I offered resigned lips, to my husband scorn and melancholy. I am forced to wander and wander, eternally, from one to the other. *To Firdusi.* Hello handsome!

FIRDUSI *without being able to see her.* Who are you? What's your name? Angel.

ANIMA. The female soul, Anima, sweet Anima.

PARROT *repetitiously.* Anima, sweet Anima.

FIRDUSI *pulls a larva out, like a dentist.* I've been through all this once already. Women have an earthly body but an immortal soul.

ANIMA *pointing to his figure.* You have an interesting view.

Firdusi, thinking that she is referring to what he has said, proudly puffs his chest out.

ANIMA. Oh, I believe that I only love you.

FIRDUSI *smiling pathetically.* If I could only respond out of my loneliness to your secret confessions, oh, to be able to place a rainbow of reconciliation over shocked sexes, *becoming hysterical,* my feelings are like so many falling stars, stars falling into the narrow fields of my soul to be extinguished—but the Word which reaches out far beyond me like a huge gesture means nothing to you.

ANIMA. Oh, but I do so love grand gestures! My dear, sweet big head. My light, my wisdom. *Shrieking she jumps on top of him.* My master, dear sweet Mr. Firdusi.

FIRDUSI. My self-respect grows by leaps and bounds.

Rubberman, panting; Anima pulls his leg up to his nose and he trembles gently.

ANIMA *quietly.* Oh, Rubberman, I think I'm in love but I'm not sure. Do you gentlemen know each other—Mr. Rubberman.

FIRDUSI *involuntarily.* Fir-du-si!

RUBBERMAN. The pleasure is all mine! *A very deep and very odd bow; Firdusi bows facing the other way for obvious reasons.*

FIRDUSI. Emanuel is getting a mother.

PARROT. Anima, sweet Anima.

Death appears in thunder and lightning; Firdusi is horrified.

FIRDUSI *screams.* Entreprise des pompes funèbres! Sex murder for ever! If you think about the future the present disappears.

Searching for Anima. I don't even have her photograph.

DEATH *knocks with a bone on the proscenium. Firdusi becomes rheumatic.* In spite of the spectacular stage effects I want to reassure the audience that death has lost all its horror now that the masculine imagination in Europe is obsessed by gynolatry.*

FIRDUSI *still upset but a little quieter.* The human soul is like a magic lantern, in the past it projected devils on the wall, now it projects our women over the whole world. *Shudders like an electric eel and destroys the pig's bladder.* That used to be the soul. *Resigned.* Oh, I'll never ever again disbelieve in fairytales, but I will laugh a little. *Laughs louder, a hundred voiced resonance, a rushing echo, then quiets down.* My method for restoring my body's balance.

He hitches up his trousers. Death follows him. Anima screams and flees with Rubberman into the Rose room. Firdusi gropes after them clumsily but he is unable to find his way. Meanwhile, the Rose room is lit up. Two shadows can be seen kissing.

PARROT. Oh, my Anima, sweet Anima. *Very clearly.* Oh my sweet Mr. Rubberman! Oh my sweet Mr. Rubberman! Oh my sweet Mr. Rubberman!

*The worship of women.

FIRDUSI. *His head snaps back as he hears the unexpected additional remarks of the Parrot; he notices the shadows, and then rushes to the telephone.* Who are you?

ANIMA. Anima, your dear sweet Anima, the female soul.

FIRDUSI. What are you up to?

ANIMA. Experiments in spiritualism, exorcism. I am having myself saved.

FIRDUSI. Who am I?

PARROT. Oh my sweet Mr. Rubberman.

Firdusi staggers to the middle of the stage, lies down flat on the floor and shoots himself with an air pistol. He sprouts horns. Johann opens a curtain which hangs below the Rose room. On it there is a painting of a gigantic cat catching a mouse. There is another curtain. On it are painted a group of gentlemen dressed in black with top hats. Instead of faces there are holes through which heads pop out. First one gentleman speaks and then quickly another answers and so on to the end.

FIRST GENTLEMAN. The Enlightenment will come to a bad end. The brain is too heavy and the pelvis much too frivolous.

SECOND GENTLEMAN. And there is no conscience to keep things balanced.

THIRD GENTLEMAN. Death gave all his power to a woman.

FOURTH GENTLEMAN. This is the way a great fantast takes all the magic out of culture.

FIFTH GENTLEMAN. Mr. Firdusi, who was supposed to have been born of woman, gave his inheritance, his masculine imagination back to his wife, and now her soul suffers.

SIXTH GENTLEMAN. He persuaded a woman to swallow her miscarriage under the impression that she could still give it a proper birth.

SEVENTH GENTLEMAN. Eat this you bird people, or die!

EIGHTH GENTLEMAN. Can't modern science help.

NINTH GENTLEMAN. It's become shameful since everyone in the elementary schools knows its ancestors.

TENTH GENTLEMAN. Man must be willing to suffer the anguish which woman causes him because he knows why she is so different from him. He wisely compensates for the "it is" through the better "it could be" and so rounds out the horizon of his experience.

Anima throws herself on Firdusi weeping.

FIRDUSI *Stirs himself for the last time.* I forgot!—Quick, a priest!

RUBBERMAN *chases after Anima, his tie is gone.* What about the wedding? *Sings.* Joy reigns supreme, conscience is dead. Yes, marriage reform, marriage reform and let us make love in front of scientists!

FIRDUSI *stirs himself for absolutely the last time.* Passion needs spirit as a filter or else it floods over the entire body and soul and dirties them both. I have faith in the genius of mankind, Anima, amen.

DEATH *with lightning and thunder.* A good, strong faith is like blindness. It covers over unpleasant things, but those things never disappear.

Death goes away with Anima.

Appendix D
Job, a Drama

1917

*Translated by Walter H. Sokel and Jacqueline Sokel**

CHARACTERS

JOB

ANIMA, *his wife*

MR. RUBBERMAN

ADAM, *the gardener*

EROS

CHAMBERMAID

YOUNG LADIES

GENTLEMEN

PARROT

Motto: A pain for a rib

When Adam slept on the green lawn,
God had pity, the sun stood at zenith
And He from boredom was about to sleep.
Awaken'd by a kick in his ribs, Adam cried: "Hi,"
And found himself wedded to Eve:
"My God, if only He had left my rib in peace."

FIRST ACT

JOB, *in nightcap and dressing gown, knocks at the door of his wife's room.*

CHAMBERMAID *sticks her head cautiously out the other door, hiding something behind her back.* I've been knocking and now I'm asking, sir, if you could not take something off my back. Madam has given it to me with two kicks on my backside; it's garnished with plumage and talons, tongue and beak. Her Ladyship herself went out already this morning with the young gentleman, he's handsome as a picture. This feathered thing here she has left you, sir, for your amusement.

She launches a PARROT *from a basket. The* PARROT *flies upon* JOB's *shoulder.*

CHAMBERMAID *exits trilling.* 'Tis the balmy summer night—
Vanished and sighing from a deep crevasse.
It lubicrates tongues, it puts the salt in tears—
The blond lock of hair weaves and spins its web behind the flickering flame—
Ensnares the heroes versed in dangers. . . .

JOB. But I thought she had just been here?

Pointing to the door.

She bartered her virginity for a soul—slipped from one man to the next. And leaves the skull when it's picked clean.

Points to his forehead.

Here where she nested she has quickly, even in her flight, deposited an egg, from which she leaps restored, like a phoenix.—I wish no sun to rise, no skies to loom with castles before which sphinxes converse! . . .

PARROT *flies with one flap onto* JOB's *head while* JOB *is pacing up and down.*

Woe to the youth whom she seeks to spiritualize, until he starts talking with my tongue.

Falls into a chair.

Once long ago, from the Creator's head leaped forth the Mother of Creation, secretly hiding in her womb his world.

PARROT *tears at his hair.*

Ai, Ai, my head! In a jiffy gone—where? Ai, *horror vacui! Sings.*

*From *An Anthology of German Expressionist Drama,* ed. Walter H. Sokel (New York: Anchor, 1963), pp. 159–71.

How love has twisted me since in this empty house a gentle woman's voice has called to me to search for her—has vexed me into a labyrinth. From it an echo teases, and a breeze of air makes me run helter-skelter everywhere. "As ye sow, ye are like to reap." Because in a moment's breath she metamorphoses by some back door into a creature that—is I myself!

ANIMA *singing behind the door.*

JOB *does not hear her, plays with the bird, entices it on his finger.* What is man's favorite—amusement?

PARROT, *imitating the female voice.* Anima—your soul, your wife—for such was meant.

JOB. My soul! Her naughtiness or flight, or whatever I call it, leaves me things to think about that . . . but . . . What name can man call his? Eh?

PARROT. Oh and Amen—Man's woe she is and—Oh, man's Ah!

PARROT *again leaps onto* JOB'S *head, and scratches him trustingly.*

JOB. That treacherous woman has gone to my head—talks after my lips, looks out of my eyes, turns my insides out.

Turns my outside in!

Shakes the impudent guest who is pecking at his ears.

In short, I'm like a pumpkinhead that must with a mystic halo putrefy in a ditch.

The bird spreads out on JOB'S *head and puffs itself up.*

Hope or treachery, you are getting too heavy! Leave me my mind so that I can bear you. I comprehend you! Help!

Softer.

Isn't that she talking? How. . . ?

ANIMA *echoes.* I can't relieve you—United are we! Eternally—One.

JOB. But tell me for once—in Heaven's name and Hell's—who you are!

ANIMA *echoes.* Anima I am—your wife! Your soul I am.

JOB. Gone is—"I am"—and what remains—I?

Shaking frantically once more at the doorknob.

I had a wife, she was my world!

With tears.

The edge of the globe I thought I was grasping, then the ground vanished from under my feet and dominion hangs in the air like—a pig's bladder! *Horror vacui!*

More composedly.

Even if it remained only a plan, yet it was my world!

Dizzy, stumbles.

ANIMA, *gently, behind the door.* He who does not take care, who errs in judgment, may lose his head!

JOB, *crossly.* Head or world! I see no difference! My own words are torn from my mouth! I wish I could believe I am learning them for the first time! As a sponge absorbs vinegar, renders it up again without retaining . . .

Outraged, JOB *turns from the door after his efforts to gain admission have remained futile.*

ANIMA, *softly.* Such a one surely was not to be host to me, he who gave vinegar while desiring wine.

SECOND ACT

JOB *flees to be alone into the bathroom where men's and women's wash is hung on lines to dry. Pulls himself up to the small window. Storm with lightning flashes outside. Wants to throw himself out, but notices something in the street.* Elements! Heavens, pour out yourselves! Flood, inundate my troubled heart! A dog . . . Come here! A faithful dog—the last solace to him in whom humankind inspires hate.

THE POODLE *runs through the hall, opens the door, jumps up on* JOB *wagging his tail.* Wow, wow, wow. A dog has a keen nose. I am a psychoanalyst! How . . . How . . . How. The Male sniffs Female's clothes!

MR. RUBBERMAN *wriggles out of the dog skin.* Forgive this foolish masquerade—I am the poodle's core!* So you have become a misanthrope.

Points to the hall.

This good maid would not turn a dog away when it rains cats and dogs! Hats off to a man in whom sensation twists through heart and kidneys. Whenever it should slacken—off with his head! To be sure, research has found that after

*This is a reference to Goethe's *Faust*, Part I. Mephistopheles appears to Faust first in the shape of a poodle. Upon the poodle's transformation into human shape, Faust exclaims: "So that was the poodle's core!"

the decapitation of poor sinners, the heart continues beating for a while, still full of feeling. But whether it felt pure joy has not been proved. For all our winding, every clock must someday cease to run! As I in another context already had occasion to remark—I am a psychoanalyst and can serve usefully with good advice. Defense attorney for the cause of life I've not become, because that could only kill the client. If he trusts in me then I have claims on him! That's only fair, agreed? An exchange of views may not be a trade-in of insights but rather a sellout of foresights.

From the window RUBBERMAN *sees returning the lady of the house, who then busies herself in the room next door. Curiously, he sniffs at the keyhole. Upon hearing her movements in the adjoining room,* JOB *turns away disgruntled and constrained.*

MR. RUBBERMAN. A beautiful woman! She's undressing! Pulling off . . . she pulls me on!

To JOB, *who with a great effort forces himself not to glance toward the ominous door.*

Besides, in case her difficult hour, requiring extraordinary endeavor even in dressing and addressing herself to . . .

Looking into the keyhole with great effort, nearly crawling into it.

I am observing a woman who, in short, turns a man's head!

JOB, *reluctant, apart.* And you a doctor, friend of the weak, do not prevent this act of violence?

MR. RUBBERMAN. The personal joy of research alone prompts me. I am no doctor.

Into the door.

Experiment interests me. . . .

Joyfully.

Eureka! I have got it! . . . Her method! . . . It's discovered! Eroditis, jealousy! The seed which a bacillus incubates, erotococcus, lumbago—the witches' dart! The one discovery my colleagues left for me! This happens in cases like yours where the patient, weakened by long suffering, no longer is immune.

ANIMA, *from the next room.* Science makes the man who cannot fit its rules easily lose his head. It separates his head from him who, twisted by ideas, confused by God's or love's power, reflective for a while, forgets the little self and turns his back on it.

JOB *sees* RUBBERMAN *cleaving to the keyhole with drooling mouth and greedy eye. The door is opening slowly;* ANIMA *steps out, stops.* JOB, *crazed by the sight, twists his neck.* JOB *is no longer able to get his head back into its customary position, clutches his ears in dread, tears out huge handfuls of hair.*

MR. RUBBERMAN *rushes to* JOB, *shocked.* Let me feel your pulse! This man will die of fright under my hands! You're suffocating! Open your collar! You are doing everything wrong! The trouble comes from your twisted view of things that won't go straight!

JOB, *roaring.* They've twisted my head! They've twisted my head!

Whimpering.

Twisted!

MR. RUBBERMAN, *fingering* JOB's *chest.* The heart is still intact! I must interrupt the double circulation

Pulling out a surgeon's saw

so that the infection won't paralyze his heart. Head off, courage! If you live headless the trouble isn't half as bad!

ANIMA. My God, if I could only help! No one pays attention to me!

JOB *dances around in circles, roars away* RUBBERMAN, *who is waving his saw about.* I no longer know where I have my head! Does this belong to me—does that one? You are nearest me. . . . That means—I must get at your throat! I'm reaching—I catch! I'm dropping—I fetch!

JOB, *shaken.* Just one more mirage, pretending to be shape that all eyes see.

To RUBBERMAN.

Why are you gaping at me so serenely? Just wait, a serene man is no match for a—deranged one!

Wanting to tear his head off his shoulders, pummeling with his fists against his forehead.

While still projected—the world rejected! The globe is turning—and rolling away! Woman has bewitched my head—twisted it. . . . It is bedeviled and possessed!

MR. RUBBERMAN, *inviting* ANIMA *to step nearer while he studies* JOB's *head.* When a woman possesses her husband's head, she always seeks a lover for it. And since I take an interest in yours—There she comes. . . . Please introduce me!

ANIMA, *innocent, bourgeois, gentle, blond.* You bad husband! You are scolding me. Me, Anima! Your wife! Born of the breath that inspired creation—whence impatience expelled Anima, before she was fulfilled.

JOB, *with hands imploring.* Anima, my soul!

PARROT, *flying into the room, screeching.* Anima, my soul!

JOB, *reaching out for* ANIMA, *who is turning to* MR. RUBBERMAN. Eluded my head, with him! And took the soul of sleepy Adam!

RUBBERMAN, *yanking* ANIMA *to his breast.* That Bible text of the old potter? Woman was not made from—your clay!

EROS *leaps through the door, precocious.* From Papa's tears in Mama's womb arose a little boy. . . .

ANIMA, *bitter;* EROS *stumbles and rubs his leg, roaring.* The mother of grief thought it would be for her joy!

RUBBERMAN. I don't understand a word! Ha, what joy to live. . . !

From now on everyone indulges in pandemonium, screaming, rushing, the PARROT *screeches incessantly,* EROS *cries.*

JOB *pacifies the child. To* RUBBERMAN. You opportunist! What seemed to her a trampoline for leaping from lust to lust is—alas—vulgarity that procreates itself! And all her seven Heavens are one Hell! An infant's birth is his fall to earth and he weeps at the entrance gate!

RUBBERMAN, *to* JOB. He's the spitting image of you. But stop this cry baby from babbling on and on. In this house everything is hexed.

Pointing to the CHAMBERMAID *and the* PARROT.

So throw out these noisy beasts!

JOB. To Hell with them from where they came.

ANIMA, *taking* EROS *by his hands and dancing in circles with him out through the door.* Let Heaven be Heaven and Hell be Hell! I love Lord Eros. With imagination I bore him—of whom I'd dreamt even as a girl. One feature I would take from this man, another from the next. To my lover I offered lips of resignation, and to my husband mocking mournfulness. From one to the other! Like a bee fickle while garnering the pollen! Until Lord Eros is arrived!

RUBBERMAN, *clamoring after the two fugitives while the general commotion subsides.* Adored lady—stay. . . . Besides, your Eros stimulates me too! . . . Purely objectively I wish to remark that the genetic development of your mythological son urges me toward an explanation by natural causes.

THIRD ACT

JOB *has fallen asleep from grief on a bench in front of his house. In the little garden there are many small flowering trees.*

FIRST YOUNG LADY, *softly, emerges with her curly head from the bed of roses, tries to awaken* JOB *and to seize his dangling hand.* Quite as you please! My God! In the wilderness the strong eat the weak. At home it's just the other way! Consequently one often has the face of a little lamb, the phlegmatic temper of a capon and . . .

JOB, *softly, in his sleep.* . . . and you the brain of a chicken.

SECOND YOUNG LADY, *softly laughing behind a tree.* Indeed, yes, when an ardent young man visits her, she goes to roost at once. She begs his pardon—does he have his red comb?

THIRD YOUNG LADY, *who has been squatting under the bench, looking up at him, softly.* You'll never again make that one lose his equilibrium! That's him all right, *Homo anthropos!* Just feel his calves!

JOB, *tickled, kicks in his sleep, so that the* YOUNG LADY *tumbles over backward.*

THIRD YOUNG LADY. Accursed frog's perspective! I'll be limping from this for the rest of my life!

FOURTH YOUNG LADY, *tickling* JOB's *ear with a flower stem, drops an apple, hiding all the while in a bush behind him.* Adam lives on in posterity because he bowed before Eve in Paradise!

JOB, *dreaming.* When one reflects how posterity is made by such worthless dalliances, he must lose faith in a better future!

FIFTH YOUNG LADY, *reaching out from the draperies of the house door for his shock of hair, softly.* 'Tis Fortune. Grab a hold! Or else she'll pull you 'round!

SIXTH YOUNG LADY, *administering him a gentle slap on the back.* As a man of the world, let him consider now which side of himself he wishes to show!

JOB, *sleepy.* Fortune is a gypsy who leads us by the nose! She wants her behind to be the object of our attention. When she performs her striptease there, beware the horn of plenty with which she might surprise you!

SEVENTH YOUNG LADY, *mockingly, from a tree.* Oh, for floating forth to meet furtive confessions and for uniting the warring sexes with the rainbow of forgiveness!

JOB, *dreaming, overcome by nostalgia.* My feelings are descending meteors hurtling down through the night of my heart and burning themselves out in it! My word, that transcends my self like the gesture of an invisible hand, remains for you mere stage effect!

ALL YOUNG LADIES, *singing softly.* Oh, how we love effects, farces and tragedies at midnight, when they hold sleep at bay. . . .

JOB, *mumbling.* Is this no demon towering in the sky who sets her heel upon me in the mud—but yet gentle angel who cools my head?

EIGHTH YOUNG LADY. Look about you, Sunday's child! Ghosts wear no clothes. What then can flesh-and-blood have on?

She comes from the path of the now dimly illuminated garden, the sun rises, she kisses his brow.

Good day, my friend! Life smiles upon you!

JOB *snarls at her, wipes off her kiss.* I have lumbago, the witches' dart. . . .

EIGHTH YOUNG LADY, *giving him up as hopeless.* That thought at once makes love freeze stiff. . . .

JOB, *touching himself in front and back to see if some new misfortune has not befallen him, staggers into the light the better to see.*

NINTH YOUNG LADY. Uprooted plants wither in the sun no less than in the shade.

JOB, *disgruntled.* To your health, Dame Fortune! The morning crows and not the cock, the game shoots the hunter down—a weary man curses the carnival and now shuts shop.

Goes into the house. Brings a bottle of poison, a skull, and two human bones to the window, contemplates the skull, lifts the bottle to his lips. The TENTH YOUNG LADY *reaches down from her tree for it and then drums gaily with the bones on the skull.*

JOB *throws the poison bottle after the* YOUNG LADY, *who retaliates with the skull and bones, which* JOB *wraps in paper.* Women, get going, out with you!

ALL YOUNG LADIES, *singing softly to the tune of the folk song, departing.* JOB *closes the store.* "Now I lay me down to sleep," *etc.*

Brief pause.

JOB, *behind closed window shutters.* The soul of man or magic lantern. . . . Times were when it projected God and Devil into the world; these days it casts women on the wall!

Humbly.

Oh, to laugh a little, to laugh . . . And not to run after these nurses who tease us children; from out there the witch looks in and can't be overlooked.

He smiles wanly; a silvery many-voiced choir echoes—cascading laughter, a hurricane—an inundation of laughter.

JOB *jumps out the window, pulls his pants tighter, stops short. In the upper story, above* JOB, *a window lights up in rosy illumination. The* PARROT *flies down from the opened window, flutters after the fugitive, opens wide her eyes, assails him, during the subsequent scene does not permit him to leave the protective wall of the house along which* JOB *runs to and fro.*

JOB *sprouts horns which develop into antlers. Whenever he rushes past the lit window, two shadows toss garments upon them so that the antlers soon become a clothes tree. Cuffs, collar, jackets, night- and under-garments of a gentleman and a lady.* JOB *grabs the doorbell and rings the house phone in deathly terror.* For pity's sake! I'm getting frightened! Anima, help! Salvation! What are they doing to me?

ANIMA, *from the window.* Conjuring spirits–do you see the plan? It's been the custom since time began.

ADAM, *the gardener, comes from the garden.* A woman, having turned his head, now makes a fool of him.

ANIMA. Mother's wit inspired me to this! An enlightened spirit has taken me to wife today, he disenchants me and now I aid him in his task!

JOB. That devil! A true enchanter he! Who bravely with kisses and fervid oaths conjures Anima up for his use. Oh, gaping Hell! Most fugitive witch! Treaties she signs, herself to surrender; confused, she blushes on bosom and neck; she opens her heart; airs secrets and skirts; and then shares in bed, in housewifely fashion, the power of the male. . . . What is it I feel? I am not like him, my opposite, that I could settle there and start begetting just like that! . . .

ANIMA *drops like a ripe apple down from the window, scantily clothed, to land with her buttocks on* JOB's *head. He collapses under* ANIMA's *weight and dies. At the window* MR. RUBBER-

MAN *is still after her virtue in an obvious way.* ANIMA, *reproachfully.* But no—dear Mr. Rubberman, what do you think?

PARROT. But no, Mr. Rubberman . . .

ADAM, *gently.* You've placed your wife too high in the heavens. Only now when she falls can you see through her and view her bottom.

ADAM *draws down a curtain which covers the house, the garden,* JOB, *and* ANIMA. *Ten gentlemen in mourning are painted on the curtain. In place of their faces they have holes through which an actor puts his head when in the following dialogue the gentleman concerned has his say.*

PARROT *explodes and drifts as pinkish cloud up through the sky.*

ADAM, *looking after it.* Once long ago in Paradise this same bird whispered a warning to me. Busy gathering apples, I failed to listen.

Sighs.

ANIMA *appears, chewing an apple.* Job, God bless him, was also eager for the apple of knowledge, alas. . . .

FIRST GENTLEMAN, *impudently.* Because the apple had its worm, Eve offered Adam his share first.

ADAM. Quiet! Keep in step, it isn't your turn yet! Each in his time. First you must stick your head through here. But don't kick around too much, or else the wall will fall on you.

In consequence of the commotion, JOB's *head rolls in front of the wall.* ANIMA, *shocked, bends over it, almost goes out of her mind.*

SECOND GENTLEMAN. Madame Sphinx got poor reward
For having brought into his world—
This enigmatic garbage-heap—the Philosophic Man—
Especially his riddle-posing head.
Madame Anima is now her other name,
She lacks imagination now to understand herself!

THIRD GENTLEMAN. Divine insanity created all.

FOURTH GENTLEMAN. The poor victim of seduction should be persuaded to take her abortion back again! Let's hope she will be pregnant once again!

MR. RUBBERMAN, *stepping forward timidly.* Modern science will help!

FIFTH GENTLEMAN. Having grown ashamed of its descent, while yet in school, it limits itself to analysing all creation, trying to see if there was need of one at all.

ADAM *drags* JOB's *body out from under the screen and neatly puts the head back on again. With an angry side glance at* RUBBERMAN. The doctor invents the disease, the patient foots the bill.

SIXTH GENTLEMAN, *to* JOB, *who lies downstage with arms outspread.* Death, who hit you with Woman right in your spine, will no longer open any hell-hole for any amount of huffing and puffing.

SEVENTH GENTLEMAN, *to* SIXTH GENTLEMAN. Even in a hell-hole a single ray refracted light into a thousand hues! Darkness falls and yields its place to this enlightened age.

EIGHTH GENTLEMAN. Too much light will never become night. Swallow this, Phoenix, and die!

ADAM, *softly, guarding* JOB, *puts a handful of earth on* JOB's *breast.* Such a multitude of flowers from a single shovelful of earth. May earth rest easy on you!

ANIMA. Is he dead?

ADAM, *calmly.* No! Only his head and heart and other things are gone.

MR. RUBBERMAN, *crying.* Mankind must be elevated genetically! Marriage reform, marriage reform! Let copulation proceed before the eyes of scientists!

NINTH GENTLEMAN. Science, unpurified by the filter spirit, oozes over life and death, besmirching both!

TENTH GENTLEMAN, *forcefully.* I believe in the genius of man! Anima—Amen!

ADAM, *gently, turning off the stage lights.* Good faith is a green eyeshade! It screens the light of truth for sickly eyes. The only good I still can do is blow out the light so that it needn't shine at all.

Exits with ANIMA.

ANIMA, *in the darkness.* Perhaps Job could never help but bear a heavy cross. I, with my own eyes, have seen here how they slandered me. Perhaps I alone slander myself—and Anima, who settled the heavy cross on Job's shoulders, is truly—Eve.

Notes

Full bibliographic citations will be found in the Selected Bibliography which follows this section.

Introduction

1. Oskar Kokoschka, *Schriften 1907–1955*, p. 407.
2. Carl E. Schorske, *Fin-de-Siècle Vienna*, p. 325.
3. Oskar Kokoschka, *My Life*, p. 20.
4. Quoted in Peter Selz, *German Expressionist Painting*, p. 149.
5. For further discussion and an English translation of the poem, see Henry I. Schvey, "Oskar Kokoschka's 'The Dreaming Youths,' " pp. 484–90.
6. Quoted in *Oskar Kokoschka: Vom Erlebnis im Leben*, p. 12.
7. Schvey, "Kokoschka's 'The Dreaming Youths,' " p. 487.
8. Kokoschka, *My Life*, p. 37.
9. Kokoschka, *My Life*, p. 67.
10. Selz, *German Expressionist Painting*, p. 163.
11. Quoted in Remigius Netzer's Postscript to Kokoschka's *My Life*, p. 217.
12. Kokoschka, *My Life*, pp. 216–17.
13. Ulrich Weisstein, Introduction, in *Expressionism as an International Phenomenon*, p. 23.
14. Werner Haftmann, *Painting in the Twentieth Century*, Vol. 1, p. 65.
15. Quoted in Paul Pörtner, ed., *Literatur-Revolution 1910–1925*, Vol. 2, p. 23.
16. J. M. Ritchie, *German Expressionist Drama* (Boston: Twayne, 1976), p. 44.
17. H. F. Garten, "Foreign Influences on German Expressionist Drama," in Weisstein, p. 61.
18. Kokoschka, *My Life*, p. 30.
19. August Strindberg, *The Father*, trans. Arvid Paulson (New York: Bantam, 1960), p. 51.
20. Ritchie, p. 44.
21. Quoted in *Schriften 1907–1955*, pp. 50–51.
22. Kokoschka, interview with author, Villeneuve, Switzerland, August 1973; hereafter cited as Kokoschka interview.
23. Kokoschka, *My Life*, p. 183.
24. Quoted in Selz, p. 162.
25. Karl Kraus, in "Franz Ferdinand und die Talente," p. 2.
26. Kokoschka, *My Life*, p. 38.
27. Quoted in Schorske, p. 339.
28. Schorske, p. 327.
29. Henry A. Lea, "Expressionist Literature and Music," in Weisstein, p. 148.
30. Kokoschka, *My Life*, p. 181.
31. Stefan Zweig, *The World of Yesterday*, pp. 72–73.
32. Zweig, pp. 71, 73, 76.
33. Kokoschka, *My Life*, p. 27.
34. Schorske, p. 224.
35. Schorske, p. 224.
36. Frank Whitford, *Expressionism*, p. 155.
37. Schorske, p. 343.
38. Kokoschka, *My Life*, p. 33.
39. Quoted in Selz, p. 165.
40. Quoted in Paul Raabe, ed., *The Era of German Expressionism*, pp. 335–36.
41. Paul Hadermann, "Expressionist Literature and Painting," in Weisstein, p. 125.
42. Regina Brandt, *Figurationen und Kompositionen in den Dramen Oskar Kokoschkas*, p. 15.
43. Bernhard Diebold, *Anarchie im Drama*, p. 319.
44. Quoted in Günther Rühle, ed., *Theater für die Republik 1917–1933*, pp. 64–65.
45. Joseph Sprengler, "Kokoschkas Bühnendichtungen," p. 677.
46. Paul Kornfeld, "Theaterzettel der Uraufführung von Oskar Kokoschkas Dramen," p. 40.
47. These include Paul Westheim, *Oskar Kokoschka*; Edith Hoffmann, *Kokoschka—Life and Work*; Hans Maria Wingler, *Oskar Kokoschka: The Work of the Painter*; Bernhard Bultmann, *Oskar Kokoschka*; and Fritz Schmalenbach, *Oskar Kokoschka*.
48. Edith Hoffmann, "*Der Sturm*: A Document of German Expressionism," p. 50.
49. The only previous study to focus on Kokoschka's "double tal-

ent" is Gerhard Johann Lischka's *Oskar Kokoschka: Maler und Dichter*. However, Lischka systematically divides his study into parts, which, instead of revealing the "mutual illumination of the arts," propagates the practice of separating Kokoschka the artist from Kokoschka the dramatist. Thus, Lischka gives examples of the theme of "man and woman" in both Kokoschka's literary work and his visual work, but does not analyze the details common to both—which would reveal the precise relationships in Kokoschka's use of the two media.

50. See Hans Schwerte, "Anfang des expressionistischen Dramas: Oskar Kokoschka," and Horst Denkler, "Über Oskar Kokoschkas Dramen."
51. René Wellek and Austin Warren, *Theory of Literature*, pp. 134, 127.
52. Wellek and Warren, pp. 128–29.
53. Wassily Kandinsky, *Concerning the Spiritual in Art*, p. 47.
54. Quoted in Hadermann, "Expressionist Literature and Painting," p. 122.
55. Otto Kamm, "Oskar Kokoschka und das Theater," p. 44.
56. Quoted in Selz, pp. 17–18.

Chapter 1

1. The date of the first performance of *Murderer Hope of Women* has not been ascertained with absolute certainty. In accepting the July 4, 1909, date, I follow Kokoschka's statement in his autobiography (*My Life*, p. 28). This date is also given in a note to the first publication of the text in *Der Sturm*, No. 20 (1910), p. 156, as well as in most of the secondary literature. The principal dissenter is Hans Maria Wingler, who, following the account of the architect Philipp Häusler, who had a small part in the original production, accepts July 4, 1908, as the date of the premiere in his edition of Kokoschka's writings (*Schriften 1907–1955*, p. 455).
2. Kokoschka interview.
3. The original title, affixed to the 1910 version, was *Mörder, Hoffnung der Frauen* (*Murderer, Hope of Women*). In the 1916 version the comma was omitted.
4. Each time the play was republished Kokoschka made slight alterations in the text. For more detailed discussion of the textual variations, see Horst Denkler, "Die Druckfassungen der Dramen Oskar Kokoschkas," pp. 101–4. For a list of the various versions of the play, see Appendix A.
5. Unless otherwise specified, all references to the text of this play are to the version published in Oskar Kokoschka, *Dichtungen und Dramen*, Vol. 1 of *Das Schriftliche Werk*, and translated by Michael Hamburger as *Murderer the Women's Hope* in *An Anthology of German Expressionist Drama*, Ed. Walter H. Sokel, pp. 17–21. Hamburger's translation (Appendix B) has been the basis for my own quotations.
6. In the first version he is actually lowered into a coffin.
7. Kokoschka, *My Life*, p. 27.
8. Kokoschka interview.
9. Paul Kornfeld, "Theaterzettel der Uraufführung von Oskar Kokoschkas Dramen," p. 40.

10. The method of killing could also be seen as a deliberate parody of Michelangelo's depiction of the Creation on the ceiling of the Sistine Chapel, suggesting the life-denying futility of the sexual conflict.
11. Paul Westheim, *Oskar Kokoschka*, p. 68.
12. For additional information on the supposed influence of Weininger on Kokoschka, see Horst Denkler, "Oskar Kokoschkas Einakter 'Mörder Hoffnung der Frauen,'" p. 47, and Hans Schwerte, "Anfang des expressionistischen Dramas: Oskar Kokoschka," p. 175.
13. This interpretation was suggested by Horst Denkler's essay cited above, p. 49f.
14. Lothar Schreyer, *Erinnerungen an Sturm und Bauhaus*, p. 96.
15. Quoted in Günther Rühle, Ed., *Theater für die Republik 1917–1933*, p. 66.
16. Bernhard Diebold, *Anarchie im Drama*, p. 318.
17. Quoted in Rühle, pp. 64–65.
18. Quoted in Kornfeld, pp. 40–41.
19. In my Kokoschka interview, he said, "Red is for me like blood. When I am dead, I am no longer red. Red is the color of life, white is the color of death." See also *My Life*, p. 28.
20. A less convincing interpretation of the title would suggest that "murderer" refers to the Woman, who, by killing the Man, gives "hope" to the other women, her followers.
21. The four illustrations appear in Nos. 20, 21, 24, and 26 of *Der Sturm*, Vol. 1 (1910).
22. Quoted in an interview with Wolfgang Fisher in *Kokoschka Lithographs*, an exhibition organized by the Arts Council of Great Britain to mark the artist's eightieth birthday (London: The Arts Council, 1966), p. 12.
23. Schreyer, p. 97.
24. Because the poster for the play had outraged both public and critics, Kokoschka felt like a criminal. As a result, he defiantly shaved his head to look like one (Fig. 7). In the illustrations to *Murderer Hope of Women* (to the extent that these are self-projections), and in a later poster for *Der Sturm*, he also depicted himself in this way. See also Kokoschka, *My Life*, p. 28.
25. Werner Haftmann, *Painting in the Twentieth Century*, p. 133.
26. Kokoschka, *My Life*, p. 33.
27. Kokoschka interview.
28. Karl Kraus, "Pro domo et mundo," p. 25.
29. Erika Tietze-Conrat, "Ein Porträt und Nachher," p. 70.
30. The assertion that the shape at the upper right of the canvas is indeed a "moon" is strengthened by a comparison with the Pietà poster (Fig. 1), where a crescent moon is executed in identical fashion and is placed in precisely the same corner of the work.

Chapter 2

1. Fearing a further scandal, the censor finally admitted that the play was banned "because of its erotic content" as well as its incomprehensible dialogue and its "abstruse, incomprehensible

images." A detailed account of the controversy is to be found in Otto Kamm's "Oskar Kokoschka und das Theater," pp. 81–83. An account in Edith Hoffmann's *Kokoschka—Life and Work,* p. 106, incorrectly maintains that the canceled performance ·was scheduled for 1911.

2. In Oskar Kokoschka, *Dramen und Bilder,* pp. 37–62.
3. The differences between *The Burning Bush* and the earlier version are very slight and will not be examined in detail. Unless otherwise specified, all references in this chapter will be to *The Burning Bush.* For further discussion of the differences between the two versions, see Horst Denkler, " 'Schauspiel' und 'Der brennende Dornbusch' von Oskar Kokoschka"; and Regina Brandt, *Figurationen und Kompositionen in den Dramen Oskar Kokoschkas,* pp. 41, 50–52.
4. The edition used is Oskar Kokoschka, *Dichtungen und Dramen,* Vol. 1 of *Das Schriftliche Werk,* pp. 89–110. The play has not been translated into English, and the translations of passages from the play are mine unless otherwise specified.
5. The translation of these lines appears in Victor H. Miesel, ed., *Voices of German Expressionism,* p. 146.
6. An English translation of Kokoschka's essay appears in Miesel, pp. 98–99. For the German text see Oskar Kokoschka, *Schriften 1907–1955.*
7. Miesel, pp. 100–101.
8. Kokoschka, *Dramen und Bilder,* p. 62.
9. Brandt, p. 21.
10. The cloth also refers to a song which the Woman sings just before the Man's entrance: "The old man draped a green cloth over the bars of the bird-cage; then the bird no longer sang cheerfully to the old man." Her song also suggests the difficulty that the Man will have in curbing the Woman's animal instincts and forcing her to look within.
11. Oskar Kokoschka, *Der gefesselte Kolumbus.* The lithographs have also been reproduced in Kokoschka, *Das druckgraphische Werk,* pp. 43–54.
12. See Kokoschka, *Dichtungen und Dramen,* pp. 18–24. There is no available English translation.
13. Hoffmann, p. 123.
14. Oskar Kokoschka, *My Life,* p. 70.
15. Hoffmann, p. 112.
16. Fritz Schmalenbach, "Kokoschkas malerische Entwicklung," p. xvi.
17. Quoted in Günther Rühle, *Theater für die Republik 1917–1933,* p. 64.
18. Quoted in Oskar Kokoschka, *Die Fächer für Alma Mahler,* p. 6.
19. Kokoschka, *Die Fächer für Alma Mahler,* p. 17.
20. Quoted in Kokoschka, *Die Fächer für Alma Mahler,* p. 6.
21. Hans Tietze, "Oskar Kokoschka," p. 87.
22. Tietze, p. 87.

Chapter 3

1. Joseph Sprengler, "Kokoschkas Bühnendichtungen," p. 676.
2. The text of *Job* appears in Oskar Kokoschka, *Dichtungen und Dra-*

men, pp. 65–88. The play has been translated by Walter H. Sokel and Jacqueline Sokel in *An Anthology of German Expressionist Drama* and by Michael Benedikt in George E. Wellwarth, ed., *German Drama between the Wars.* The translation used in this chapter is by the Sokels (reprinted in Appendix D).
3. Kokoschka interview.
4. These two versions will henceforth be designated *I* and *II.* For a list of various versions of the play, see Appendix A.
5. The first version of *Sphinx and Strawman* was published in *Wort in der Zeit,* 2 (1956), pp. 145–48. There is no precise documentation of the 1907 performance, although Edith Hoffmann (*Kokoschka—Life and Work,* pp. 54–56) gives a detailed account, presumably based on conversations with the author. The translation used for *Sphinx and Strawman II* appears in Victor H. Miesel, ed., *Voices of German Expressionism,* pp. 119–25, and is reproduced in Appendix C.
6. Oskar Kokoschka, *My Life,* p. 183.
7. Hoffmann, p. 55.
8. For other allusions suggested by the name Firdusi, see footnote to first page of Appendix C. The name Lilly evokes Wedekind's temptress Lulu and Adam's first wife, Lilith.
9. Hugo Ball, *Flight out of Time: A Dada Diary,* p. 106.
10. Tristan Tzara, "Chronique Zurichoise," pp. 237–38.
11. Heinz Herald, "Der Kokoschka Skandal," p. 163.
12. Kokoschka, *My Life,* p. 103.
13. Horst Denkler, "Die Drückfassungen der Dramen Oskar Kokoschkas," p. 99.
14. The word "myth" is employed in the broad sense in which Northrop Frye uses it in his *Anatomy of Criticism: Four Essays.*
15. For example, Faulkner's *The Sound and the Fury,* O'Neill's *Mourning Becomes Electra,* Joyce's *Ulysses,* Eliot's *The Waste Land,* and Kafka's *The Castle,* among others.
16. Camill Hoffmann, "Kokoschkas Dichtung und Theater," p. 221.
17. Quoted in Günther Rühle, ed., *Theater für die Republik 1917–1933,* pp. 64–65.
18. Wingler, ed., *Schriften 1907–1955,* p. 465.
19. Kokoschka, *Schriften 1907–1955,* p. 465.
20. Kokoschka, *My Life,* p. 183.
21. Quoted in Rühle, p. 64.
22. Originally published by Paul Cassirer in Berlin in 1917, the illustrations to *Job* have also appeared in Oskar Kokoschka, *Das druckgraphische Werk,* pp. 87–100.
23. Kokoschka, quoted in Hoffmann, p. 167.
24. Hoffmann, pp. 167–68.
25. Hans Maria Wingler, *Kokoschka—Fibel,* p. 34.
26. John Russell, *Oskar Kokoschka: Watercolours, Drawings, Writings,* p. 15. In describing his work on this painting in *My Life* (p. 117), Kokoschka compares himself to Job: "When I painted *The Emigrants [The Exiles],* I had argued with God like Job, beseeching him to send me a ray of light in a world devastated by war."
27. Russell, p. 16.
28. Hoffmann, p. 173.

Chapter 4

1. *Orpheus and Eurydice* has not been translated into English. The text used is found in Oskar Kokoschka, *Dichtungen und Dramen*, pp. 111–73. The translations are mine.
2. Oskar Kokoschka, *My Life*, p. 96.
3. I am grateful for the suggestion by Olda Kokoschka that the idea of the bark of Hades may have been inspired by Kokoschka's introduction to Wagner's opera *Tristan und Isolde* by Alma Mahler.
4. The words *Allos Makar* also form the title of a poem, with five accompanying lithographs; it dates from 1914 and has been translated into English in Victor H. Miesel, ed., *Voices of German Expressionism*, p. 146.
5. Kokoschka employed this same technique to stress the identification of the Woman and the virgin at the conclusion of the third scene of *The Burning Bush*.
6. Oskar Kokoschka, *Schriften 1907–1955*, pp. 432–33.
7. Oskar Kokoschka, *A Sea Ringed with Visions*, p. 68.
8. Alma Mahler, *And the Bridge Is Love*, pp. 74–75.
9. Alma Mahler, *Mein Leben*, p. 118.
10. *A Sea Ringed with Visions*, p. 26. For the connection between *Orpheus and Eurydice* and Kokoschka's Italian trip with Alma Mahler, I am indebted to Otto Kamm's "Oskar Kokoschka und das Theater," p. 26.
11. Hans Maria Wingler, in Kokoschka, *Schriften 1907–1955*, p. 470. Although Wingler correctly perceives the regenerative function of Hades in the play and sees the eternal bond between Eurydice and Hades as the "key to the entire play," he assumes that Kokoschka identifies himself (rather than Mahler) with this regenerative power. Instead, it seems clear that at the period in which the play was written Kokoschka identified himself with Orpheus. See also n. 12 below.
12. Because Kokoschka was suffering physical and mental anguish at the time of the writing of *Orpheus and Eurydice* (1915), it seems highly unlikely that he identified *himself* with Hades, as Wingler (n. 11 above) suggests (see Kokoschka, *Schriften 1907–1955*, p. 470). Wingler's evidence, that Hades is depicted with Kokoschka's features in the triptych *The Prometheus-Saga* (1950), hardly qualifies as an appropriate clue for the analysis of a work conceived in 1915 at a time when Kokoschka—unwell both physically and spiritually—would not have identified himself with the principles of "creative regeneration."
13. Kokoschka, *My Life*, p. 77.
14. Mahler, *And the Bridge Is Love*, p. 77.
15. Kokoschka, *My Life*, p. 77.
16. *Oskar Kokoschka*, catalogue, Hamburg, 1965, p. 48.
17. *Oskar Kokoschka*, catalogue, Hamburg, 1965, p. 48.
18. Karl Kerényi, Introduction, p. 15.
19. Kerényi, p. 32.
20. Quoted in *Oskar Kokoschka*, catalogue, Hamburg, 1965, p. 48.
21. Kokoschka, *Schriften 1907–1955*, pp. 50–51.
22. Kerényi, p. 33.
23. Robert Graves, introduction, Lucius Apuleius, *The Golden Ass* (Harmondsworth: Penguin, 1950), p. 18.
24. Joseph Sprengler, "Kokoschkas Bühnendichtungen," pp. 677–78.
25. By the playwright Paul Kornfeld in his *Expressionismus, Literatur und Kunst, 1910–1923*, p. 40.
26. Kamm, p. 48.
27. Lia Secci, *Il mito greco nel teatro tedesco espressionista*, p. 168.
28. Erich Neumann, *Amor and Psyche*, p. 158.
29. In both *The Burning Bush* and *Orpheus and Eurydice*, fire is used in a double sense: initially as a symbol of physical passion, then later as a symbol of the purgation of that passion. In the visual image of Orpheus digging into the ruins of his house, both meanings are suggested: for Orpheus it is primarily orgasmic (the result of the friction created by his digging); for Eurydice it represents the cleansing fire of Hades.
30. Quoted in Mahler, *And the Bridge Is Love*, p. 77.
31. For this point, I am indebted to Regina Brandt, *Figurationen und Kompositionen in den Dramen Oskar Kokoschkas*, pp. 79–80.
32. Six of the illustrations have been published in Oskar Kokoschka, *Das druckgraphische Werk*, pp. 120–25. Two more of the illustrations (nos. 4 and 5 discussed here) appear in Kokoschka, *Schriften 1907–1955*, p. 272. In 1956 he executed a series of eight pastel sketches as suggestions for a proposed production of the play, but as these illustrations, created almost forty years after the play was written, do not belong to the same stylistic period as the play or works contemporary with it, they are excluded from this discussion. Four of these sketches have been reproduced in *Oskar Kokoschka*, catalogue, Hamburg, 1965.
33. Oskar Kokoschka, *Die Fächer für Alma Mahler*, p. 26.
34. Edith Hoffmann, *Kokoschka—Life and Work*, p. 119.
35. Kokoschka, *My Life*, p. 137.
36. Quoted in Bernhard Bultmann, *Oskar Kokoschka*, p. 62.
37. The correspondence between Kokoschka and the dressmaker was published by Paul Westheim under the title of "Der Fetisch."
38. Kokoschka, *My Life*, p. 117.
39. Kokoschka, *My Life*, p. 118.
40. Kokoschka, *My Life*, p. 117.
41. Oskar Kokoschka, *Vorträge, Aufsätze, Essays zur Kunst*, p. 319.
42. Kokoschka, *Vorträge, Aufsätze, Essays zur Kunst*, p. 319.

Chapter 5

1. Actually *Comenius* was begun in 1936. Kokoschka worked on it from 1936 to 1938. However, the play remained a fragment and was completely rewritten in 1972. See Appendix A.
2. This comment should not imply that Kokoschka sticks rigidly to historical fact in *Comenius*. In fact, he often alters events to suit his purpose.
3. *Comenius* is nearly a hundred pages long, almost as long as the previous four plays put together, an indication of the greater role assigned to discourse here.

4. Oskar Kokoschka, quoted in Hans Maria Wingler, "Kokoschkas pädagogische Konzeption," pp. 46–49.
5. Oskar Kokoschka, *My Life*, p. 11.
6. Oskar Kokoschka, *Schriften 1907–1955*, p. 337. The translation is from Victor H. Miesel, ed., *Voices of German Expressionism*, p. 98.
7. Kokoschka, *Schriften 1907–1955*, p. 345.
8. Kokoschka, *Schriften 1907–1955*, p. 352.
9. Oskar Kokoschka, *Vorträge, Aufsätze, Essays zur Kunst*, p. 13.
10. Kokoschka, *My Life*, p. 110.
11. Comenius' *Didactica Magna* was written in Czech in 1627. It was translated into Latin by Comenius in 1638, when all hope of instituting reforms in his native Bohemia had vanished. In 1657 it was published in Amsterdam, together with other didactic works, under the title *Opera Didactica Omnia*.
12. Jean Piaget, ed., *John Amos Comenius: Selections*, pp. 80–81.
13. In 1941 Kokoschka wrote: "The essential principle of his [Comenius'] educational plan translated into modern language demands from World Democracy an international scientific control of mass-education by a board of internationally minded education experts and scientists." Such was the plea Jan Amos Comenius addressed to the Conference of Breda (1667), when the ideological wars of his time were ending. See Kokoschka's essay "Comenius, the English Revolution, and Our Present Plight," p. 69, and *Das Schriftliche Werk*, Vol. 4, pp. 231–41.
14. Kokoschka, *My Life*, p. 156.
15. Quoted in Edith Hoffmann, *Kokoschka—Life and Work*, p. 212.
16. Published in Kokoschka, *Schriften 1907–1955*, pp. 309–34. There is no English translation.
17. Her name is spelled "Hannah" in the final version of the play.
18. Kokoschka interview.
19. Kokoschka, *Vorträge, Aufsätze, Essays zur Kunst*, pp. 252–53.
20. Kokoschka, "Comenius, the English Revolution, and Our Present Plight," pp. 65–66.
21. See the year 1937 in the chronological table at the end of Hans Maria Wingler's *Oskar Kokoschka: The Work of the Painter*.
22. Quoted in Edith Hoffmann, *Kokoschka—Life and Work*, p. 212.
23. Hoffmann, *Kokoschka—Life and Work*, p. 213.
24. Hoffmann, *Kokoschka—Life and Work*, p. 214.
25. Quoted in *Kokoschka—Life and Work*, p. 236.
26. Quoted in Gerhard Johann Lischka, *Oskar Kokoschka: Maler und Dichter*, p. 35.
27. Kokoschka, *Schriften 1907–1955*, p. 378.
28. Kokoschka, *My Life*, p. 176.
29. This is the title of the final chapter of Kokoschka's autobiography, *My Life*.
30. Kokoschka interview.
31. Kokoschka interview.
32. Although no specific dates are given in the text, most of the events which take place in act 1 correspond roughly with historical events which occurred in 1618 and 1619.
33. *Comenius* appears in Oskar Kokoschka, *Dichtungen und Dramen*, pp. 175–272. There is as yet no English translation of the play.
34. Comenius also revisited the town on several other occasions.
35. This speech could be said to contain some of Kokoschka's own, more recent, misgivings about Comenius' thought.
36. Comenius declined an offer from Richelieu to found a Pansophic College in France, made at approximately the same time, in favor of the Swedish proposal. He also visited London in 1641 in an (unsuccessful) effort to found a similar institution.
37. The painting known as *The Night Watch*, the largest and most famous of Rembrandt's paintings, actually bears the title *The Company of Captain Frans Cocq and Lieutenant Willem van Ruytenburch*. Its popular title is based on the false assumption that the scene depicted takes place at night. In fact, it is a daytime scene, as was discovered when the painting was stripped of its varnish and dirt for cleaning following World War II. Nevertheless, it continues to be known as *The Night Watch*.
38. There is some ambiguity as to whether we should identify Christl and Hannah. On the realistic level, it is clearly impossible that Hannah is Christl, since in the play Christl the foundling is a little girl in 1628, and Comenius dies in 1670 in Amsterdam. On the other hand, Hannah is obviously not intended as a realistic character but as an allegorical representative of the "inner light" for which Comenius (and Rembrandt) had been searching. In support of the point of view that Hannah and Christl are one is the fact that there is only a single entry in the list of characters: "Hannah, a little Jewish girl who, as Comenius' foster-child, is named Christl." In the film version of the play (for which Kokoschka was consulted), the two roles are distinct (although played by the same actress), suggesting that Comenius is mistaken in his suggestion that the two girls are the same. Since Hannah is rarely seen (and then indistinctly) in her appearance in act 4, and is often only present as a disembodied voice, the director is free to choose his own interpretation. I think that it is essential to retain some ambiguity, although the Christl of act 2 should be played more as a person of flesh and blood than the mysterious child of act 4, whose function is almost entirely symbolic.
39. There is no use of color symbolism in *Comenius*.
40. Kokoschka, *My Life*, p. 208.
41. Kokoschka interview.
42. Kokoschka, *Vorträge, Aufsätze, Essays zur Kunst*, p. 110.
43. Kokoschka, *My Life*, p. 209.
44. This moment of rebirth was prefigured by the children's celebration of the death of winter and the rebirth of spring in the second scene of act 2. In both cases, it is significant that *children* are the ones who commemorate this rebirth (a vital concept throughout Kokoschka's work, which he borrows from Comenius via romanticism), and that they do this in the springtime and by means of light (e.g., the candles inside the hollow eggs and the light which Hannah brings to Rembrandt).
45. Four of Kokoschka's plays move from darkness or night toward morning or light, suggesting the development from blindness to sight. Only *Job*, Kokoschka's tragicomedy, parodies this process by moving from night (act 1) toward morning (act 3) but concludes with the stage in total darkness.

46. Kokoschka, *Schriften 1907–1955*, p. 50.
47. Kokoschka, *Schriften 1907–1955*, p. 373.
48. Kokoschka interview.
49. Although executed in 1942, this pen-and-ink drawing was signed only in 1957 for a planned Czechoslovakian production of the *Comenius* fragment. A reproduction appears in the 1975 Hamburg catalogue, p. 86. In 1973, Kokoschka made six sketches for the film version of *Comenius*, directed by Stanislav Barabas, for German television. In 1975 he made an additional six portrait drawings for the play. However, the first six sketches were designed specifically for the film version of the play, and the latter six are not concerned with the events of act 4, which has been the focus of the present discussion. They cannot be said to illuminate the play's visual elements; therefore, they have been omitted here.

50. The cartoon for the mosaic was executed by Kokoschka in 1972. Following its completion by a craftsman from Ravenna, the mosaic was unveiled at the St. Nicolai Church in Hamburg in 1974.
51. For this observation I am indebted to Heinz Spielmann, *Oskar Kokoschka*, p. 86.
52. Spielmann, *Oskar Kokoschka*, p. 71.

Conclusion

1. Carl E. Schorske, *Fin-de-Siècle Vienna*, p. 335.
2. Martin Esslin, *The Theatre of the Absurd*, p. 7.
3. Antonin Artaud, *The Theatre and Its Double*, p. 28, 93, 71.

Selected Bibliography

Artaud, Antonin. *The Theatre and Its Double*. Translated by Mary Caroline Richards. New York: Grove Press, 1958.

Ball, Hugo. *Flight out of Time: A Dada Diary*. Translated by Ann Raimes. New York: Viking, 1974.

Benedikt, Michael. *"Job*. By Oskar Kokoschka." In *German Drama between the Wars*, edited by George E. Wellwarth. New York: Dutton, 1964.

Böttcher, Kurt, and Mittenzwei, Johannes. *Dichter als Maler*. Stuttgart: W. Kohlhammer, 1980.

Brandt, Regina. *Figurationen und Kompositionen in den Dramen Oskar Kokoschkas*. Munich: UNI—Druck, 1967.

Bultmann, Bernhard. *Oskar Kokoschka*. Salzburg: Galerie Welz, 1960.

Denkler, Horst. "Die Druckfassungen der Dramen Oskar Kokoschkas." *Deutsche Vierteljahrsschrift für Literaturwissenschaft und Geistesgeschichte*, 40, (1966), pp. 90–108.

———. "Oskar Kokoschkas Einakter 'Mörder Hoffnung der Frauen.'" In *Drama des Expressionismus*, edited by Horst Denkler. Munich: Fink, 1967.

———. " 'Schauspiel' und 'Der brennende Dornbusch' von Oskar Kokoschka." *Deutschenunterricht*, 17 (1965), pp. 34–52.

———. "Über Oskar Kokoschkas Dramen." *Jahrbuch der Evangelischen Akademie Tutzing*, 15 (1966), pp. 288–306.

Diebold, Bernhard. *Anarchie im Drama*. Frankfurt: Frankfurter Verlagsanstalt, 1921.

Esslin, Martin. *The Theatre of the Absurd*. 2d ed. New York: Doubleday, 1969.

Fechter, Paul. *Das europäische Drama*. 3 vols. Mannheim: Bibliographisches Institut, 1956–58.

Haftmann, Werner. *Painting in the Twentieth Century*. 2d ed. Vol. 1. Translated by Ralph Manheim. London: Lund Humphries, 1968.

Herald, Heinz. "Der Kokoschka—Skandal." *Das junge Deutschland*, 2 (1919), p. 163.

Hoffmann, Camill. "Kokoschkas Dichtung und Theater." *Das Kunstblatt*, 7 (1917), pp. 219–21.

Hoffmann, Edith. *Kokoschka—Life and Work*. London: Faber and Faber, 1947.

———. "*Der Sturm*: A Document of German Expressionism." *Signature*, 18 (1954), pp. 44–55.

Hofman, Werner. "Oskar Kokoschka." *Wort in der Zeit*, 2 (1956), pp. 129–39.

Kamm, Otto. "Oskar Kokoschka und das Theater." Ph.D. diss., University of Vienna, 1958.

Kandinsky, Wassily. *Concerning the Spiritual in Art*. New York: George Wittenborn, 1970.

Kerényi, Karl. Introduction. *Orpheus und Eurydike*. Munich: Langen/Müller, 1963.

Kokoschka, Oskar. "Comenius, the English Revolution, and Our Present Plight." In *The Teacher of Nations*, edited by Eduard Beneš. Cambridge: Cambridge University Press, 1942.

———. *Dichtungen und Dramen*. Vol. 1 of *Das Schriftliche Werk*. Hamburg: Christians, 1973.

———. *Dramen und Bilder*. Leipzig: Kurt Wolff, 1913.

———. *Das druckgraphische Werk*. Edited by Hans Maria Wingler and F. Welz. Salzburg: Galerie Welz, 1975.

———. *Erzählungen*. Vol. 2 of *Das Schriftliche Werk*. Hamburg: Christians, 1974.

———. *Die Fächer für Alma Mahler*. Edited by Heinz Spielmann. Hamburg: Christians, 1969.

———. *Der gefesselte Kolumbus*. Berlin: Gurlitt, 1916.

———. "Mörder, Hoffnung der Frauen." *Der Sturm*, No. 20 (1910), pp. 155–56.

———. *Mörder Hoffnung der Frauen*. Berlin: Der Sturm, 1916.

———. *Mörder Hoffnung der Frauen*. Leipzig: Kurt Wolff, 1917.

———. *My Life*. Translated by David Britt. New York: Macmillan, 1974.

———. *Politische Äusserungen*. Vol. 4 of *Das Schriftliche Werk*. Hamburg: Christians, 1976.

———. *Schriften 1907–1955*. Edited by Hans Maria Wingler. Munich: Langen/Müller, 1956.

———. *A Sea Ringed with Visions*. London: Thames and Hudson, 1962.

———. "Sphinx und Strohmann." *Wort in der Zeit*, 2, No. 3 (1956), pp. 145–48.

Selected Bibliography

————. *Variationen über ein Thema.* Vienna: Lanyi, 1921.

————. *Vorträge, Aufsätze, Essays zur Kunst.* Vol. 3 of *Das Schriftliche Werk.* Hamburg: Christians, 1975.

——— *Oskar Kokoschka.* Catalogue of an exhibition at Museum für Kunst und Gewerbe, Hamburg, April 29–June 20, 1965. Hamburg: Museum für Kunst und Gewerbe, 1965.

——— *Oskar Kokoschka.* Edited by Heinz Spielmann. Catalogue of an exhibition at B.A.T. Haus, Hamburg, 1970.

——— *Oskar Kokoschka: Vom Erlebnis im Leben.* Edited by Otto Breicha. Catalogue of an exhibition at Künstlerhaus, Vienna, May–June, 1976. Salzburg: Galerie Welz, 1976.

Kornfeld, Paul. "Theaterzettel der Uraufführung von Oskar Kokoschkas Dramen." *Expressionismus, Literatur und Kunst, 1910–1923.* Catalogue of an exhibition at Schiller-Nationalmuseum, Marbach, 1960. Munich: Langen/Müller, 1960.

Kraus, Karl. "Franz Ferdinand und die Talente." *Die Fackel,* 400 (1910), p. 2.

————. "Pro domo et mundo." *Die Fackel,* 300 (1910), p. 25.

Lischka, Gerhard Johann. *Oskar Kokoschka: Maler und Dichter: Eine literarästhetische Untersuchung zu seiner Doppelbegabung.* Berne: Lang, 1972.

Mahler, Alma. *And the Bridge Is Love.* London: Hutchinson, 1959.

————. *Mein Leben.* Frankfurt-am-Main: Fischer, 1960.

Miesel, Victor H., ed. *Voices of German Expressionism.* Englewood Cliffs, N.J.: Prentice-Hall, 1970.

Neumann, Erich. *Amor and Psyche.* Translated by Ralph Manheim. New York: Pantheon, 1956.

Piaget, Jean, ed. *John Amos Comenius: Selections.* Translated by Iris Unwin. Paris: UNESCO, 1957.

Pörtner, Paul, ed. *Literatur-Revolution 1910–1925.* 2 vols. Neuweid: Luchterhand, 1961.

Raabe, Paul, ed. *The Era of German Expressionism.* Translated by J. M. Ritchie. London: Calder and Boyars, 1974.

Reisinger, Alfred. *Kokoschkas Dichtungen nach dem Expressionismus.* Vienna: Europaverlag, 1978.

Ritchie, J. M. *German Expressionist Drama.* Boston: Twayne, 1976.

Rühle, Günther, ed. *Theater für die Republik 1917–1933.* Frankfurt: Fischer, 1967.

Russell, John. *Oskar Kokoschka: Watercolours, Drawings, Writings.* London: Thames and Hudson, 1960.

Schmalenbach, Fritz. "Kokoschkas malerische Entwicklung." Catalogue of an exhibition at Haus der Kunst, Munich, 1958.

————. *Oskar Kokoschka.* Königstein im Taunus: Karl Robert Langewiesche, 1967.

Schorske, Carl E. *Fin-de-Siècle Vienna.* New York: Knopf, 1979.

Schreyer, Lothar. *Erinnerungen an Sturm und Bauhaus.* Munich: Langen/Müller, 1956.

Schvey, Henry I. "Oskar Kokoschka's 'The Dreaming Youths.' " *Books Abroad,* August 1975, pp. 484–90.

Schwerte, Hans. "Anfang des expressionistischen Dramas: Oskar Kokoschka." *Zeitschrift für Deutsche Philologie,* 83 (1964), pp. 171–91.

Secci, Lia. *Il mito greco nel teatro tedesco espressionista.* Rome: Bulzoni, 1969.

Selz, Peter. *German Expressionist Painting.* Berkeley and Los Angeles: University of California Press, 1957.

Sokel, Walter H., ed. *An Anthology of German Expressionist Drama.* New York: Anchor, 1963.

Spielmann, Heinz. *Oskar Kokoschka.* Hamburg: B.A.T. Haus, 1975.

————. "Oskar Kokoschkas Drama 'Comenius.' " In *Begegnung mit Kokoschka.* Pöchlarn: Oskar Kokoschka-Dokumentation, 1973.

Sprengler, Joseph. "Kokoschkas Bühnendichtungen," *Hochland,* 2 (1922), pp. 670–78.

Strindberg, August. *Three Plays.* Harmondsworth: Penguin, 1958.

Tietze, Hans. "Oskar Kokoschka." *Zeitschrift für bildende Kunst,* 29 (1918), pp. 83–96.

Tietze-Conrat, Erika. "Ein Porträt und Nachher." *Bekenntnis zu Kokoschka.* Edited by J. P. Hodin. Mainz: Kupferberg, 1963.

Tzara, Tristan. "Chronique Zurichoise." In *The Dada Painters and Poets: An Anthology,* edited by Robert Motherwell. New York: George Wittenborn, 1967.

Weisstein, Ulrich. *Comparative Literature and Literary Theory.* Translated by William Riggan. Bloomington: Indiana University Press, 1973.

————, ed. *Expressionism as an International Phenomenon.* Paris and Budapest: Librairie Marcel Didier and Akadémiai Kiadó, 1973.

Wellek, René, and Warren, Austin. *Theory of Literature.* 3d ed. New York: Harcourt, Brace and World, 1956.

Westheim, Paul. "Der Fetisch." In *Kunstlerbekenntnisse.* Berlin: Prophylaen, 1925.

————. *Oskar Kokoschka.* 2d ed. Berlin: Cassirer, 1925.

Whitford, Frank. *Expressionism.* London: Hamlyn, 1970.

Wingler, Hans Maria. *Kokoschka—Fibel.* Salzburg: Galerie Welz, 1957.

————. "Kokoschkas pädagogische Konzeption." *Das Kunstwerk,* 5 (1951), pp. 46–49.

————. *Oskar Kokoschka: The Work of the Painter.* Trans. F. S. C. Budgen, J. P. Hodin, and Ilse Schreier. Salzburg: Galerie Welz, 1958.

Zweig, Stefan. *The World of Yesterday.* Lincoln: University of Nebraska Press, 1964.

Subject Index

Name Index

Henry I. Schvey, associate professor of English at Leiden University, The Netherlands, holds a Ph.D. from Indiana University. He is the author of several scholarly articles on Oskar Kokoschka and on modern drama.

The manuscript was edited by Jean Spang. The book was designed by Richard Kinney. The typeface for the text is Palatino, designed by Hermann Zapt about 1950. The display face is Windsor, designed by Stephenson Blake about 1905.
   The book is printed on S. D. Warren's 80-lb. Lustro Dull Enamel coated paper and bound in Holliston Mills' Linen finish cloth over binder's boards. Manufactured in the United States of America.